GALLIPOLI

GALLIPOLI
THE END OF THE MYTH

ROBIN PRIOR

YALE UNIVERSITY PRESS
NEW HAVEN AND LONDON

For Mark, Cathy and Isabella

For information about this and other Yale University Press publications, please contact:
U.S. Office: sales.press@yale.edu   www.yalebooks.com
Europe Office: sales@yaleup.co.uk   www.yaleup.co.uk

Set in Minion by IDSUK (DataConnection) Ltd.
Printed in Great Britain by TJ International Ltd, Padstow, Cornwall

Library of Congress Cataloging-in-Publication Data

Prior, Robin.
    Gallipoli : the end of the myth / Robin Prior.
      p. cm.
    Includes bibliographical references and index.
    ISBN 978-0-300-14995-1 (ci : alk. paper)
    1.   World War, 1914-1918—Campaigns—Turkey—Gallipoli Peninsula. 2.   Gallipoli Peninsula (Turkey)—History, Military. I. Title.
    D568.3.P76 2009
    940.4'26—dc22   2008044682

A catalogue record for this book is available from the British Library.

10 9 8 7 6 5 4 3 2 1

Contents

Illustrations

Illustrations reproduced with the kind permission of the Australian War Memorial. Nos 21–4 are from their special collection.

Maps

Acknowledgements

I wish to acknowledge both the institutions and the many people who have helped me in the research and production of this book.

First, I would like to thank my colleagues at the Australian Defence Force Academy for their support, which has been much appreciated. In particular, I would like to thank Elizabeth Greenhalgh for help in obtaining sources, especially those in French, and for many fruitful discussions on Gallipoli. I would also like to thank John Coates, John Reeves and Vice Admiral James Goldrick.

To John Baird, Rector of UNSW@ADFA, I am grateful for the provision of money to make myself acquainted with the Gallipoli Peninsula. My trip to Gallipoli was made much more fruitful and constructive by the expert guidance of Mehmet Ali Oneren and Aykut Degre.

I would also like to thank Professor David Lemmings and my new colleagues at the University of Adelaide for making me so welcome.

I wish to thank the National Maritime Museum, Greenwich and the Liddell Hart Centre at King's College, London and the Churchill Archives for granting access to their collections and for permission to quote from them. The National Archives, Kew deserves particular praise. Surely it is the most efficient research centre in the world; it is a real pleasure to work there.

As always, I owe a special thanks to Rod Sudderby and his staff at the Imperial War Museum. Rod drew my attention to several collections, access to which has improved this book immeasurably.

The Australian War Memorial deserves a special thank you. Steve Gower, Helen Withnell, Ashley Ekins and their staff came to my aid and allowed me access to the AIF war diaries at a difficult moment. This would have been a quite different book and a poorer one but for their intervention. They also allowed me privileged access to their photographic collection for which I am very grateful. The debt owed by me to this splendid institution is immense.

Ashley Ekins deserves special mention. He has always been available for help and advice in his position as Principal Historian in the Australian War Memorial. His encyclopaedic knowledge of the AWM collections is truly remarkable.

Jay Winter has been an enthusiast for this book from the moment I commenced writing. His encouragement and confidence in the manuscript have meant more to me than he knows. Any author with a friend such as Jay is very fortunate.

This is the fourth book with which I have been associated for which Keith Mitchell has drawn the maps. For once again bringing clarity to a very basic scrawl, I owe a great debt to Keith.

I would also like to express my gratitude to Robert Baldock and his expert team at Yale University Press, London. Richard Mason has been a copy editor *par excellence* and has saved me from many an error. Robert, as ever, has been an encouragement throughout the project. His wise counsels have invariably proved correct. I regard him as my friend as well as my publisher.

My wife Heather has been my greatest supporter, acting as guide, critic and researcher. She has read the entire manuscript (more than once) and her suggestions have invariably led to a better and more readable book. This book belongs to her as much as it belongs to me.

My daughter Megan has been a source of joy and a lift for sagging morale.

Cleo and Georgia were my constant companions while I was typing this book. Any errors belong to them.

Introduction

Military history is replete with tales of battles and campaigns, even whole wars, that hung in the balance by the slenderest of threads, the outcome only reached by the commitment of the last reserves or a final effort of willpower by the commander or his troops. Thus we are led to the 'narrow margin' by which many conflicts are said to have been decided. In this way of thinking the battle of Waterloo was 'a close run thing' which might well have gone the other way had Napoleon only persisted with his cavalry charges.

The Second World War provides a particularly rich harvest of examples of this kind. The Battle of Britain is widely regarded as an action that Britain only won because a misguided Luftwaffe turned its attentions in September 1940 to the bombing of London. Had the Luftwaffe kept up their attacks on the airfields of Fighter Command, the story goes, it might well have won the battle. In keeping with this popular view, Park's famous response to Winston Churchill's enquiry about fighter reserves, 'We have no reserves', is far more likely to make it into print than the figures that show Britain out-producing Germany in aircraft by an ever increasing margin.

In the same vein it is suggested that if the Germans had started their eastern campaign one or two weeks earlier in June 1941, Moscow and perhaps the entire Soviet state might well have fallen before the Russian winter ground the blitzkrieg to a halt. Similarly, one more push at Stalingrad in August 1942 and the Germans would have been across the Volga. Only Rommel's failure to realize that he was on the brink of success in early 1942 allowed the British to hang on in the Western Desert. (The failure of Montgomery to realize later in the same year that he had Rommel on the ropes prolonged the desert campaign into 1943, and thus delayed D Day into 1944.) The list goes on.

The military history of the First World War has, in general, been free of this kind of brinkmanship in the literature. There have been few suggestions that many of its battles were close run. On the contrary, at the Marne in September 1914 the Germans are portrayed as exhausted, fortunate to have proceeded as far as they had. In the great French battles of 1915 in the Artois (spring) and Champagne (autumn), historians have not discovered any actions by which the commanders could have turned defeat into victory; indeed, the consensus is that these battles should not have taken place at all.

Similar views have been expressed about the great British battles of 1916 and 1917. Whether authors are pro- Haig or anti-Haig, there has been little discussion along the might-have-been lines enumerated for the Second World War battles. Some have suggested that if Haig had acted differently on 1 July 1916, or on 14 July or on 15 September, the British might have made greater progress at less cost to human life. But no one has suggested that these actions would have delivered great victories that would suddenly have ended the campaign or the war. Similar remarks could be made about the Passchendaele offensives of July to November 1917; no historical alchemists have been tempted to transmute this campaign into an action that might have won the war. As for the final campaigns in 1918, the consensus seems to be that all that was achieved by the Ludendorff offensive was the attrition of his own armies. When, later in the year, the Allies did finally win, they achieved victory through a series of relentless yet individually unspectacular advances. There was no narrow margin here, the German army and war economy just collapsed under the accumulated strain of four years of total war.

The one outstanding exception to this tendency in the historiography of the First World War is the Gallipoli campaign. Reading about Gallipoli over a number of years, it seems to me that the literature of this one campaign is as replete with alleged turning points as is that of the Second World War. So, at the Dardanelles, one more push by the British navy after

18 March 1915 would have seen the ships through to Constantinople. At Gallipoli, had the military campaign not been preceded by the naval attack or had the military landed earlier than 25 April, the Turkish defenders would have been caught napping. A rapid Turkish surrender must have followed. Later, if a few thousand Anzac troops had been landed in the correct place, there would have been victory, or at least a major advance towards it. Competent middle-ranking officers would have seen Sari Bair captured in August. Had there been some general other than Sir Frederick Stopford at Suvla Bay, great things would have been accomplished. Had Constantinople fallen, the war would probably have been shortened by a coalition of Balkan armies advancing along the Danube and catching Austria–Hungary and Germany in the rear. Gallipoli, it seems, was the great lost opportunity of the First World War.

What led to this retrospective portrayal of Gallipoli as a missed opportunity is difficult to say. Some possible reasons include the dramatic setting of the Gallipoli Peninsula; an ingrained belief that, as Prime Minister Asquith said, Britain and France must have been able to defeat Turkey; or the desperate wish for a battle that could provide the momentum so lacking on the Western Front.

What I have endeavoured to do in this book, as well as tell the story of the campaign, is investigate these so-called lost opportunities.[1] It is my claim that I have been able to bring new perspectives to some of these long-standing controversies and to dispatch some of them to the dustbin of history. Whether this claim has substance is for others to judge.

I have also taken a different approach to much of the recent writing on Gallipoli. In the last ten or so years the naval, military and political events central to the campaign have rather taken a back seat to books that seek to explain why remembrance of Gallipoli has undergone such an emphatic revival, or to reveal the personal experience and often agony that the ordinary soldier underwent on the Peninsula. Such books are to be welcomed. The best of them add breadth to our understanding of the First World War and of the times in which we live.[2] Nevertheless, it seems to me that there is a danger of forgetting the events we claim to be remembering and of narrowing our focus of attention to the limits of a single soldier. Lack of a good grasp of the events around and on the Peninsula also runs the risk of sentimentalizing the experience of the men who served there. Unwittingly, much of this type of literature portrays the troops as helpless victims of great impersonal political forces of which they were either ignorant or contemptuous. In my view this does damage to the past by allowing the intrusion of current political concerns. The veterans of Gallipoli, I believe, would have been some of the most vociferous critics of this approach.

This book is, however, not neglectful of the sailors and troops who fought at Gallipoli in 1915. Indeed, the questions it asks are central to the experiences of these men. I seek to understand whether they were well led by officers both junior and senior, whether the high command gave them a decent chance of success and whether they fought to any purpose. These are difficult questions but they are vital to an understanding of the campaign.

Much military history is misunderstood on this point. The movements of armies and their components, the firepower they have at their disposal and the actions of their commanders can seem to some to be far removed (or indeed irrelevant) to the concerns of the ordinary soldier. In truth these matters most often decide which soldiers and how many of them will survive a particular action or the campaign. In war soldiers die. It is necessary to scrutinize the actions of commanders to determine whether so many needed to die and to what end they forfeited their lives. These are very human concerns and the best military history places them at the heart of its investigations.

In my choice of source material, I have relied on accounts that are as close as possible in time to the actions they describe. These sources are to be found in the naval case studies, the war diaries and in the after action reports in the National Archives in London. For Australian accounts I have used similar military material in the priceless archives of the Australian War Memorial (AWM). Whatever the shortcomings of this contemporary material (and it has many), it has the advantage of being fresh and unencumbered by expectation or knowledge of the final outcomes of the campaign, and it can be cross-checked with like material. I have sought to supplement this material with first-hand accounts found in the Imperial War Museum, London, and in the AWM. Finally, I have had access to a wealth of private papers including those of Churchill and his admirals, of many political figures and to the papers of staff officers who accompanied Sir Ian Hamilton and other commanders. Where a document has appeared in published form, I have substituted the archival reference for the published one. This will allow readers to check these references with relative ease. I wish to emphasize, however, that all documents have been viewed in their original form. I have also used such important technical documents as the Mitchell Committee Report (1921) into the failure of the naval attack. I have not neglected the secondary sources but have used them selectively. The British and Australian official histories contain essential detail often not available elsewhere. However, it is my contention that the British official history is partial because the historian, as General Hamilton's staff officer, was an important participant in the campaign. As for C.E.W. Bean's account, it was as much about creating the story of how a nation 'found itself' on the beaches and hills of Turkey as it was a straight history of the campaign. Both works therefore remain essential but are partial and dated.

A word on Turkish sources. A number of works have claimed to use Turkish sources and I could make the same claim here. I have used the Turkish General Staff History which has been translated into a kind of English and some useful translated articles in the Rayfield Papers in the Imperial War Museum. In addition to the memoir literature available in English (Mustafa Kemal, Liman von Sanders, Hans Kannengiesser), I have also used the ground-breaking work of Edward Erikson to whom all scholars in the area owe a debt.

However, it is still the case that there is no depth to sources in Turkish, or more accurately Ottoman. We just do not have the war diaries, after action reports and operations orders on the Turkish side to place against those on the Allied side. Thus, we know little about the organization of the disastrous Turkish counterattacks of 19 May and 9 August. Neither do we know whether the Turks were aware that the Allies were about to evacuate the Peninsula in December 1915 and January 1916. I am in fact part of a team which is endeavouring to obtain Turkish military documents that might throw light on these issues. To date the signs are promising, but as the documents have to be translated first from Ottoman to Turkish and then into English, the project is of necessity an effort of years. Future scholars may, as a result of this work, be able to correct some of what appears here.

In summary, this book seeks to do a number of things. It seeks to restore some kind of balance to the treatment of the different national contingents of troops who fought at Gallipoli. So, in as much as the sources allow, attention is paid to the French and Indian troops as well as to those from Britain, New Zealand and Australia. The book also seeks to place the campaign in the context of the war as a whole, an approach that can help explain why the campaign was first undertaken and why, at various times, it seemed to be starved of resources. The text also tries to explain the political context in which the battle was fought and why at times the need to give due consideration to allies had such a profound effect on events on the Gallipoli Peninsula, though not, I believe, on the outcome of the campaign. Finally, I am concerned to strip away the weight of mythology that has so hampered the development of a sophisticated historiography of Gallipoli. As a consequence I have dealt with the campaign as an important episode in the First World War, where men fought each other in an exotic setting but where no nations except modern Turkey were created— and even that event would be delayed by almost a decade after Gallipoli. The romance of war is largely absent from this account, but in truth war is about the most unromantic occupation imaginable. The time for sentimentalizing Gallipoli has long passed. It should be treated as the men experienced it—as a bloody episode in a bloody war.

CHAPTER 1

The Origins of the Naval Offensive

Britain declared war on Germany on 4 August 1914 in response to the German assault on the Western democracies of France and Belgium. The military assistance Britain offered to its continental allies was, in the first instance, small. During the first weeks of the war the Royal Navy escorted just four divisions of infantry to France. This British Expeditionary Force, or BEF was puny compared to the hundreds of divisions deployed by each of the main European antagonists.

Lord Kitchener, the Secretary of State for War, had no doubt that this small force would have to be increased to continental proportions. He thought the war would be a protracted struggle and set about raising a large volunteer army which might reach a million men by 1917.

Others in Britain sought a way of avoiding the cost of a long war. They reasoned that while the four divisions of the army might be puny, Britain had a far more effective instrument already to hand. The Royal Navy had ruled supreme since Trafalgar. In the early years of the twentieth century its position had been tested by the rapid growth of the German fleet. But at the outbreak of war the Royal Navy was still dominant. The British possessed 24 of the latest type of battleships (Dreadnought was their popular name) while the Germans had just 13. Moreover, 13 more dreadnoughts were under construction in naval dockyards around Britain. In contrast, the Germans were building just two. In addition, the British had

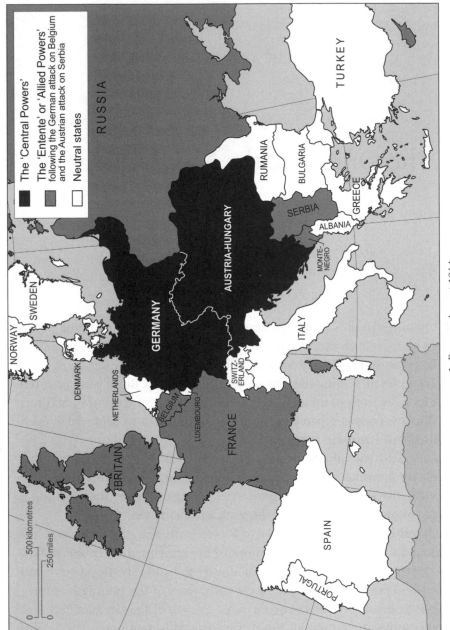

1 Europe, August 1914

some 40 older battleships, much less powerful than dreadnoughts but still formidable enough, while the Germans had a mere handful of these older vessels.

The political master of the great British armada was Winston Churchill, First Lord of the Admiralty. Churchill had been given this post in October 1911 to ensure that a reluctant navy would comply with the army's plans for it to escort an expeditionary force to France in the event of war, rather than pursue its preferred goal of capturing an island off the German coast. By September 1914 the escort had been accomplished without the loss of a single soldier. Naval units were then engaged in sweeping up small squadrons of German ships in distant seas, ensuring that vital supplies of food and war materiel of all kinds carried in unarmed merchant ships arrived safely in Britain, and in maintaining offensive patrols in the North Sea to keep watch on the German fleet.

None of this proved very congenial to Churchill. Since the outbreak of the war his restless mind had been devising a series of what he considered to be more offensive operations for his ships. Although his schemes were many and various they had one factor in common: they sought not just to defeat the German fleet but to use British naval power to exploit such a victory and shorten the duration of the war on land.

During the first four months of the war Churchill devised three schemes by which the navy could materially affect the entire course of the war.

The first of these schemes, ironically, was the seizure of an island close to the German north coast, the islands most often mentioned being Sylt or Borkum. The plan proceeded as follows. Heavy units from the fleet would obliterate the enemy island defences and their garrisons. The fleet would then escort sufficient troops to hold the island against attack. After that the island would be converted into a base from which torpedo craft and submarines could operate. The Germans would find the activities of these craft such a threat to their main fleet and its nearby bases that they would attempt to recapture the island, using the greater part of their dreadnoughts. This would provoke the hitherto elusive decisive naval battle, which the British would win.

Subsequent operations would follow to capitalize on the victory. With the German fleet removed as a threat, British heavy units could enter the Baltic, establish control of that sea and be in a position to land contingents of Russian troops on the German north coast—just 90 miles from Berlin. The Germans would be forced to react by removing troops from the

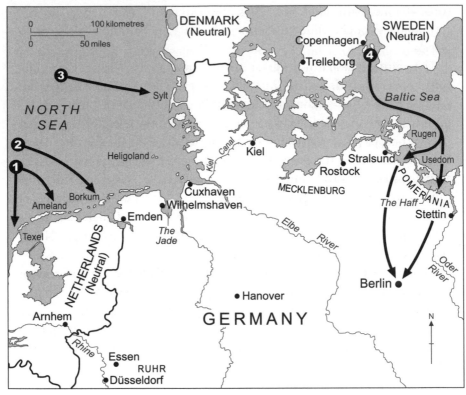

2 Naval plans against Germany, 1914–15

Western Front, thus laying that vital area open to penetration by British and French troops.[1]

The problem for Churchill's plan was that none of his admirals now thought it feasible and most thought it dangerous. Lord Fisher, the irascible and erratic septuagenarian whom Churchill in November had brought back from retirement as First Sea Lord, seemed at times to favour the scheme. Indeed, in November 1914 he wrote a long paper pressing the scheme in very Churchillian terms.[2] But his support may have arisen from the fact that the navy had not so far accomplished anything dramatic (on 21 December he wrote to Churchill, 'Do something!!!!! *We are waiting to be kicked!!!*'[3]). Or his support might have been more apparent than real, a delaying tactic that masked underlying misgivings. A naval staff officer (Captain Herbert Richmond) reported a colleague's view that Fisher 'didn't intend to have the Borkum business done'. The colleague said 'they can go on getting out their plans as much as they like, but Jacky [Fisher] is simply not going to do them in the end'.[4]

The reason that the admirals were reluctant to do the 'Borkum business' is not difficult to discern. The island to be attacked lay in mine-infested waters and was further protected by submarine and torpedo-boat flotillas. The British bombarding squadrons would be exposed to attack from all the heavy units of the German fleet. Troops would have to be landed under heavy machine-gun and artillery fire. Even if the island was captured, supplying the garrison by merchant ships passing through minefields and running the gauntlet of submarines would be a precarious affair.

As for the Baltic aspect of the scheme, it was even more hazardous. Even if the island phase saw the destruction of the entire German fleet, British dreadnoughts operating in the confined waters of the Baltic would encounter extensive minefields and the permanent squadrons of submarines and torpedo boats that were stationed there. Moreover, landing Russian troops on the north German coast presupposed that the Russians had troops available; that these troops were skilled in combined operations; that logistic support in the form of artillery and stores was available in sufficient quantity; that any language problems could be overcome; and that the Russians were willing to risk such a highly trained, well-supplied force well away from their own main theatre. A compounding issue was that the Germans, in possession of an excellent rail network, could have moved reserves northward at a faster rate than the attacking army could have been reinforced from the sea. Not surprisingly, the admirals were unwilling to risk Britain's main fleet in an operation that contained so many hazards and so little chance of success.

Churchill's second scheme involved moving the BEF to the Belgian coast. The proximity of the navy would then allow it to support the army with naval gunfire, addressing to some extent the shortage of heavy land-based artillery in the early months of the war. The British troops could then advance along the coast towards the enemy-occupied port of Zeebrugge, close to the western border of Holland. Such a manoeuvre might even influence the attitude of the neutral Dutch towards the war. After discussions with Sir John French, the commander-in-chief of the BEF, Churchill became very enthusiastic about the coastal advance. By early December he was describing it to French as 'a good & brilliant operation [which would aid] the general success of the war'.[5] Eventually, however, General Joseph Joffre, the commander-in-chief of the French army, turned against the scheme. He was reluctant for the BEF to move to the coastal flank because he thought it might prove a tempting position from which the British could embark for home. Later, opinion in Britain also turned against the plan. It was thought that in the confined waters of the Channel the heavy ships of the fleet would be at great risk from mines and torpedoes, and that in any case the BEF would not have sufficient guns and ammunition for an advance sufficiently dramatic to justify the risk.[6]

As for bringing Holland into the war, there was some initial enthusiasm. Fisher took up the idea with alacrity. He considered that it 'will sweep the field'.[7] But his call for 750,000 men for the purpose and his wild exhortations to land them at 'Antwerp, Amsterdam and all the other spots . . . along the Dutch coast—LAND EVERYWHERE AT ONCE!'[8] perhaps indicated that his support for this operation was conditional on it never being carried out. Moreover, there was the matter of Dutch national interest. Significant units of the German army stood within striking distance of Holland. These formidable hordes could invade much faster than any British force landed from the sea, even if it landed 'everywhere at once'. As with the Baltic scheme, the Germans could also reinforce their men at a faster rate than could a seaborne landing. No doubt bringing in Holland was a good idea but this scheme was not going to do it.

The third Churchillian scheme involved Turkey and harked back to the beginning of the war. Two German ships, a battlecruiser (the *Goeben*) and a lighter vessel had eluded two larger British squadrons in the Mediterranean and sailed through the Dardanelles to Constantinople in

August 1914. At the time this action was thought to have resulted in the German-Turkish alliance, which was announced soon after the ships' arrival. It is now known that the ships were directed to Constantinople in support of an alliance already concluded. But Churchill and the navy had attracted some odium over the incident and the First Lord of the Admiralty was not disposed to look kindly upon the Turkish government.[9]

Churchill therefore set up with the concurrence of the Secretary of State for War (Kitchener) a joint planning group to work out a scheme for the seizure of the Gallipoli Peninsula by means of an army supplied by Greece to admit 'a British Fleet to the Sea of Marmara'.[10] What the fleet was to do once it arrived in the Marmara was not specified. Major-General Charles Callwell, the Director of Military Operations, encapsulated the deliberations of this group in a memorandum on 3 September. He considered it 'an extremely difficult operation of war' but thought that an army of 60,000 Greeks might do the job.[11]

The problem with this plan was soon obvious. There was no Greek force available. The offer had been made by Prime Minister Eleatherios Venizelos against the wishes of his own pro-German king, Constantine I, and without taking note of the state of the Greek army. In 1914 it was being re-equipped. It was short of all types of materiel and was in no state to rectify this position rapidly because Greece had no armaments industry. Nor were the Allies in a position to make up the Greek deficiencies. The Greek army was therefore in no position to take the field against any foe.[12]

The option of operations against Turkey spluttered on for some time. In early November the Turks had bombarded Russian ports in the Black Sea, precipitating a war between the two countries. A few days later Britain and France declared war on Turkey. Churchill had already anticipated these events. Two days before the British declaration of war he had ordered a squadron stationed near the Dardanelles to bombard the forts at the entrance. So were fired the first shots in the long war between Britain and Turkey.

After that flurry Turkey dropped off the British agenda. Then on 25 November, in the context of a discussion about the defence of Egypt, Churchill noted that 'the ideal method of defending Egypt was by an attack on the Gallipoli Peninsula. This, if successful, would give us control of the Dardanelles, and we could dictate terms at Constantinople.'[13] He also noted, however, that this was a 'very difficult operation requiring a large force', and the discussion soon meandered into the question of whether wells in the Palestinian desert could be destroyed behind a Turkish force advancing on the Suez Canal.[14]

Churchill did not cease to think aggressively about Turkey. Asquith reported in early December that Churchill's 'volatile mind' was 'set on Turkey & Bulgaria, & he wants to organise a heroic adventure against Gallipoli and the Dardanelles'.[15] Nevertheless, despite Churchillian enthusiasm to punish the Turks no plans were made, and Britain's major commitment to the war remained the few (but increasing) number of divisions on what was beginning to be called the Western Front.[16]

It was a series of alarming developments on that front that gave new impetus to the search by Britain for an alternative theatre of war in which to deploy the millions of men being trained in what were called the 'New' or 'Kitchener' armies. The war of movement in the West, which had begun with the German Schlieffen Plan and continued at the Marne and the so-called 'race to the sea', had come to a halt. Now any attempt at mass advance could be halted by small groups of soldiers in rudimentary defences and armed only with bolt action rifles. The appearance of trenches and a few machine guns reduced even further the chances of advancing troops. 'Stalemate' started to enter the vocabularies of the general staff.

Politicians on all sides greeted the spectacle of war without end with consternation. Most concerned was Churchill. For some months now he had been devising the schemes just detailed that aimed to use the navy to shorten the war. All had failed, either because they risked Britain's main fleet (Borkum) or were impractical (Holland) or were opposed by allies (Zeebrugge), or because they lacked the military force with which to carry them through (Gallipoli). Yet Churchill had by no means given up on his projects. Indeed, the new developments in warfare on the Western Front caused him to redouble his efforts.

His inclinations were reinforced by a letter from a friend at the front, Valentine Fleming, who was serving in the Oxfordshire Hussars. In late November he wrote to Churchill about the nature of the fighting on the Western Front. In part the letter said:

Let me give you some general impressions of this astounding conflict:-
1: First and most impressive the absolutely indescribable ravages of modern artillery fire, not only upon all men, animals and buildings within its zone, but upon the very face of nature itself. Imagine a broad

belt, ten miles or so in width, stretching from the Channel to the German frontier near Basle, which is positively littered with the bodies of men and scarified with their rude graves; in which farms, villages and cottages are shapeless heaps of blackened masonry; in which fields, roads and trees are pitted and torn and twisted by shells and disfigured by dead horses, cattle, sheep and goats, scattered in every attitude of repulsive distortion and dismemberment. . . . Along this terrain of death stretch more or less parallel to each other lines and lines of trenches, some 200, some 1,000 yards apart, hardly visible except to the aeroplanes which continually hover above them. . . . In these trenches crouch lines of men, in brown or grey or blue, coated with mud, unshaven, hollow-eyed with the continual strain unable to reply to the everlasting rain of shells hurled at them from 3, 4, 5 or more miles away and positively welcoming an infantry attack from one side or the other as a chance of meeting and matching themselves against *human* assailants and not against invisible, irresistible machines. It's going to be a *long long* war in spite of the fact that on both sides every single man wants it stopped *at once*.[17]

This letter made a profound impression on Churchill. He passed it on to his wife Clementine with the comment, 'What wd happen I wonder if the armies suddenly & simultaneously went on strike and said some other method must be found of settling the dispute'.[18] Churchill now had another impulse for searching out an alternative front suited to naval operations. To his desire to use the navy to shorten the war generally was now added the specific goal of ending the carnage on the Western Front.

Churchill was not alone in his anxiety about the course of the war. Other members of the War Council were also expressing concern. In late December the Prime Minister was bombarded by no fewer than three proposals for a counter-strategy to the Western Front.

First in the field was Lieutenant-Colonel Maurice Hankey. An ex-marine and Secretary of the War Council, he had written a strategic paper which became known as the 'Boxing Day memorandum' (though it was dated 28 December). In it, he drew attention to what he called 'the remarkable deadlock' in the west. Hankey suggested a number of mechanical devices (including the first suggestion for the weapon that eventually evolved as the tank) that might help reduce casualties in assaults against the Germans. But he considered that other theatres offered more attractive prospects. He too conjured up an alliance of Balkan states, including

Greece and Bulgaria. He suggested that with these states on board it might be possible 'to weave a web round Turkey which shall end her career as a European Power'.[19] He thought that if Rumania and Russia could be enticed into the coalition, 'the occupation of Constantinople, the Dardanelles and the Bosphorus' could be accomplished. Thus communications would be restored with Russia via the Black Sea, allowing munitions to flow into the country and wheat out. Three British army corps combined with the Balkan and Russian forces should be sufficient to achieve these ends.[20]

We have already noted the deficiencies in Churchill's various plans. Hankey's plan was hardly less problematical. It ignored the fact that while these states had fought as one against Turkey in the first Balkan war (1912–13), they had later turned on each other. Bulgaria in particular had lost much territory to Rumania and was looking for any excuse to win it back. The idea that these states would allow troops from the others to traverse their territories was a pipe dream. Finally the 'web' strategy was desperately vague. No detail was given as to how the Allied armies would capture Constantinople. Furthermore, even if the 'web' scheme was successful and communications were opened with Russia, Hankey did not address the vital issues attendant on this. In particular, because of the unexpected intensity of the fighting on the Western Front, the Allies had no surplus munitions with which to supply their eastern ally and there was no surplus shipping to transport Russian wheat to the west.

Hankey's paper to Asquith was followed the next day by a missive from Churchill to the Prime Minister which also addressed the problem of stalemate on the Western Front. He wrote:

> I think it quite possible that neither side will have the strength to penetrate the other's lines in the Western theatre. . . . Without attempting to take a final view, my impression is that the position of both armies is not likely to undergo any decisive change—although no doubt several hundred thousand men will be spent to satisfy the military mind on the point. . . . Are there not alternatives than sending our armies to chew barbed wire in Flanders? Further, cannot the power of the Navy be brought directly to bear upon the enemy? If it is not possible or unduly costly to pierce the German lines on existing fronts, ought we not, as new forces come to hand, to engage him on new frontiers, and enable the Russians to do so too?[21]

He then went on to restate his scheme for capturing a German island as a preliminary to entering the Baltic and landing a Russian army on the German coast.[22] This was the same scheme that had been resolutely opposed by his admirals since the beginning of the war.

On New Year's Eve Lloyd George, the Chancellor of the Exchequer, entered the debate. He also noted the stalemate on the Western Front, arguing 'that any attempt to force the carefully prepared German lines in the west would end in failure and in appalling loss of life'.[23] As for alternatives, Lloyd George was opposed to the German island option because of the excessive risk to the Grand Fleet, but he put forward two other propositions. The first was that the Kitchener volunteers gathering in Britain should be used in conjunction with the Serbs, Rumanians, Greeks and Montenegrins to attack the weaker enemy—Austria—by the landing of a combined force of 1.4 to 1.6 million men at Salonika or, more promisingly, on the Dalmatian coast. This would force Austria to move troops from Carpathia, which would give the Russians their chance. Alternatively it would force the Germans to shift forces from the Western Front, which would provide opportunities for the British and French.

Lloyd George's second scheme, which was of a minor nature, was designed against Turkey. Here he thought that the Turks should be allowed to advance on the Suez Canal and a force landed behind them near Alexandretta in Syria. This would cut off and destroy the Suez contingent, relieve pressure on Russia in the Caucasus where Tsar Nicholas II's forces were being driven back by the Turks, secure Britain's lines of communication with India as well as secure Syria for Britain. His entire purpose was to bring 'Germany down by the process of knocking the props under her'.[24]

Lloyd George's paper was no less deficient in its clarity than Hankey's or Churchill's. At its base lay the remarkable proposition that Germany was in some way 'propped up' by such second-rate powers as Austria and Turkey. His proposed landing on the Dalmatian coast (or was it Salonika?) faced impossible logistical difficulties because of the mountainous terrain and the lack of railways. The problem of uniting the Balkan states was left un-argued. Nor was any detail supplied about the minor operation against Turkey in Syria.

Given their content, these papers were to have a cumulative effect that was distinctly odd. Only Hankey's paper had placed operations against

Turkey at its centre. Churchill was still focused on capturing a German island and Lloyd George wanted the main effort to be made against Austria-Hungary. Yet as soon as Churchill read Hankey's memorandum, his attention seemed to swing back towards Turkey. He told Asquith that he and Hankey were 'substantially in agreement and our views are not incompatible. I wanted Gallipoli attacked at the Turkish declaration of war.' Did this mean that Churchill's ambitions for Borkum/Sylt had subsided? As we will see, it did not.

Fisher meanwhile provided enthusiastic support for the Turkey plan. He wrote to Hankey:

> The more I think of your paper the more I like it. Winston spontaneously gave me [it] . . . and I went for it 'tooth & nail'! he against it! He says it's too far from the main theatre of war . . . all rot!
> This is my advice to you and then you will win!
> I Go in for Sir W Robertson commanding the expedition.
> II That all Indian Troops should be taken from France to form part of the expedition.
> III That at least 75,000 seasoned troops from Sir John French's army should [be part?] of the Expedition.
> III [sic] That (II and III) should embark at Marseilles ostensibly all for Egypt.
> On no account take fresh troops from England for the Expedition.
> IV That feints should be made at Haifa & Alexandretta and the latter (Alexandretta) made a real expedition so as to establish ourselves there & oust the Germans and being commanded by the sea with the railway under ships guns all this is easy and it's a vital spot for us in view of the Mesopotamian oil fields the most abundant in the world . . .
> V The main landing of our army to be at Besika Bay.
> VI The Greeks to land 100,000 men on the Gallipoli Peninsula.
> VII Our Fleet to force the Dardanelles when our Besika Army makes its main attack & the Greeks go for Gallipoli.
> You must do spade work vigorously with Lloyd George, Balfour, Crewe, Grey & the Prime Minister. I will undertake Kitchener & Winston.[25]

Despite Fisher's explosive language, this document should be interpreted cautiously. Fisher supposed that extensive operations in south-eastern

Europe would tie up so many troops as to make any plan to capture a German island in the Baltic fall off the agenda. For the First Sea Lord this had great advantages. He had never clarified to Churchill his opposition to the northern plans. Operations against Turkey might obviate this necessity, while at the same time conveying the impression that he was the daring sea dog of popular imagination.

No doubt hoping to cement Churchill's commitment to the southern option, Fisher continued to extol the Turkey plan to him. 'I CONSIDER THE ATTACK ON TURKEY HOLDS THE FIELD!—But ONLY if it's IMMEDIATE!' He went on to reiterate his plan as outlined to Hankey with the added detail: '[Admiral] *Sturdee forces the Dardanelles at the same time* [as the other military operations] *with Majestic class and Canopus class! God Bless him!*'[26]

This, it may be noted, was the first specific mention to Churchill of an operation designed to 'force' the Dardanelles, admittedly as part of a much larger design. But the class of ships that Fisher recommended may well have caught Churchill's attention. In a memorandum in late December 1914 Fisher had singled out the Canopus class of pre-dreadnoughts for scrapping, and the Majestic class were of the same vintage. 'Scrap them all' he had exhorted, '*The scrapheap cries aloud!* A multitude of splendid seamen butchered in ships that can neither fight or run away!'[27] Here then was an operation using ships clearly superfluous to the needs of the Grand Fleet but expendable in an operation against the Turks.

At the same time that Churchill was being bombarded by 'Turkey' memoranda from Fisher, other events were directing his thoughts towards the Dardanelles. On 1 January 1915 the British ambassador in Russia, Sir George Buchanan, had telegraphed to the Foreign Office that the Grand Duke Nicholas of Russia had informed him that Russian forces were being hard pressed by the Turks in the Caucasus, and that the Grand Duke had asked whether 'it would be possible for Lord Kitchener to arrange for a demonstration of some kind against the Turk elsewhere, either naval or military [to] ease the position of Russia'.[28]

Kitchener asked Churchill for his opinion, making the point that 'we have no troops to land anywhere' and enquiring whether a naval 'demonstration' at the Dardanelles might be the most effective way of preventing more Turkish troops being sent east.[29]

A summary of Churchill's position and the events that led him to it is now in order. Since the outbreak of war he had recommended the use of the navy to affect the land war. All his schemes had come to nothing, often for the very good reason that they were impracticable, or risked the ships that maintained Britain's naval supremacy, or both. Yet the impulse to find an alternative theatre of operations had become more urgent since he had been alerted to the fact that action on the Western Front was likely to be protracted and bloody. At this moment Hankey and Fisher's fulminations about Turkey arrived. Churchill knew that Fisher's grandiose plan for several armies to be deployed against the Turks was wildly impracticable (had not Kitchener stated that there were no troops to land anywhere?). But Fisher had mentioned using some ships that he himself had previously described as useless to force the Dardanelles. And Kitchener had also drawn attention to the Dardanelles as the one place where Britain might usefully take action to ease the pressure on the Russians in the Caucasus. As we have seen, Churchill was not averse to action against the Turks and it seems certain that Hankey, Fisher and Kitchener had reinforced his hopes that something might be done in that region. As a result then of all these influences Churchill called a meeting of the Admiralty War Group for 3 January to discuss possible operations against Turkey.

This group consisted of Admirals Fisher (First Sea Lord), Sir Henry Jackson (a retired admiral brought back as an informal consultant), Henry Oliver (Chief of the Naval Staff), Wilson (a former First Sea Lord also employed in a consultative capacity), Captain Charles de Bartoleme (Churchill's Naval Secretary) and Churchill himself. We do not know what transpired at that meeting for no minutes were kept. But its secretary, Graham Greene, later stated that usually the group discussed 'a great variety of questions . . . & many decisions [were] embodied in Minutes by [the] First Lord & concurred in by First S L. (that is Fisher)'.[30] He went on to say that at the meeting in question the subject of operations against Turkey 'was brought forward by the First Lord' and thoroughly discussed.[31] It is difficult to believe, therefore, that the telegram sent by Churchill to Admiral Carden, commanding the squadron off the Dardanelles, did not have the approval of Churchill's main naval advisers. It said:

Do you consider the forcing of the Dardanelles by ships alone a practicable operation.
It is assumed older Battleships fitted with minebumpers would be used preceded by Colliers or other merchant craft as bumpers and sweepers.

Importance of results would justify severe loss.
Let me know your views.[32]

There are a number of interesting facets to this message. First, it is hard to avoid the conclusion that it was framed to encourage a positive response, for if severe losses were justified what commander would say that the operation should not be attempted? Why Churchill wrote in this vein is not difficult to divine. So far all his senior admirals, both within the Admiralty and the Grand Fleet, had opposed his schemes for offensive operations; he was not going to give such a relatively lowly commander as Carden the luxury of refusal. Second, the operation specified by Churchill was neither the demonstration mentioned by Kitchener nor a large combined operation as suggested by Hankey, Fisher and Lloyd George. What Churchill had done was to draw out those aspects of Fisher's plan which did not involve the use of non-existent armies and did not risk vital units of the Royal Navy. It therefore met Kitchener's objections that there were no troops to land and the admirals' objections to all of Churchill's other schemes. What perhaps the admirals did not notice (on 3 January anyway) was that the operation ran counter to long-standing naval orthodoxy which stated that ships were at a fatal disadvantage when they attacked land fortifications.

Evidence that Churchill's interest in an operation by the navy alone would not preclude interest in other schemes came the day after the War Group meeting. On 4 January he wrote to Admiral Jellicoe, commander of the Grand Fleet, that 'everything convinces me we must take Borkum'.[33] On the same day he reiterated the importance of Borkum to Fisher and warned him that 'we had better hear what others have to say about the Turkish plans before taking a decided line. I wd. not grudge 100,000 men because of the great political effects in the Balkan Peninsula; but Germany is the foe, & it is bad war to seek cheaper victories & easier antagonists.'[34] These communications effectively ended Fisher's strategy of fixing Churchill's attention on Turkey in order to deflect him from Borkum.

This situation goes far towards explaining an utterly bizarre event that took place the next day. The First Sea Lord resigned, not on naval operational grounds but because no official announcement had been made warning the public of impending Zeppelin raids[35] (equally bizarrely the Admiralty was responsible for the air defence of London). Churchill ignored the resignation and no more was heard of it, but it was surely the sign of someone under great pressure. Captain Richmond, a member of the naval war staff and a close observer of Admiralty personalities, certainly thought so. He wrote of Fisher at this time:

> This is the mastermind which his worshippers would have us believe to be so steeped in strategy! In reality he does nothing: he goes home and sleeps in the afternoon. He is old & worn out & nervous. It is ill to have the destinies of an empire in the hands of a failing old man, anxious for popularity, afraid of any local mishap which may be put down to his dispositions.[36]

This is an acute observation from Richmond. Clearly the thought of both Borkum and the Dardanelles proceeding was driving Fisher to the brink. The only way out might be resignation on whatever grounds he could find.

Others on the Admiralty War Group were also rethinking their position. Jackson was in the process of putting figures to what the 'severe loss' mentioned by Churchill might mean. He calculated that a squadron of eight battleships rushing the Dardanelles could expect six to be sunk and the other two severely damaged. A second squadron following close behind might then get through with much less damage. But he recommended instead a more methodical operation to reduce the forts one by one so that a squadron with depleted ammunition supplies and with some ships out of action did not diminish the effect of its arrival before Constantinople.[37] He did not go further than this but it was a severe qualification of the Churchill plan to rush the Straits.

Soon after Jackson had penned his memorandum, Carden's reply to Churchill's enquiry of 3 January arrived. Carden was in agreement with Jackson's position. He did 'not consider Dardanelles can be rushed. They might be forced by extended operations with large numbers of ships.'[38] On the following day Churchill telegraphed back: 'Your view is agreed with by high authorities here. Please telegraph in detail what you think could be done by extended operations, what force would be needed and how you consider it should be used.'[39] Clearly Churchill was absolutely determined that an operational plan be produced by Carden, yet the main focus of his strategic thinking still remained in northern Europe. Just two days after receiving Carden's reply he reintroduced his German island plan and urged the War Council to adopt it. Despite an ominous remark from

Fisher that the navy would not be ready to carry out the plan for some months, the War Council, which also seemingly disposed of the Zeebrugge operation at this meeting, concluded:

> The proposed attack on an island is approved in principle, subject to the feasibility of the plan when worked out in detail. The Admiralty to proceed with the making out of plans.[40]

British strategy thus seemed to be settled: most divisions would still proceed to the Western Front while Carden developed his Dardanelles plan and the Admiralty worked on the German island scheme. Yet there was obviously still great unease among Britain's decision makers about future strategy for Asquith called another meeting of the War Council for the next day to discuss this very subject.

This meeting proceeded to canvass many of the operations rejected earlier in the week. Lloyd George led off with a long statement on the dangers of undertaking frontal attacks on the Western Front. 'Was there,' he asked, no alternative theatre in which we might employ our surplus armies to produce a decisive effect?' He then answered his own question by suggesting (as he had done in late December) that southern Austria would be the ideal theatre. Kitchener quickly scotched this idea by reading out two War Office memoranda showing that such operations were logistically impossible. Lloyd George then switched discussion to the Mediterranean:

> The Dardanelles appeared to be the most suitable objective, as an attack here could be made in co-operation with the Fleet. If successful, it would re-establish communication with Russia; settle the Near Eastern question; draw in Greece and, perhaps, Bulgaria and Roumania; and release wheat and shipping now locked up in the Black Sea.

Lloyd George was immediately supported by Hankey, who pointed out that if successful the operation would provide a jumping-off place from which central Europe could be penetrated by way of the Danube Valley.

The discussion then turned towards a landing at Alexandretta which Lloyd George had also suggested in his earlier paper and which had been greeted with stunning indifference by his colleagues.

Churchill meanwhile was clearly concerned that the War Council was drifting away from the main game—operations in northern Europe. While agreeing that plans should be prepared for operations at the Dardanelles, he 'urged . . . that we should not lose sight of the possibility of action in Northern Europe'. He argued that if Holland could be brought in, an island could be obtained as a base for future operations in the Baltic without having to fight for it. The problem with this plan was that no one could think of how the Dutch could, while surrounded by the German army, be induced into the war on the Allied side. And no conclusions were reached.[41]

In the next few days, however, it must have become clear to Churchill that his island scheme had little chance of fulfilment. On 8 January he received a note from Jellicoe emphasizing the difficulties and dangers of the plan; Fisher now stressed the importance of Alexandretta (a minor operation at best) while continuing to wax enthusiastic about Holland (a strategic dead end, as he must have known), and remained silent about Borkum.[42]

At this moment Carden's plan for forcing the Dardanelles arrived. In truth it was not so much a plan as a list of the order in which the Dardanelles defences would be attacked, starting with the outer forts and working towards the series of forts at the Narrows. The only new factors were requests from Carden for seaplanes to direct the fire of the ships' guns onto the forts, the provision of battlecruisers to deal with the *Goeben* and the supply of the large amounts of ammunition required to complete the task.[43]

At last Churchill had an operational plan. He lost no time in placing it before the War Council which met again on 13 January. He emphasized that the guns of the Fleet were more modern than those in the Turkish forts and outranged them. What the Fleet would do when it cleared the Narrows was left rather vague. All Churchill had to say on this aspect was that 'it would proceed up to Constantinople and destroy the "*Goeben*"'.

The discussion that followed Churchill's exposition was remarkable for its incoherence. Lloyd George and Kitchener thought the plan worth trying, Kitchener making the additional point that 'we could leave off the bombardment if it did not prove effective'. So far the War Council was sticking to the point, but then Sir Edward Grey turned the discussion towards bringing Italy into the war. Sir John French (who was in London for talks with Kitchener) suggested that Lloyd George's plan against Austria should be considered. Churchill again emphasized the importance of Holland. Grey countered by stating that the conditions for Dutch entry were not propitious. Lloyd George (obviously encouraged by French) returned to his

Austrian plan, whereupon French retreated from his earlier foray with the observation that Joffre 'would not like it if we were to divert troops to some theatre of war other than France'. Churchill, who had not so far deigned to comment on Lloyd George's strategic fantasies, urged that preparations for the Austrian venture should be made. Kitchener then noted that a good scheme had been worked out to capture Alexandretta, but added that there were no trained troops with which to carry it out. Churchill, who had to this point also paid little heed to Alexandretta, intervened to note that the navy saw no difficulties with such an operation.

This was the War Council at its worst—unable to stick to a thorough discussion of any subject, discursive, rambling, incoherent, the Prime Minister preoccupied with a letter from Venetia Stanley. Not surprisingly the War Council's conclusions reflected the discussion. It decided that the Zeebrugge plan, thoroughly discredited a few days before, was to be reviewed, the Admiralty was to try to take some kind of (unspecified) action to bring Italy into the war, a subcommittee was to be set up to consider other theatres in which British troops might be deployed and, most importantly for our story, 'That the Admiralty should also prepare for a naval expedition in February to bombard and take the Gallipoli Peninsula, with Constantinople as its objective'.[44]

Most of these resolutions were never implemented. The French once more put paid to British plans for an advance along the Belgian coast towards Zeebrugge, the Admiralty had no ideas about influencing Italy and so did nothing, and the subcommittee set up to examine other theatres never decided on anything.

Only the conclusion concerning the Dardanelles was followed through. Churchill ordered his admirals to give effect to Carden's requests. Other plans might still be discussed but from 13 January on there was no doubt that a naval offensive at the Dardanelles would go ahead. It is worth noting that even if this outcome was reached mainly by default, it must have seemed to the War Council that there was little to be lost in an option that diverted no troops or ships (of any consequence) from the main theatre of war. In that sense Britain's decision makers had not made any decision of vast consequence.

CHAPTER 2

From Ships to Troops

The decision of the War Council on 13 January gave political authorization at the highest level for an attack by the navy alone. Yet just six weeks later the same body authorized troops to be on hand at the Dardanelles to fulfil a purpose that was never specified.

As far as Churchill was concerned there was no talk of troops in the aftermath of the decision made on 13 January. He was now determined that despite continuing discussions about Borkum and other offensives, naval operations against Turkey would be pursued. Soon after the meeting on the 13th, he drafted instructions to Fisher and Oliver that 'detailed proposals should be worked out by C O S [Oliver] and orders drafted both as regards the concentration of the ships and the regulation of the gunnery'.[1] He also noted:

Admiral Carden's proposals should be carefully analysed by an officer of the War Staff in order to show exactly what guns the ships will have to face at each point and stage of the operations, the character of the guns, and their range; *but this officer is to assume that the principle is settled, and all that is necessary is to estimate the force required.*[2]

Initially, some members of the Admiralty War Group were attracted by the possibilities of the naval expedition. Richmond considered Carden's plan 'excellent'.[3] Oliver expressed a wish to command the bombarding squadron.[4] Moreover, in his unpublished autobiography written after the war he stated that he thought it right to go ahead with the naval attack.[5]

Others, such as Jackson, were more hesitant. Soon after Churchill had sent his first telegram to Carden, Jackson had warned the First Lord that the operation would require a large amount of ammunition, be costly in ships and that the shore batteries would need to be destroyed as well as the guns in the forts.[6] After Carden's plan arrived, Jackson stated that he concurred 'generally' with the scheme but again warned about the large amount of ammunition required (3,000 rounds of heavy ammunition would be needed to destroy the large Turkish guns and a similar amount of lighter shells for the smaller enemy ordnance). He suggested that only the destruction of the forts at the entrance of the Straits be approved in the first instance.[7] These statements considerably qualified his endorsement of the plan, although it is noticeable that Jackson did not condemn it as impracticable. Probably he was hedging his bets.[8]

Fisher was, as always, an enigma. He approved the Admiralty War Group's telegram to Carden and then on 12 January, the day before the crucial meeting of the War Council, suggested adding the *Queen Elizabeth*, the most powerful battleship in the world, to Carden's squadron.[9] While this hardly seemed the act of one opposed to the operation, the addition of a powerful battleship could have indicated doubts about the strength of the Dardanelles fleet.

Yet Fisher, in so far as he endorsed any plan for a naval offensive in his public utterances, had always insisted that troops in large numbers accompany the fleet to ensure success. So on the same day that he added the *Queen Elizabeth* to British naval forces in the Mediterranean, he had written to Sir William Tyrell at the Foreign Office: 'if the Greeks land 100,000 men on the Gallipoli Peninsula in concert with a British naval attack on the Dardanelles I think we could count on an easy and quick arrival at Constantinople.'[10] Such wishes were daydreams but perhaps Fisher was hoping that a powerful force of battleships off the Dardanelles would concentrate the minds (and the armies) of some of the Balkan states such as Greece. It is notable, however, that on the actual merits of Carden's purely naval plan he was silent.

If it is possible to sum up Admiralty opinion on the naval attack at around mid-January 1915, it could be said that some were enthusiastic, others thought the plan worth trying and no one had said (as they had in relation to Borkum) that it was impossible or too dangerous. There were lurking doubts. A close reading of Jackson's memoranda reveals them. At this point only a reading of Fisher's correspondence could have detected his hesitations. There seemed reason to think, therefore, that on 13 January the Admiralty was generally supportive of the War Council's decision to carry out operations at the Dardanelles.

As for the War Council itself, there was no dissenting voice. Most members had been born between 1850 and 1876 when British imperialism and its main instrument, the Royal Navy, were at their height. If in their eyes there seemed little that sea power could not accomplish, it should be no matter for wonder. Moreover, as no naval voices had yet spoken a word against the Dardanelles operation, they had no peg on which to hang opposition to the project, even had it existed.

In any case, no one had yet agreed to anything large. A group of old battleships was to attempt to blast their way through the Dardanelles to Constantinople. If operations in the Straits prospered, well and good; if they did not, all seemed to agree that the ships could sail away. This might make a slight dent in British prestige, but it could then be emphasized that these ships were in the second or third rank, as could the probing nature of the attack.

*   *   *

The sanction of the War Council for the naval attack resulted in a flurry of activity at the Admiralty. On 15 January Churchill informed Carden that his plan had been accepted, that he would receive, in addition to the bombardment fleet of pre-dreadnought battleships, the dreadnought *Queen Elizabeth* and two capital ships (later reduced to one) to deal with the *Goeben*. Admiral John de Robeck was appointed second in command.[11]

The next day the French were informed of the operation and on 19 January the Russians. The French were asked to contribute a squadron of battleships to the bombardment fleet and another squadron to assist along the Syrian coast should the landing at Alexandretta take place.[12] They readily agreed to both requests, possibly to watch what the British were doing in an area they regarded as being within their sphere of influence, rather than for any intrinsic merit they saw in the operation. The Russians were asked to provide a naval force to operate at the mouth of the Bosphorus to distract Turkish naval forces, but they declined on the rather specious grounds that their fleet was not ready.[13]

On 25 January Oliver announced that the fleet was being assembled. It consisted of 10 (later 12) pre-dreadnought battleships, 1 dreadnought battlecruiser, the dreadnought *Queen Elizabeth*, 4 light cruisers, 16 destroyers, 1 primitive aircraft carrier and 6 seaplanes, 21 trawlers for minesweeping, 6 submarines and attendant craft.[14] This seemed a mighty array, yet apart from the two dreadnoughts, most of the other ships were too old to face the fire of modern enemy units and were therefore useless for action in the North Sea. So whatever the merits or demerits of the plan, it would hardly risk British naval superiority.

However, even as orders were being sent around the world for these ships to assemble off the Dardanelles, there was growing concern at the Admiralty that the naval operation should be assisted by troops. Richmond, once so gung-ho for the naval attack, was soon writing to the Director of the Operations Division at the Admiralty, Admiral Arthur Leveson, 'urging the Greeks to assist at once in the Dardanelles operations with an army, which they should land on the northern side of the Gallipoli Peninsula [while] our fleet is occupying the forts on the Dardanelles side'.[15] This was a notable shift in opinion by Richmond. The naval attack was now regarded only as a means of distracting the fire of the forts while an army landed and captured them.

The key figure, however, as far as the Dardanelles or any other operations involving the navy were concerned, was the First Sea Lord. Fisher, though, was playing a very oblique game. He was uneasy about the naval plan because he could see no army in sight to assist it, but chose to hide these fears from Churchill. At the same time he tried to undermine the Dardanelles by indirect means. Thus on 18 January 'while not minimizing the coming Dardanelles operation', he pleaded with the First Lord to concentrate on bringing in Holland, '[which] would finish the War'.[16] Then on the 20th he warned Churchill that Jellicoe had sunk into 'a temporary depression', partly because of the fleet's weakness in destroyers, noting that 16 were on their way to the Dardanelles.[17] These were arguments that were easily disposed of by Churchill. He knew that Fisher was aware that bringing in Holland represented insuperable diplomatic difficulties. As for Jellicoe, Churchill suggested a reorientation of destroyers in home waters which he thought should ease Jellicoe's mind. Fisher, however, remained obdurate. He insisted that the 16 destroyers heading for the Dardanelles be brought home and be replaced by French vessels—an impossibility, as he must have known that the French had no such force to spare.[18]

Had Churchill but known it, however, Fisher was being much more direct with others in his correspondence about the Dardanelles. On 19 January, just six days after the crucial War Council meeting, Fisher wrote to Jellicoe:

> And now the Cabinet have decided on taking the Dardanelles solely with the Navy, using 15 battleships and 32 other vessels, and keeping out there three battle cruisers and a flotilla of destroyers—*all urgently required in the decisive theatre at home!* There is only one way out, and that is to resign! But you say '*no*' which simply means I am a consenting party to what I absolutely disapprove. *I don't agree with one single step taken,* so it is fearfully against the grain that I remain on in deference to your wishes.[19]

It is difficult to know what was passing through Fisher's mind at this point. So far from disagreeing with a single step (at least at the War Council), it was he who had added the *Queen Elizabeth* to the bombardment fleet, agreed to the concentration of the other ships, including the destroyers, and approved Carden's plan. As for staying on in deference to Jellicoe, there is no evidence that he had canvassed the issue of resignation with the commander-in-chief of the navy. What then was the cause of this outburst?

There seems to have been a number of pressures operating on the First Sea Lord, intertwined and acting in combination. The first was the sheer pressure of the job. It would be easy to conclude that Fisher had been driven to distraction by the stress of presiding over Britain's vital instrument of war and that no further explanation need be sought for the erratic nature of his actions. To the stresses of the job, however, should be added Richmond's insight that Fisher enjoyed his popularity and did not want it jeopardized by what he saw as extraneous, risky operations, be they at Borkum or the Dardanelles. However, against this he wished to maintain the persona of the daredevil sea dog in the Nelson tradition (one of his favourite, yet meaningless, aphorisms was 'think in oceans, shoot at sight'). This internal conflict did not help Fisher deal with the pressure of his job.

Publicly, anyway, since the beginning of the war Fisher had projected the apparently consistent position that no ships should be committed to peripheral naval operations without accompanying troops. This had been the essence of his 'Turkey Plan', his 'Holland Plan' and the basis for his objection to the bombardment of the Belgian coast if the British army was not to advance in step with it. Yet he had agreed to Carden's troopless enterprise. Why? Probably because he thought that an army would be found from somewhere and act in conjunction with the fleet, and because of the assurances from Churchill, Kitchener and most members of the War Council that the operation could immediately be broken off in the event of failure. In addition, despite his lamentations to Jellicoe, he knew that the ships to be used were surplus to requirements and that the operation, even if it failed, would not endanger British naval supremacy. How could he veto a seemingly riskless operation that he admitted might succeed through the sheer ineptitude of the Turks?[20] So Fisher consented to the operation, but he consented reluctantly and his fears were growing. However, late in January he had not conveyed these fears to his political master.

He had, however, conveyed his opinions to other members of the War Council, no doubt in the hope that they would bring the required pressure to bear on Churchill—in short, that they would do the job he feared to face. Apart from Jellicoe, Fisher had expressed reservations about the operation to Hankey, who told Asquith.[21] This should have alarmed Asquith but apart from asking Venetia Stanley for her views, he did nothing.

This inactivity on the part of the Prime Minister finally forced Fisher to act. During the early hours of 25 January he composed a long memorandum to Churchill. When the First Lord arrived at work at 10.00 a.m., it was on his desk.

Fisher's paper was entitled 'Memorandum by the First Sea Lord on the Position of the British Fleet and its Policy of Steady Pressure'.[22] Briefly, its argument was that Britain should husband its fleet (including the old ships because they contained reserve manpower for the Grand Fleet) for a decisive encounter with the Germans in the North Sea. This battle was only a matter of time because the pressure of British sea power would compel the Germans to seek a decision or be blockaded out of the war. As for 'coastal bombardments', their sole justification was 'to force a decision at sea' and it was the 'first function' of the British army to assist the navy in achieving this result. This was what happened in the Napoleonic Wars and what should happen now. He was therefore opposed to such operations as the Dardanelles and Zeebrugge because they did not contain the necessary military component. If troops were provided he would have no complaint but he understood that this was not to happen and that 'the English [sic] Army is apparently to continue to provide a small sector of the allied front in France, where it no more helps the Navy than if it were in Timbuctoo'. He concluded that the influence of sea power on warfare was a slow process that required much patience and that Britain 'being already in possession of all that a powerful fleet can give a country we should continue quietly to enjoy the advantage without dissipating strength on operations that cannot improve the situation'.[23]

This document was a curious construction. It contained much specious argument but was also the key to the First Sea Lord's deeply held, but seldom publicized, strategic views. To dispose of the speciousness first: Fisher seemed to imagine that the climactic episodes of the wars against Napoleon were the Battles of the Nile, Copenhagen and Trafalgar, and that the contribution of the British army was to facilitate those battles. The fact was that the real climacterics were Leipzig, Moscow and finally Waterloo. And at Waterloo, so far from relying on sea power, Britain had to involve itself directly in the land war to assist its allies in delivering to Napoleon the knock-out blow.

Fisher's view of the war that he was actually fighting was equally bizarre. The supremacy of Britain at sea provided the context in which it could fight the war and Fisher was correct in pointing to this matter as vital. However, it was hardly the fact that the Dardanelles squadron in any way endangered that supremacy. Apart from one modern battleship and a battlecruiser, the remainder of the squadron could not fight in a line of battle against the main units of the German navy. The units of the Grand Fleet that could undertake this task were in such overwhelming superiority in the North Sea that all the Germans had managed was a tip-and-run bombardment of Scarborough and Whitby. Nor was Fisher's point about reserve manpower well made. The navy already had men surplus to requirements. Twelve thousand of these men had in fact been formed into a division of infantry by Churchill. As for coastal bombardments being justified only to force a decision at sea, this was nonsense. In fact, all of Churchill's plans had been in the direction of using the navy to influence the land war. This had been behind Borkum, operations in the Baltic, Zeebrugge and now the Dardanelles. In as much as anyone had suggested an end target for the bombarding squadron, it was probably imagined that its appearance before Constantinople would overawe the Turks and force them out of the war.[24] One prop, in this view, would have been knocked from under Germany. In brief the end result would positively (or so its advocates imagined) effect the *land* war.

Fisher's statement that the army in France was of no use to the navy is astonishing. The army, it hardly needs stating, was in France not to assist the navy but to help prevent the German army (which was also in France, if Fisher had not noticed) overrunning Western Europe. In short, Fisher's idea that Britain was fighting a naval war with some military add-ons was quite wrong. It *was* fighting a naval war but it was also fighting a deadly war on land which looked like being endlessly protracted. Churchill had at least grasped that much. Fisher had not.

Nevertheless, it was probably the title of the paper and its last paragraph that caught Churchill's attention because they both implied that Fisher was opposed to *any* extraneous naval operations, whether troops were a component of them or not. Sea power, he was saying, was a matter of slowly strangling an enemy over a long period of time. It enabled Britain to keep its supply lines open while closing those of the enemy. For the navy this should be enough. There should be no adventures involving even a fragment of the force that was accomplishing that feat.

After reading this Churchill was quick to realize that, despite the verbiage with which it was surrounded, Fisher's paper represented a dire threat not just to the Dardanelles operation but to all his other schemes as well. As a countermove he wrote a short letter to Fisher urging him to put his views privately to the Prime Minister before the meeting of the next War Council, scheduled for 28 January.[25] This did not prove sufficient to mollify the First Sea Lord. Fisher replied to Churchill suggesting that he (Fisher) resign and 'revert to roses at Richmond', his London home. He now stated clearly his opposition to any modern battleships being diverted to the Dardanelles and reiterated his determination not to see Asquith or to attend the War Council.[26] In a letter written later the same day he expressed the same views to Asquith.[27]

Eventually Asquith ordered Fisher to attend the War Council and to meet him and Churchill beforehand. At this meeting Asquith thought he had hammered out a compromise. Fisher would not circulate his paper to the Council, Churchill would withdraw the battleships currently bombarding the Belgian coast, and the Dardanelles would go ahead.

At the meeting of the Council, Asquith was quickly disabused of the notion that Fisher had accepted a compromise. Churchill opened proceedings by stating that preparations for the naval attack were in hand and asked whether 'the War Council attached importance to this operation, which undoubtedly involved some risks.'[28] At this point Fisher immediately interjected. He said 'that he had understood that this question would not be raised to-day. The Prime Minister was well aware of his own views in regard to it.' He then left the table and walked towards the window. Kitchener quickly followed and after an animated discussion persuaded Fisher to return.

This was an extraordinary incident but nothing flowed from it. No member of the Council asked Fisher to enlarge on his statement or even why he had left the table. In fact most members already knew of Fisher's reservations about the naval attack. Churchill, Asquith and Kitchener obviously knew; the Marquess of Crewe, Lloyd George and Arthur Balfour testified later that they knew; and Grey and Lord Haldane (the remaining two members of the Council) probably knew. The fact is, as is made manifest by the subsequent discussion, members' enthusiasm for the naval operation overrode the reservations of a First Sea Lord whom many thought slightly potty. Balfour summed up what were the views of most about the Dardanelles attack:

It would cut the Turkish army in two;
It would put Constantinople under our control;
It would give us the advantage of having Russian wheat, and enable Russia to resume exports;
This would restore the Russian exchanges, which were falling owing to her inability to export, and causing great embarrassment;
It would also open a passage to the Danube;
It was difficult to imagine a more helpful operation.

At which point Grey chimed in with the comment that 'it would also finally settle the attitude of Bulgaria and the whole of the Balkans'.[29]

Against attitudes such as these Fisher hardly stood a chance. The War Council was just not interested in his views.

Churchill, however, was concerned that Fisher's views might threaten his determination that the navy could materially assist in shortening the land war. After the meeting he spoke to Fisher alone and urged him to support the Dardanelles plan. According to Churchill, Fisher agreed but it was only agreement under pressure. And it was short-lived, for the next day found him writing to Churchill:

Not a grain of wheat will come from the Black Sea unless there is military occupation of the Dardanelles! And it will be the wonder of the ages that no troops were sent to cooperate with the Fleet with half a million . . . soldiers in England![30]

* * *

While Fisher was losing his fight with the War Council, preparations for the attack were moving forward. Oliver outlined the method by which the forts would be attacked—slow, methodical bombardment from the larger vessels while the smaller ships, together with seaplanes, spotted for the fall of shot.[31] He was in no doubt that the fleet could get through. He then passed the plan over to Jackson for a more detailed examination. Jackson reported on 13 February. He thought that some battleships would get through but went on to say:

> The provision of the necessary military forces to enable the fruits of this heavy undertaking to be gathered must never be lost sight of . . .. To complete the destruction [of the forts at the Narrows], strong military landing parties with strong covering forces will be necessary. It is considered, however, that the full advantage of the undertaking would only be obtained by the occupation of the Peninsula by a military force acting in conjunction with the naval operations, as the pressure of a strong field army of the enemy on the Peninsula would not only greatly harass the operations, but would render the passage of the Straits impracticable by any but powerfully-armed vessels, even though all the permanent defences had been silenced.
>
> The naval bombardment is not recommended as a sound military operation, unless a strong military force is ready to assist in the operation, or, at least, follow it up immediately the forts are silenced.[32]

The trajectory of this memorandum was clear enough. Some battleships might get through the Straits but this would serve little purpose as many Turkish guns would be left intact and could therefore prevent unarmoured supply ships from following the warships with essential stocks of ammunition and other provisions. The only way of ensuring that all enemy guns were dealt with was to land a military force to destroy them. So Jackson was saying that the fleet could get through but that it would reap no benefit without soldiers to occupy the Gallipoli Peninsula.

At about the same time Richmond had reached a similar conclusion. The day after Jackson's paper he wrote a memorandum entitled 'Remarks on Present Strategy', in which he called for an army to be landed at

Gallipoli to convert what might only be a 'local success' into something more permanent.[33] What the local success actually was remained unspecified by Richmond. Probably he agreed with Jackson that some heavily armoured ships could get through, but their operations would be short-lived if they could not be resupplied.

The thrust of the Jackson/Richmond papers was definitely opposed to an operation by ships alone. Together with Fisher's hesitations (only Oliver still thought that the ships would need no military help), it might be thought that their papers should have proved fatal to the purely naval plan. But it needs to be emphasized that neither Fisher nor Richmond nor Jackson had explicitly stated that a naval attack was impossible. Indeed, Fisher had not argued this case at all. As for Jackson and Richmond, both, although with considerable equivocation, thought that some battleships could get through. For most of the War Council (including Churchill) this was deemed to be the crucial factor. It was the appearance of such a force before the Turkish capital that they believed would compel the government to capitulate or bring about a revolution. In this happy instance no soldiers would be needed except for occupation duties after the surrender. Matters of supply and reinforcement in this scenario did not enter the equation. By dangling the prospect of a force of battleships appearing before Constantinople, Churchill's naval advisers therefore allowed the War Council to arrive at their preferred conclusion, namely, that a cheap operation from which it was easy to disengage could be undertaken.

It would not do, however, to think of the War Council as a body with firm, well-thought-out views on matters strategic. There was a distinct tendency for them to be convinced by the last military man who spoke to them. By mid-February quite a few military and naval personnel had made their views about the Dardanelles known to War Council members, and it was obvious to the civilians that these views had undergone considerable change.

It all started with Fisher and others at the Admiralty convincing the Secretary of the War Council, Maurice Hankey, that a purely naval attack was futile. Hankey, therefore, now started putting pressure on members of the War Council to send troops to the Dardanelles.

Soon after his meeting with Fisher, Hankey told Balfour that 'from Lord Fisher downwards every naval officer in the Admiralty who is in the secret believes that the Navy cannot take the Dardanelles without troops'.[34] He added he had informed Asquith that Churchill's opinion that a 'ships alone' operation could still succeed was not to be trusted. Asquith was much influenced by Hankey and agreed that a 'fairly strong military force' should be assembled to assist the fleet.[35]

In fact by this time Churchill was also having second thoughts. He had read Jackson's memorandum which asserted that the ships could get through but would achieve nothing of importance without troops. He was certainly aware of Fisher's doubts and perhaps had seen Richmond's memorandum recommending 30,000 men be landed on the Gallipoli Peninsula.[36]

Indeed, such was the strength of feeling on the issue of military support for the naval undertaking that another impromptu War Council was summoned, on 16 February. Just Asquith, Lloyd George, Churchill, Fisher, Grey and Kitchener were present. They decided to send the 29 Division (the last of Britain's prewar Regular divisions) and a contingent of troops from Egypt to the island of Lemnos in the northern Aegean 'in case of necessity to support the naval attack on the Dardanelles'.[37]

So by 16 February most politicians on the War Council were coming to the view that troops would be needed to support the fleet after all. But this did not mean that the addition of troops would convert the naval-only plan into a combined operation.

For one thing, the naval bombardment was scheduled to start on 19 February, so neither the 29 Division nor the other forces would be present or ready with an operational plan to be carried out in conjunction with the naval attack. In fact no thought had been given by the War Council as to what these troops were to do. Members of the Council probably thought that they might mop up a number of guns not destroyed by the fleet (as recommended by Jackson) or be used as occupation forces after the Turks had surrendered. None of this was stated, however: all was left desperately vague.

Moreover, the proponents of troops seemed to be overlooking one large fact. Most had suggested landing the troops on the Gallipoli Peninsula in order to deal with the guns that might not be destroyed by the ships. Yet there were many guns on the Asiatic side of the Straits. The Mitchell Committee identified a total of 111 guns on the European side of the Straits and 121 on the Asiatic side.[38] Neither Jackson nor Richmond nor Fisher had suggested landing troops in Asia Minor to take care of the larger number of guns there. But how could unarmoured ships ply the Straits, either to pass troops through the Narrows or to maintain the fleet before Constantinople, if the Asiatic guns were not destroyed? In other words, occupying one side of the Straits would be useless. This aspect of the military component of the plan, which would have proved fatal to its prospects, was not considered by anyone at the Admiralty.

The first definite statement about what these troops might do came from Churchill. On 18 February he urged Kitchener to place 50,000 men in reach of the Dardanelles, in order to occupy the Peninsula once the Turks had evacuated it and then to occupy Constantinople if a revolution took place. In short, he was arguing for troops to carry out occupation duties in some weeks time rather than for operations to assist the fleet immediately as part of a combined operation. Yet he also argued that an essential part of the troop deployment be the Regulars of 29 Division.

This did not make sense. There was no need for Regular troops to be used for occupation duties; Anzac forces then training in Egypt would do admirably. What lay behind Churchill's thinking? Two explanations suggest themselves. First, Churchill might have thought that by the time Carden was advancing on Constantinople it would be a prudent matter if a British Regular division accompanied him, because the troops might prove the decisive factor in convincing the Turks that Britain was indeed serious and thus add to the forces compelling them to surrender. Or he might have been shaken in his view that the fleet could get through unaided, that real fighting might take place on the Peninsula or before Constantinople, and in these scenarios only British Regulars would do.

Whatever the impulse behind Churchill's thoughts, they immediately put him at odds with Kitchener. At a meeting of the War Council on 19 February, Kitchener surveyed the position in the east. He noted that the Turks were retreating from the line of the Suez Canal and considered that this would free the 39,000 Australian and New Zealand troops, training and carrying out garrison duties near the canal zone, for occupation duties at the Dardanelles. He was therefore retaining the 29 Division in Britain in case the weakening Russian position resulted in a transfer of more German troops to the Western Front.[39] Churchill's reaction to this news perhaps revealed his changed position regarding the prospects of the purely naval attack. He said:

> It would be a great disappointment to the Admiralty if the [29] Division was not sent out. The attack on the Dardanelles was a very heavy naval undertaking. It was difficult to overrate the military advantages which success would bring. . . . In his opinion, it would be a thrifty disposition

on our part to have 50,000 men in this region. . . . He was sending out ten trained battalions of the Naval Division. Neither these, however, nor the Australians and New Zealanders could be called first-rate troops at present, and they required a stiffening of regulars . . . .. We should never forgive ourselves if this promising operation failed owing to insufficient military force at the critical moment.[40]

Asquith tried to come to the aid of Churchill by reading out some extracts from a 1906 report on the Dardanelles (no doubt provided by Hankey), which noted that any operation without military co-operation was bound to fail. (The report also stated that even a combined operation stood little chance, but it seems certain that this section was not read out by Asquith.) Kitchener, however, would not budge. He reluctantly agreed that transports could be made ready for the 29 Division if the situation on the Western Front improved, but that was all.[41]

In one sense this was a distinctly odd decision by Kitchener. He was apparently arguing that hordes of German troops from the east could be stemmed by the arrival of just one British division on the Western Front. In other ways, however, the decision was not odd at all. What Kitchener was doing at the meeting was reflecting the views of a War Office that happened to take seriously the assurances given by Churchill about the naval attack. A memorandum written in February by the Director of Military Operations, General Calwell, stated that the navy would no doubt succeed in forcing the Straits and 'that all the troops will be required to do . . . will be landing . . . to finally destroy works or to render them useless supposing that the garrison should subsequently return. This means comparatively small landing parties of infantry and engineers.'[42] He concluded by stating that further progress by the navy would lead to a more favourable position in Constantinople, and that it was therefore doubtful if any more troops than were already present in the east would be required at all. There was therefore no urgency in making a decision about the 29 Division.[43] This left Churchill and some members of the War Council in an awkward position, for Calwell was merely using arguments that they had used to initiate the naval attack. After all, Churchill had promised that the navy could get through alone. Why was he now calling for a large army to be assembled to assist it?

Nor was it clear that Churchill did not already have what he required. He had called for 50,000 troops. Kitchener had offered 39,000 Australians and New Zealanders, to which could be added the 10,000 men from the Naval Division; that is almost exactly the number Churchill was saying was needed. Yet he now deemed these troops to be unsuitable, even for the occupation duties he claimed were the maximum that they would be called upon to perform. Clearly he had come to accept that troops would be required to fight in order to occupy the Peninsula and allow the fleet through. For this purpose it would be useful to have a 'stiffening of regulars' to support the untested colonial and naval troops. Why did he not simply admit to a change of opinion on troops? Possibly he was unaware of how many of his colleagues on the War Council were coming to the same conclusion, and he was worried that they would withdraw support for the naval attack if they considered large military operations to be in the offing. Perhaps he was reluctant to admit that his first opinions on the operations had been wrong. In any case that admission would now create a difficulty. As the War Council met on 19 February the opening shots of the naval attack had already been fired. To halt operations now would reveal the British design to the Turks and give them ample time to reinforce the Peninsula. Churchill probably hoped that the ships might still get through, a position that Jackson, Richmond and Oliver all supported, though with varying degrees of qualification.

And if the fleet did force the Narrows it was at least a reasonable bet that the Turks might throw in the towel. Should the naval attack be checked however, due to unexpected Turkish resistance, an army would perforce be assembled to deal with it. Churchill would therefore push ahead with naval operations while at the same time pressing for Regular troops. These tactics would cover all contingencies and have the added advantage (so he thought) of keeping Fisher on side. All now depended on the success or otherwise of the naval attack.

As for the War Council as a whole, they had now taken a fateful step. Initially, they had agreed to a naval attack which could be broken off at any time with minimal loss. Now they had dispatched troops to the area. What they were to do was uncertain but troops of varying quality and numbers would be in the vicinity if the naval attack faltered. The slippery slope to the Gallipoli operation had begun.

CHAPTER 3

The Worst-Laid Plans

The defences that an attack at the Dardanelles had to overcome were formidable. First and most obviously were the large-calibre guns situated in a series of forts which ran from the entrance to the Narrows. In all, these contained 108 heavy and medium guns, fairly evenly distributed between the Gallipoli Peninsula and the Asiatic coast. The main concentration of guns (72), however, was in the forts at the Narrows.

In addition to this heavy ordnance, there were 87 more guns protecting the minefields—47 on the European side and 40 on the Asiatic shore. Many of these guns were mobile and could be shifted to danger spots as required.[1]

Then there was the minefield. At the outbreak of war it had consisted of 5 lines of contact mines—a total of 191 mines laid to a depth of 14 feet. By the opening of the naval attack these had been increased to 9 lines containing 271 mines, and by the great attack on 18 March to 11 lines and a total of 344 mines. The minefields were also protected by 12 searchlights.[2]

Adding to this formidable array of weaponry was the nature of the Straits themselves. The prevailing northerly wind blew strongly down the Straits, adding a speed of approximately 4 knots to the already strong current. This might not matter to battleships but would be a considerable factor for smaller, slower craft. The wind also increased the turbulence of the waters which swirled around the entrance to the Straits.

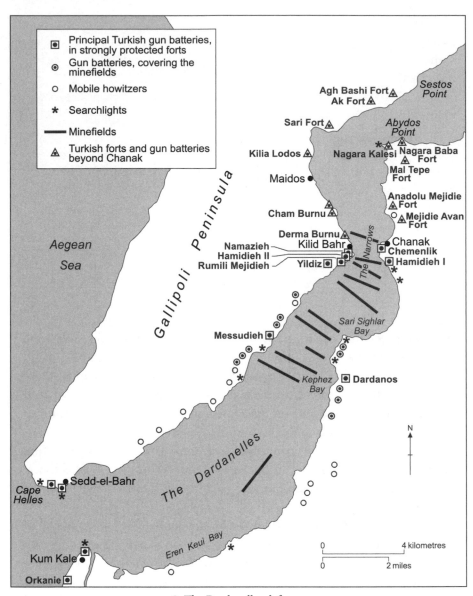

Legend

- ▣ Principal Turkish gun batteries, in strongly protected forts
- ◉ Gun batteries, covering the minefields
- ○ Mobile howitzers
- ✳ Searchlights
- ▬ Minefields
- ▲ Turkish forts and gun batteries beyond Chanak

Sestos Point

Agh Bashi Fort ▲
Ak Fort ▲

Sari Fort ▲

Abydos Point

Kilia Lodos ▲

Nagara Kalesi

Nagara Baba Fort
Mal Tepe Fort

Maidos ●

Anadolu Mejidie Fort

Cham Burnu ▲

Mejidie Avan Fort

Aegean Sea

Gallipoli Peninsula

Derma Burnu ▲
Namazieh
Hamidieh II
Rumili Mejidieh

Kilid Bahr

Yildiz

Chanak
Chemenlik
Hamidieh I

The Narrows

Sari Sighlar Bay

Messudieh

Kephez Bay

Dardanos

The Dardanelles

N

Sedd-el-Bahr

Cape Helles

Eren Keui Bay

| 0 | 4 kilometres |
| 0 | 2 miles |

Kum Kale

Orkanie

3 The Dardanelles defences

Moreover, the Straits are very narrow. At their widest point ships can easily be seen from either side; at the narrowest, large ships seem only a stone's throw away and provide massive targets for even the lightest shore-based artillery.

How was Carden to overcome these considerable obstacles? His first plan, which arrived at the Admiralty on 11 January, had the following features. He would assail the outer forts by 'indirect' bombardment, by which he presumably meant bombardment from long range, with either an aircraft or another ship spotting the fall of shot for accuracy. The mine-field at the entrance (non-existent as it happened) would then be cleared and the fleet would move into the Straits to deal with the guns protecting the successive rows of mines. While this action was proceeding, the forts at the Narrows would be attacked by ships firing across the Peninsula from off Gaba Tepe on the west coast. The minefields would then be swept and any guns remaining be dealt with from close range by the battleships. Carden estimated that the amount of ammunition required would be 'large'; that he would require 12 battleships, 3 battlecruisers (2 of which should enter the Marmara to deal with the *Goeben*), 3 light cruisers, 16 destroyers, 12 minesweepers (including 'perhaps' 4 fleet sweepers), 4 sea-planes and various other attendant ships. With this force he thought he 'might do it all in a month about'.[3]

This plan was very short on anything but the barest details. However, as it happened the Admiralty had no intention of allowing the admiral on the spot to develop it any further. Instead, in what must be deemed a peculiar process indicating a lack of confidence in Carden, the plan was given to Admirals Jackson and Oliver to complete.

Over the next few weeks Jackson and Oliver wrote four papers on the operation. All were dispatched to Carden. Although, in total, the length of these papers was considerable, the insights they contained were not. At the end of the day they added little to Carden's first plan and in some instances confused the issues confronting him.[4]

There were some basic points of agreement, however. Jackson and Oliver both endorsed Carden's plan to carry out the bombardment of the forts at long range. Salvo firing was forbidden. The ships would anchor and fire from just one gun to simplify spotting for the fall of shot. Oliver realized that the spotting aspect would present considerable difficulties at extreme range. He suggested placing other ships close in and the use of seaplanes, both for signalling corrections. Carden's plan to bombard the Narrows forts from across the Straits off Gaba Tepe was endorsed as a trial.

Neither admiral commented in detail on the minefield or its defences. Jackson considered the mines should be swept at night and searchlights on the protecting warships be used to blind the Turkish land-based lights. The only mention of the minefield batteries was a statement that these could be dealt with by the guns of the supporting battleships or cruisers.

As for the amount of ammunition required to deal with the defences, the two admirals differed considerably. Jackson identified 200 guns that had to be knocked out, which happened to be very close to the mark. He then concluded, on what evidence we do not know, that the November bombardment of Turkish forts at the entrance to the Dardanelles had expended 64 heavy shells and destroyed 6 guns. On this calculation 10 rounds would be sufficient to destroy each gun, so 2,000 heavy shells should demolish the Turkish heavy ordnance. To this he added a safety margin of 50 per cent, making a total of 3,000. He also suggested that as the secondary armament of the battleships would be much in use when the fleet closed to decisive range, a similar number of lighter shells should be provided.

On the subject of shells Oliver was all confusion. He argued it was the forts, not the guns they contained, that were to be destroyed. Using the German experience in 1914 against the forts of Antwerp as a guide, he concluded that the *Queen Elizabeth* could demolish all 24 Dardanelles forts with about 10 shells for each fort—a total of just 240×15-inch shells. Yet he also stated that the older battleships should play a considerable role in the bombardment to save wear on the *Queen Elizabeth*'s guns, but was not specific on exactly what this role should be.

Carden's requirements regarding ships were confirmed by Oliver and Jackson, except in two instances. Because of the power of the *Queen Elizabeth* he would receive two dreadnoughts, not three. And there would be no fleet sweepers in the minesweeping force, just 21 North Sea trawlers, manned by civilian crews.

What Carden made of all these papers with their contradictions and lacunae is not known. As far as can be determined he never drew the Admiralty's attention to any aspect of the Jackson/Oliver planning papers. However, it is hardly the case that these documents constituted, either together or separately, a well-thought-out plan. In fact, as products from the senior staff of the largest navy in the world, they represented a lamentable failure to get to grips with most of the important issues confronting Carden.

First, let us consider the matter of shells. Jackson had estimated, on the alleged result of the November bombardment, that 3,000 each of the heavy and lighter armament might be sufficient. However, this figure was the merest guesswork. Jackson had no certain intelligence as to how many Turkish guns the British had destroyed on that occasion. (Even after the war, Turkish estimates varied from one to six guns).

In sharp contrast, Oliver had specified that only several hundred shells from the *Queen Elizabeth* would be needed, but had then gone on to suggest that the older, less accurate ships would also be firing. It is therefore virtually impossible to establish what quantity of shell he thought Carden should receive, except that it was less than Jackson's estimate. In any case Oliver was quite misguided in believing that even accurate shelling of a fort would render its guns useless. Most of the forts were low earthworks of considerable dimensions. Any number of shells could fall within their perimeter without disturbing the guns at all.

Indeed, Oliver's whole Antwerp analogy was not well chosen. At Antwerp, the forts stood out as giant protuberances in a flat landscape—targets that could be seen for miles. So the German howitzers that demolished them not only had the advantage of a stable platform (the land) as against an unstable one (the sea), but their targets were not concealed behind low earthworks as with most forts at the Dardanelles. Finally, the plunging fire of a howitzer was much more accurate at hitting distant targets than the flat trajectory of naval shells.[5]

Was it not possible to be more precise in calculating shell requirements than either the guesswork of Jackson or the false analogies of Oliver indicated? As it happens it was. Indeed, this task was undertaken by the Mitchell Committee specifically to demonstrate that there *was* a scientific method available at the time to estimate the number of shells required to hit small targets at long distance. Briefly, the logic is this. If a gun fires 100 shells in identical conditions of weather, wind and temperature, *and* if the wear on the barrel of each gun is known with some precision, then all 100 shells will land not in the same place but in an area called the 100 per cent zone of the gun (say a rectangle of 50 × 200 yards). The number of shells that will hit a small target like a gun located within that area is therefore very small. Range tables produced for the *Queen Elizabeth* suggest that at 20,000 yards it would obtain a 0.55 per cent hitting rate on a gun and that at 12,000 yards this would increase to 3.1 per cent. So even under ideal conditions, the most modern British battleships (of which there were just two at the

Dardanelles) at quite close range could expect just 3 shells in 100 to hit a gun. If any of the factors (such as wind speed) varied and no corrections were made, the hitting rate would of course be reduced. For the 10 older ships the rate was much lower, about 1.6 per cent at 12,000 yards. Therefore taking all ships together, on average their shells could, on an optimistic assessment, be expected to hit a gun from a distance of 12,000 yards on just 2 occasions in 100. Each enemy gun would therefore require 50 shells on average to destroy it, and as there were 200 guns a total of 10,000 heavy shells would be needed. In fact the total would be much greater than that because in actual operations of war the factors of weather and wear on the guns would not remain constant. Any prudent calculation would have at least doubled this figure, giving a total in the order of 20,000 shells. It is lamentable that no one at the Admiralty thought to make a methodical calculation of the shell requirements at the time.

Had these calculations been carried out, however, an unpalatable conclusion must have followed. The gun barrels of the pre-dreadnoughts were already worn (to differing degrees) when the ships arrived at the Dardanelles. The firing of over 1,500 shells by each ship in the course of the attack would have wrecked their gun barrels many times over. So a calculation that 20,000 rounds or more were needed would have revealed the need for a huge supply of new or re-bored gun barrels. As no such stock existed, this fact alone might have put paid to the whole conception of an attack by the navy alone.

On the difficult matter of spotting, neither Oliver nor Jackson provided a workable solution. They suggested that seaplanes be used to establish the fall of shot but failed to recognize that seaplanes lacked sufficiently powerful engines to undertake this task. When radios were fitted to the seaplanes to allow instant communication with the ships, the weight of the radios prevented the planes from reaching the altitude needed either to spot or to avoid the fire of the Turkish guns. Indeed, even Turkish rifle fire was able to threaten the planes.

Yet without radios, the planes would be almost useless. After observing a fall of shot, they would have to fly back to their ship and drop the necessary corrections in a waterproof pouch which the ships would have to retrieve. By that time the required adjustment to the gun would, in all probability, be out of date, as conditions of wind and weather would have changed.

What was needed for the ships was a large number of the more powerful aeroplanes whose pilots had gleaned some operational experience from the

Western Front. Whether any could have been made available is another matter, but in the planning stage of the operation the question was not asked.

As it happened, therefore, the fleet had no reliable spotting force. What this meant was that the ships had no sure way of correcting their fire because the decision to engage the forts at distances of 13,000 yards meant that they could not be certain exactly where their shells were falling. This reduced most of their firing to a matter of chance.

The question of minesweeping was another issue that did not receive sufficient attention from either Jackson or Oliver. Both men seemed to assume it was a minor matter that could be carried out at night while attendant ships kept down fire from the minefield batteries. This was a gross underestimation of one of the most difficult problems facing Carden. The batteries protecting the minefields were carefully located behind ridges or folds in the ground where the fire from flat trajectory guns could not hit them. No matter how much fire was poured in their general direction by the fleet, these enemy batteries could be assured of their safety and concentrate all their efforts on sinking the sweepers.

The composition of the sweeping force provides another indication that the Admiralty was not taking this problem seriously. Carden had asked (if tentatively) for some fleet sweepers. These were relatively fast vessels that could sweep for mines at the head of a fleet without impairing greatly the speed at which it could proceed. Instead he received 21 North Sea fishing trawlers, which could barely make 5 or 6 knots with their sweeps out and which were manned by civilian crews. This meant that they could hardly make headway against the Dardanelles current, especially when that was strengthened by the prevailing wind. The result was that on many days the trawlers struggled even to reach the minefields inside the Straits. Moreover, the ineffectiveness of the guns of their supporting ships ensured that on those occasions when they were able to sweep, they did so under heavy fire. And in this motley force, not only were the crews amateurs. The naval commander put in charge had the distinction of having had no minesweeping experience at all.[6]

That minesweeping was no minor matter in this operation can be illustrated by the use of a counter-factual scenario. Jackson and Oliver had spent a great deal of time considering how the ships were going to demolish the forts or the guns which they contained. But let us imagine for a moment that there were no forts at the Dardanelles. Without them Carden's force could certainly have safely entered the Straits to a point near the edge of the first line of mines. But then the problem of how the mines were to be swept to clear a path for his fleet would have reasserted itself. And in this matter it was not fire from the forts that prevented progress being made, it was fire from the minefield batteries (assuming that the pitifully weak minesweeping force ever reached the minefield to provide them with targets). Thus, even without the forts to distract him, Carden had not been provided with a force appropriate to deal with the real obstacle at the Dardanelles—the minefield and its protecting batteries.

Simple matters of seamanship were also neglected by Oliver and Jackson. Both men had agreed that it would be necessary to anchor the ships to provide as stable a firing platform as possible. What neither of them considered was that the strong current flowing down the Dardanelles would make this a difficult task. Anchors, fore and aft, would stabilize a ship to some extent but would not be sufficient to negate the effect of the current. No matter how well anchored they were, the ships would still bob and pitch, making accurate firing at long distance something of a lottery.

Even had Carden's fleet forced the Straits, it faced formidable obstacles. Carden had asked for three dreadnoughts, two of which were to steam through and deal with the formidable German battlecruiser *Goeben*. The Admiralty only supplied him with two, one of which, the *Queen Elizabeth*, was forbidden to go through the Straits. This would have left Carden with the *Inflexible* as the only British ship capable of fighting the *Goeben*. The result of this contest is speculative but design flaws in the *Inflexible*'s class of battlecruiser meant it was not a foregone conclusion that it would have prevailed, a fact that might have left the *Goeben* free to pick off at will the older ships in Carden's force.

Furthermore, had Carden's squadron reached Constantinople, in all probability he would have achieved little. In keeping with the more civilized standards of those times, he had been forbidden to bombard the city. All, then, hinged on the Turks surrendering at the appearance of the British squadron. Had they not obliged, what might Carden have done? The most likely scenario is that he would have been forced to retreat down the Straits, confronting along the way those defences that had not been obliterated. In this instance it is highly unlikely that any of his ships would have returned unscathed.

So, to summarize, the Admiralty sent Carden to do battle with the formidable defences of the Dardanelles using assumptions that were false, with an inappropriate force structure (particularly in regard to minesweepers and aircraft), with major matters such as spotting neglected, with uncertain estimates of the amount of ammunition required and a basic ignorance of the strength of the minefield defences.

We can only speculate about the reasons why the naval advice was so poor. There is some evidence that Oliver thought little of the Turks and considered that in the end questions of morale would decide the issue. In early February he noted:

> It is expected that the slow, irresistible destruction of the forts by vessels which cannot be reached effectively by their fire will have a great effect on the morale of the garrisons of whose forts have yet to be attacked, and will go far to shake the confidence of the Turks in their German advisers, and it may possibly result in the overthrow of the German rule in Constantinople.[7]

In short, the appearance of a mighty array of battleships off the Dardanelles would crack Turkish morale. Further details were therefore unnecessary.

Jackson's advice concentrated on the question of ships fighting forts and seems rooted in the nineteenth century, where modern weapons such as minefields protected by complex land defences did not exist. Perhaps this is the clue—the changed nature of war in 1915 was beyond him.

While we may never be able to fathom the pitiful quality of Jackson's and Oliver's analyses, what we can say with more certainty is that had the naval advice been of a higher calibre and identified all the difficulties detailed above, and drawn them to the attention of the Admiralty War Group, it is a reasonable proposition that the operation would have met the same fate as Borkum, the Baltic and other Churchillian schemes. After all, trenchant criticism from admirals such as Jellicoe had stopped those adventures in their tracks. It is therefore probable that had good naval advice been tendered there might have been no naval attack at the Dardanelles and no land campaign at Gallipoli.

CHAPTER 4

The Rise and Fall of the Naval Attack

The first naval attack began at 9.51 a.m. on the morning of 19 February. No fewer than seven battleships were involved (*Inflexible*, *Triumph*, *Vengeance*, *Cornwallis* from the Royal Navy and *Suffren*, *Gaulois* and *Bouvet* from the French squadron). Later, the *Queen Elizabeth*, *Agamemnon* and *Albion* joined in. On paper this seems a formidable force but apart from the *Inflexible* and *Queen Elizabeth* all the ships were of ancient vintage. The older ships had all been built around the turn of the century before the all-big-gun ship revolution brought about by the *Dreadnought*. Their armament therefore consisted of a mixture of heavy guns and lighter pieces, but no ship had more than 4 big guns and none of those was larger than 12-inch. None had been fitted with modern systems of fire control whereby the big guns could be simultaneously fired by a central controller. More importantly, it is likely that all the gun barrels of ships of this age had worn, making consistently accurate firing impossible. It can also be assumed that the crews of these vessels did not represent the cream of the British and French services. De Robeck, Carden's second in command, called them 'grandfathers' and noted that they 'should hardly have been sent out during a "show" of this sort'.[1] Admiral Wemyss, at this time Governor of Lemnos, agreed, lamenting the state of the crews and concluding 'the whole lot are quite finished'.[2] The best crews were of course on first-rate ships in the North Sea watching the Germans.

Just to look at photographs of the Dardanelles squadron must have been unsettling, even at the time. The ships seem to have come from another age, their odd shapes and paucity of heavy guns giving them an almost pre-modern appearance. The French ships looked decidedly odd. Each was different, the French at this time not designing classes of ships like the British.

The opening of the attack was not auspicious. The first shot was fired by the *Cornwallis* at Fort Orkanie on the Asiatic side of the entrance to the Dardanelles. It missed by a considerable distance. *Cornwallis* then broke down and had to be replaced by the *Vengeance.* This ship, *Suffren* and *Triumph* then opened fire at the same fort and again missed by a wide margin. Oddly, given his instructions, Carden had ordered all his ships to fire while under way. The lack of results led him to obey the Admiralty directions and anchor.[3] Lamentably for the Allies this brought no improvement. Not a hit was landed on any of the forts at the entrance. However, this was not apparent to Carden who interpreted the feeble Turkish response as evidence of great damage being inflicted on their guns. After maintaining steady fire until 2.00 p.m., Carden considered that the forts had been sufficiently destroyed for the ships to close in so that their secondary armament could be brought into play. The entire squadron then closed and poured a hail of fire into the forts. By the end of the day, however, even though the forts had been under bombardment for eight hours by ten battleships, often at close range, the results were derisory. Two Turkish officers and four men had been killed, but of the 27 guns in the entrance forts not a single one had been put out of action.[4]

In fact, if the 'hail of fire' is analyzed it did not amount to very much. Because of the restrictions placed on the use of ammunition and the ban placed on salvo firing, only 139 shells from the ships' primary armament had been fired. It will be recalled that these old ships had about a 1.6 per cent chance of hitting a small target from long range with their heavy shells, if conditions and the state of their guns were perfect. This means that of the 139 × 12-inch shells fired, about 2 shells would be expected to hit a gun. As it happened, on this first day they did not. The ships did fire 760 rounds from their smaller guns but many of these shots were fired at lesser targets such as field batteries. Other shells were too small to do significant damage to the forts and their guns even had they hit them.

Carden's summary of the day's action was a mixture of insight and obtuseness. He noted:

The effect of long-range bombardment on modern earth work forts is slight; Forts No. 1 and 4 appeared to be hit on many occasions by 12-in common shell well placed but when ships closed in all four guns of these forts opened fire.[5]

The admiral had at least grasped that the day had not gone well, but his remarks on the inability of the ships to demolish earthwork forts indicate that his thinking was as wide of the mark as his gunnery. His task was not to demolish the forts whether they were made of earth or brick or stone but to destroy the guns which they contained. He might have reflected (but did not) that if he could not destroy the forts, any chance he had of destroying their guns was weepingly remote. The other group that also might have grasped this point, the 'high authorities' at the Admiralty, made no comment. The bombardment would be renewed on the morrow.

As it happened there was no action by the fleet on the next day or on the four subsequent days.[6] The weather (a factor to which only Carden seems to have paid any attention, warning the Admiralty that favourable conditions could not be expected before the end of February) turned rough almost as soon as the ships had dropped anchor on 19 February.[7] On the 20th, according to an eyewitness on the *Albion,* it was 'blowing like billioo'.[8] By the 24th the same eyewitness was venting his frustrations in his diary: 'I wish the weather would get calm & let us get on with the work. It is all in favour of brer Turco [sic] having a breathing space.'[9]

That breathing space came to an end on 25 February. The weather cleared sufficiently to allow the bombardment to resume but not sufficiently for the seaplanes to spot for the fleet, thus depriving the ships of their eye in the air. Nevertheless, this was to prove the most successful day of the naval attack. Fire was opened at 10.00 a.m. and within 40 minutes the 15-inch guns of the *Queen Elizabeth* had hit two guns of Fort No. 1 at Helles. Shortly after that (and much more surprisingly) the 12-inch guns of the pre-dreadnought *Irresistible* destroyed two guns at Kum Kale on the Asiatic shore. Many more hours of firing from various ships followed but there were no more successes. Notwithstanding that, it had been a good day. The *Queen Elizabeth* had only fired 31 shells and the *Irresistible* 35, and 4 long-range Turkish guns were no more.[10] A mood of euphoria swept through the fleet. Admiral Guepratte, commanding the French squadron, wrote: 'An excellent day . . . allowing us to auger well for the success of the campaign'.[11] A moment's reflection, however, should have had a sobering effect. The range tables for the guns of the *Queen Elizabeth* and *Irresistible* indicate that the modern ship had, at the distance, about a 3 per cent chance of hitting and the older ship a 2 per cent chance—an average chance of 2½ per cent. Yet on this day they had achieved three times this rate of success. There is nothing to indicate that the ships had done anything different in their gunnery on the 25th or that the weather conditions were particularly favourable. Neither could accurate spotting have been a factor because on that day the weather did not allow for spotting. In other words no conclusions at all should have been drawn from the fact that out of a small number of shells fired, four had found a target.

Indeed, there is every indication that any mood of optimism was short-lived. Carden was well aware that despite the destruction wrought on 25 February, many guns still remained in action at the entrance to the Straits. He therefore arranged for demolition parties to be landed the next day to complete the work.

At 2.30 p.m. on 26 February the demolition parties and a group of forty-five marines to ward off any Turkish attack landed near Seddelbahr. As soon as the men landed, twenty or thirty Turks commenced sniping from behind the village, forcing the marines to pull back to the fort. At this moment the *Irresistible* opened fire at the enemy and drove them away. Meanwhile the demolition party had found that only one or two guns had been damaged by the bombardment. They set about laying charges against the six largest guns and blew them up. Then they withdrew and re-embarked under the cover of the ships' guns. At the same time a similar scene was being enacted on the Asiatic coast. There the marines landed near Kum Kale but were stopped by a strong group of Turks on a nearby ridge. Some skirmishing followed and casualties were suffered, so it was decided to confine operations to two 4-inch guns and one of the larger guns in Fort No. 4. These were blown up and the force withdrawn. Three guns had been destroyed but the guns at Kum Kale had not been touched.[12]

Nevertheless, Carden decided to persist with landing parties. After all, the relative lack of response from the Turks (who had a division of troops on the Gallipoli Peninsula and who could therefore have intervened in much greater force) and the fact that more guns had been destroyed on that day than in the three-day bombardment by the fleet, gave cause for hope. In fact, subsequent landing parties proved spectacularly successful. On 27 February six howitzers were destroyed at Seddelbahr; on 1 March ten heavy guns and six lighter pieces were blown up at Kum Kale; and on

3 March six light guns (all that remained at Seddelbahr) were dealt with. In all, 48 guns of which 16 were heavy were destroyed by the landing parties. This was a much better rate of return than had been accomplished by the ships and in fact had accounted for all of the major guns in the forts at the entrance to the Straits.[13]

A further demolition party was landed on 4 March to check on the destruction. This time, however, the Turks responded in force. The demolition group at Seddelbahr, though strengthened to 250 men, ran into Turkish soldiers in considerable strength and were forced to withdraw. At Kum Kale a similar group ran into entrenched Turks firing machine guns. After failed attempts by the guns of the supporting ships to deal with the trenches, this force too was withdrawn.[14]

While all this had been going on, desultory operations were taking place inside the Straits. On 26 February *Albion*, *Triumph* and *Majestic* (with escorting destroyers) entered the Straits. Their intention was to cover some minesweepers clearing the entrance (not a difficult task as there were no mines in this area) and to commence the destruction of Forts Nos 7 and 8 (Fort Dardanos on the Asiatic side) located halfway between the entrance and the Narrows. Let Lieutenant W. Gibson, our eyewitness on the *Albion*, describe in some detail what was to become a typical day for the ships during this period:

The destroyers went ahead. We came under fire from a light battery & also a 6″ howitzer battery on N Shore, position unknown probably No 7. . . . We opened fire with fore turret at 13000 [yards] on No 8 Fort Dardanos & planted several . . . 12″ common [shell] bang on top. They did not reply. We were out of range I suppose & I expect they dipped[?] The Majestic now came up & also fired at No 8. The 6″ howitzer unseen battery now began to drop salvos between us and Majestic, nearer her, eventually one almost hit her & she moved. They still continued to plonk them into the same place. She was close to a red buoy & it is believed they use them as ranging marks so we sent a destroyer to sink it . . .. A field gun battery very well mounted half way up a hillside which was covered with small trees & scrub opened fire on the destroyers. The latter steamed about replying. We tried to knock them out but it was impossible to get gunlayers to see them & there were no prominent objects we could use either as description points or aiming marks. So I gave it up. The minelayers [sweepers] coming under fire from supposed No 7 & this field battery were told to retire. A pause ensued then while we went on firing at No 8 with 12″, the field battery stopped. We had drifted down with current perhaps a thousand yards when from the south shore a howitzer battery I should think 4.7″ or perhaps 6″ mounted on a ridge about a mile inland began to fire at us. We were portside on & as soon as I could get the guns on I opened fire. Point of aim was a building with a red roof. This was on the ridge too but to the right so I had 45 knots [degrees][15] left deflection on. Got the range with second salvo [obviously the ban on salvo firing either did not apply to the secondary armament of the battleships or *Albion* was ignoring the order] & let them have it. Several very good salvos. They [the enemy shells] were coming all round. One passed very close over foretop [where Gibson was located] & fell about 50 yards over the ship. Another just before foretop. One went just abaft funnels & one about 3 yards short under [turret] B2 nearly drowned them in B1 and B2. Spray and bits of shell came all over the ship. It was lucky we weren't hit. We burst 8 or 10 x 6″ right on the ridge & silenced them. . . . It was now about 5pm. . . . Signal now came for two ships to relieve Albion and Triumph who were to go to Tenedos & I not sorry.[16]

Here, in this entry, are outlined all the problems that would beset the naval attack: the difficulty of the gunlayers, low down in the ships, to see targets on distant heights; the lack of aiming points on which to lay their guns when the targets were seen; the accuracy of the harassing fire of the mobile howitzers and field batteries, which kept craft of all descriptions moving; and the habit of the Turks of abandoning their guns when the ships found their range, thus rendering it almost impossible to tell whether shells had found their target.

Most notable is the unwillingness of the ships to run much risk, for in Gibson's graphic account, despite the fire on the *Albion* the ship was never actually hit. This policy was of course imposed on such ships as the *Albion*. Oliver at the Admiralty had insisted that few risks be run during the course of the bombardment and Carden, as we know, agreed with this policy. Of course this 'safety first' approach entirely negated one of the basic premises of the whole operation, namely, the expendability of the old ships.

In the days that followed, operations against the inner defences of the Dardanelles therefore took on a most peculiar pattern. On each day (weather permitting) only three or four ships would enter the Straits, fire a few shells at various forts and then retire. Certainly, this was in line with the policy of not risking the ships. But when we investigate the number of shells fired by these ships an additional puzzle emerges. On those days where the numbers of heavy shells fired can be established we have the following:[17]

Date	Shells fired (10-inch and above)
1 March	19
2 March	74
3 March	47
4 March	Nil
5 March	33
6 March	7
7 March	104
8 March	11
Total	**295**

Now we know there were more heavy shells fired at the forts than is indicated in the table. On 5 and 6 March only those shells fired across the Peninsula by the *Queen Elizabeth* were counted. On the 8th we only know for certain that the *Queen Elizabeth* fired 11 shells. Yet on that day the *Vengeance, Canopus, Irresistible* and *Cornwallis* were also firing. So to the 295 heavy shells we know were fired over this period we have to add an additional number of unknown dimension. In these circumstances, let us be generous. Let us suppose that at least another 205 heavy shells were fired in the period. That would give a round figure of 500 shells fired at the Dardanelles defences in the eight days under discussion.

The point to be made is that even this number is pitifully small. Given that only about 1.6 per cent of shells would find their target, Carden could have expected, under perfect conditions, to destroy about 8 of the heavy guns in the forts. Yet he knew with some accuracy that for the defence of the Narrows the Turks had 72 guns of 15-cm and upwards, not counting such formidable intermediate positions as Fort Dardanos. Thus the method being adopted by Carden offered no prospect of early success. Why then was Carden obsessively conserving ammunition?

The obvious answer is that he was following orders. He had been told by Oliver not to hurry operations or to run great risks, and he was therefore proceeding cautiously. Another explanation might be the weather. On some days firing was restricted by an early morning mist or by other unfavourable conditions such as a strong cross wind. Nevertheless, it must be said that on most of the days in question the weather would have accommodated much more firing than actually took place.

A further factor was the difficulty in aerial spotting. Initially, the aircraft sent to the Dardanelles were not supplied with any kind of wireless telegraphy, so communication between the ships and planes was by messages dropped from the air to the vicinity of the ships. Then there was the problem that the crews of both ships and aircraft had had no experience of working together. This resulted in directions given to the gunners being so vague that an appropriate response was not possible or that changes in bearings were not fully understood. In addition, when wirelesses were provided, they proved unreliable and there were no technicians on hand to adjust or repair them. All of this tended to slow down shooting while the difficulties with the aerial spotters were being resolved.[18]

The factor that most authorities have accepted as an explanation for Carden's actions was that he was chronically short of ammunition and obliged to limit its expenditure, especially from his heavy guns. There does seem to be evidence for this. Even before the naval attack commenced, Carden issued an order that 'strict economy of ammunition must be practised on all occasions'.[19] Then after the bombardments of 25 February and 3 March Carden found it necessary to censure the commanders of individual ships for expending too much ammunition.[20]

Yet if the figures noted earlier are even approximately correct in suggesting that Carden had fired just 500 heavy shells, he could not have been experiencing an ammunition shortage. In all he had 12 battleships, so if the firing between ships was about even, each ship had expended just over 40 shells. However, the magazines of these ships held between 250 and 400 shells when full, and it is unlikely that Carden entered the battle with half-empty magazines.

There is further evidence that Carden had plenty of ammunition. On 18 March, the day of the main attack, every battleship available to him took part in the operation, and although we do not know the number of shells fired it must have been considerably more than was fired on any other day. Then on the 19th, after the big attack had failed, Admiral de Robeck (who by then had replaced Carden) telegraphed to Churchill that he was willing to resume the bombardment as soon as possible. Presumably, therefore, he would have been prepared to undertake an attack similar in scope to that of the 18th. In addition, the Admiralty signalled to de Robeck that there was a plentiful supply of 15-inch shell; this was an indication that if such a rare calibre (the *Queen Elizabeth* was the only ship in the British fleet with 15-inch guns) was in plentiful supply, the amount for more common calibres should also have been plentiful. Moreover, there must have been an expectation on de Robeck's part that if by chance the second attack succeeded, he would be arriving in the Marmara with sufficient shells to deal with the *Goeben* and other forms of Turkish resistance. In brief, Carden might have been somewhat short of shells but he was not so short that this would account for his actions (or lack of them) inside the Straits in early March.

There might be a fourth factor. Perhaps Carden's lethargic actions in March were brought about by what he regarded as the minimal chance of success. He had been given very little option by Churchill other than to agree to the operation, and since it had opened Carden had warned the First Lord that the effect of shells on the Turkish defensive works was slight. Knowing this, he might well have been going through the motions in early March while hoping that the continuing discussion about the use of troops (of which more later) would come to fruition.

In any case Carden was not about to get away with these desultory operations for much longer. Back in London, Churchill had noticed the lack of vigour in proceedings at the Dardanelles. Carden was ordered forthwith to prepare for a major attack using the great bulk of his fleet.[21] But before that operation is discussed we must turn our attention to those other operations that had been proceeding inside the Straits—the attempts to clear the Dardanelles minefields.

It will be recalled that although Carden had asked for purpose-built fleet sweepers in his original plan, his wishes had been ignored by the Admiralty and he had been provided with 21 North Sea fishing trawlers manned by civilian crews. Of all the military operations carried out in the benighted Gallipoli campaign, none reached the level of high farce attained by the efforts at minesweeping, although that was hardly the fault of those unlucky enough to be involved in them.

The 'minesweepers' had been in operation since the first day of the attack. They swept off the entrance to the Straits to clear the way for the attack on the outer forts, and they swept off Gaba Tepe in advance of the operations of the *Queen Elizabeth* in that area. These actions were held to have been a success, but the fact is that no mines existed in either area. Therefore when the sweepers first entered the Straits they were, as far as the actual clearing of mines was concerned, something of an unknown quantity.

The element of farce revealed itself from the very beginning. On 27 February, as the trawlers prepared to enter the Straits, a north-easterly gale sprang up and actually drove the ships out towards the entrance. It was a similar story on the 28th. Two days had therefore passed and not a single sweeper had reached the start line for its operations. On the next two nights the trawlers actually entered the Straits but found no mines and retreated in good order. It was not, then, until 3 March that action was joined. On this night the main Kephez minefield was approached by the trawlers with destroyers in close support. Two searchlights were switched on by the Turks which fully illuminated the ships. A barrage of fire from the batteries protecting the minefield followed. The destroyers, blinded by the searchlights, were quite unable to locate the batteries and suppress their fire. The trawlers, unprotected and uncertain of their position, retired. They had not even entered the minefield and consequently had swept no mines. In fact, with their sweeps out they had hardly been able to make headway against the Dardanelles current.

On the days that followed many more attempts were made to sweep the mines. The sweepers were on some occasions accompanied by destroyers which endeavoured to silence the minefield batteries and destroy the searchlights. On other nights the heavier fire from escorting battleships tried to accomplish the same objectives. They failed. Overall 17 attempts were made to sweep the mines of which 12 were directed at the main Kephez minefield. On only two occasions did the sweepers even reach the minefield (on 10 and 13 March), after the civilian crews had been replaced by naval volunteers from the fleet. And on these two occasions the results were hardly rewarding. In total just 2 mines had been swept out of the 387 in the minefield. Ironically, 3 other mines had been swept in the area of Eren Keui Bay. Although this was some distance south from the main field at Kephez and the mines seemed to be at right angles to the lines laid across the Straits, no conclusions were drawn from the experience. This oversight was to have dire consequences.[22]

Finally, on 13 March, under pressure from Churchill, and faced with the absolute failure of the minesweeping operations, Carden called a council of war. All the captains attended and such was the desperation of the situation that an attempt to rush the minefields was considered. After a 'certain amount of hot air' had been talked, the meeting was adjourned to the next day. Then, to the relief of the junior officers present, a rush at the Straits was rejected and a plan for a major bombardment in conjunction with an all-out effort to sweep the mines was substituted. The day of the big attack was fixed at 18 March.[23]

The plan drawn up by Carden's staff was possibly as good as could have been devised in the circumstances. The challenge was to deploy as many of the 16 capital ships against the defences simultaneously as the confined waters of the Straits would allow. The idea developed was to use the ships in three lines. The first line would consist of the most modern ships (*Queen Elizabeth, Agamemnon, Lord Nelson, Inflexible*) with *Prince George* and *Triumph* acting as flank guards. These ships would engage the large forts at the Narrows. The second line, consisting of some of the older French ships, would be placed one mile astern of the advanced group. When considerable damage had been inflicted on the Narrows forts, these second line ships would pass through the first line, complete their demolition at close range and keep the minefield batteries suppressed. After four hours' firing these second-line ships were to be relieved by a similar group of British pre-dreadnoughts placed at the entrance of the Straits.[24]

Two hours after the commencement of the bombardment the sweepers would advance and, taking advantage of the hail of fire directed at the Turkish guns, sweep the mines up to Sari Siglar Bay north of Kephez. Then, on the following day, 19 March, a group of ships would place themselves in this protected stretch of water and deal with any remaining Turkish resistance at the Narrows. Picket boats to search out floating mines would precede each battleship.[25]

In the event these proceedings would not be directed by Carden. Two days before the main attack he collapsed, officially due to nervous dyspepsia, actually because the strain of command had become too much for him.[26] Admiral de Robeck, his second in command, was immediately appointed by Churchill and took charge of the largest British naval operation since Trafalgar in 1805.

There have been many descriptions of the naval attack on 18 March, but a vivid account by a junior officer on the *Prince George* has just come to light and deserves to be cited at length:

18 March. A Big Day indeed. About 10AM Queen Elizabeth, Inflexible, Agamemnon, Lord Nelson moved into Straits line ahead. Prince George & Vengeance on flanks. Four French ships a mile astern. Six destroyers proceeded ahead and attempted to sweep but had to retire under fire from Field Batteries—Turks quite ready. Nearly every ship in action with Field batteries the whole way up.

Four first named ships eventually formed line abreast & proceeded to bombard 5 forts and were also engaging Field Batteries on either flank. Undoubtedly the Turks disclosed a good many new batteries. Nos 8, 9, 13, 19, 20 Batteries [actually forts] were bombarded and the Fleet did some splendid shooting. Saw what was probably a magazine go up. The Forts were shooting much better than previously but still pretty badly, good enough however to get hits on pretty well every ship judging by such opportunities to look around. We were to engage Field batteries and [forts] 7 and 9 . . . on Port Side. Ran into the area again of those beastly howitzers, which are evidently well behind a hill as we failed to locate them in any way. These howitzers are evidently laid on [map] squares and fired when the ships enter their areas. They would undoubtedly do great havoc if more accurately served—missed us and two French ships by feet—would not want one of these on deck. Seem pretty accurate in themselves as 3 and 4 shell invariably fall in quite a small area—Shell have a deafening detonation, undoubtedly high explosive and well detonated. Should consider them the best weapons the Turks have, tho' probably limited range. One Battery or Fort firing pretty good shrapnel with black bursts. One of these burst over Inflexible foretop—Saw the foretop later, the roof was battered in and penetrated in about a dozen places. Part of the roof appeared to have fallen just in front of funnel. Learn later all the control party finished. We had two wounded in crows nest by one of these shell. Got a small splinter in my right temple at the same time. Each ship had a picket boat out in order to deal with mines. Ours had very narrow escapes. Could not but admire them—the picket boat of the Queen Elizabeth particularly was always ahead of the ship, acting as a pilot boat. Even remained about 50 [yards] ahead with the 15″ going over her from Q.E.

We gradually forged ahead of the first line who however continued firing. The French boats came along two on either flank. The two on the port side had each to pass thro' the howitzer area and it was marvellous to see the shell bursting closely around each in turn. I put in the best of my time trying to locate those howitzers but without result. One of these Frenchmen was particularly well handled, steamed up close to the port shore, and put in a rapid and I judged an accurate fire, engaging 8 & 9 Forts and Field Batteries in addition. She got so far up as to interfere with our fire on 9.

Trawlers were to have come in at this time for sweeping operations but the fire was much too hot.

We were hit twice. One just above net shelf port side under bridge. Burst outside luckily but burst a hole about 3″ diameter in ships side. Fragments frequently scattered thro Artificers Mess, piercing bulkheads etc. One in after corner bridge starboard side. Burst on Signalman's box, tore large hole in and out of W Cs under bridge. Fragments got thro' slit of Conning Tower, slightly wounding Captain and Signalman. An Artificer entering W C wounded in side, leg & wrist.

Shortly after this as we were crossing to retire, the Frenchman 'Bouvet' was mined. We saw a tremendous quantity of black smoke arise just abaft funnels on starboard side. Then she commenced gradually to roll towards us, we were about 400 yards to starboard of her. The roll steadily continued till she was keel uppermost then her stern steadily settled down and just as steadily she went under in about 3 minutes from when first struck. It was awful & unnerved us all in the top. There was no time to do anything. Our picket boat was away quickly and we lowered a cutter. Other boats sent their picket boats & a destroyer came along but all survivors were picked up by our picket boat—35 officers and men only. I never want to see the like again.

We were glad when our relief the Majestic came along and we could retire, which we did soon after 2 pm to the entrance of the Straits from where we could see the Fleet firing.

Queen Elizabeth, Inflexible, Agamemnon & Lord Nelson remained in—don't know what others went in. About 3.30 we saw destroyers closing round a Frenchman the Gaulois which was badly down by the bows. It looked as tho' she would sink before she could be beached but eventually she made her way back to shallow water near Rabbit Island.

Later we learn that Irresistible is sinking & Inflexible in a bad way. Destroyers ordered to close round Irresistible & Ocean to tow her. We see the Inflex steaming out briskly with a list to starboard. She anchors in shallow water at Tenedos where we follow her at dusk. 19 March. Awake to learn Irresistible and Ocean are both sunk. Official account mines. As far as I can learn happened in same place as Bouvet . . .. Few casualties on Ocean but about 200 on Irresistible. Crew mustered on deck then subjected to shrapnel & Lyddite [high explosive] fire. Must have been awful.

Three ships sunk, two disabled—no knowledge of effect on shore. Saw a personal message, 16, 19, 20 Forts silenced, only one Fort firing at dusk. Further operations postponed. . . . General despondency.[27]

In fact, events did not unfold quite as described by Hepburn. The *Bouvet* had possibly been struck by a shell from a fort as well as running into the Eren Keui minefield, but in general terms he was correct: three ships had been sunk—*Bouvet*, *Ocean* and *Irresistible*, and three badly damaged—*Inflexible*, *Gaulois* and *Suffren*. Others had sustained more superficial damage. In addition, the silence of the Turkish forts did not mean that the guns had been put out of action. In fact, just one heavy gun had been destroyed by the bombardment and four more temporarily put out of action.[28] No mines had been swept. In short, for no gain, a third of de Robeck's squadron was either at the bottom of the sea or facing extensive repairs.

De Robeck immediately offered to renew the naval attack announcing that 'we are all getting ready for another "go" & not in the least beaten or down-hearted'.[29] However, the renewal of the naval attack had now become a political rather than a naval matter, as we will see in the next chapter. But the decision to veto another attack at the Narrows threw up one of the questions that would dog the historiography of the campaign to this day. Would a renewed attempt have worked and rendered all subsequent operations at Gallipoli unnecessary? It is to this question that we now turn.

There are several factors to be considered in speculating whether a renewed naval attack might have succeeded: the state of the Turkish forts and their ammunition, the state of the minefields and the state of the British fleet after 18 March.

Many authorities (including Churchill) have alleged that the Turkish forts had fired most of their ammunition on 18 March and that a renewed attack would have found them bereft of shells. This is hard to sustain. Various estimates have been made about ammunition supply for the forts and although they differ in detail, a general consensus emerges. There would seem to have been about 55 heavy shells per gun, and between 70 and 250 shells per gun for the lighter calibres. This would have enabled the Turks to sustain a good rate of fire to meet a further two British attacks on the scale of 18 March. But it is also clear that these figures apply to modern armour-piercing shells and that the Turks also had a plentiful supply of older powder-filled shells. While these latter shells would not have inflicted any damage on the warships, they would have been sufficient to keep the ships underway and thereby lessen the accuracy of their fire.[30]

Moreover, despite its longevity in the literature, the matter of shells is irrelevant to the chances of the fleet. What really mattered was the mine-field and on 18 March this had not been touched; nor had its protecting batteries. The main barrier to de Robeck's force therefore remained intact.

As for the Allied fleet, it has to be remembered that one third of it had been sunk and another third put out of action. In addition, because of the damage to the *Inflexible*, there was now no dreadnought available to confront the *Goeben*. Accordingly, the British fleet was in no condition to renew the attack on 19 March, whatever the state of the Turkish forts and their ammunition supply.

What then are we to conclude about the great naval attack? It is hard to avoid the conclusion that it was one of the most poorly thought-out oper-ations of the war. The ships were not equipped to deal with land-based defences, especially those that could not be directly observed. Little thought had been given to the minefields and their protecting batteries, although they formed the key to the entire defensive system at the Dardanelles. The leadership of the bombarding squadron, in the persons of Carden and his staff, performed an impossible task with lamentable inefficiency. The only scintilla of a chance of success that the attack ever had was that the Turks might abandon their defences in the face of a protracted onslaught by the fleet. This was of course the very type of operation eschewed by Carden from the beginning, on the quite spurious grounds that he had a chronic ammunition shortage. Why he behaved in this manner is still puzzling today. If he was trying to ensure that his ships entered the Marmara with full magazines, his supine operations in early March guaranteed that such an event would never take place. In the end, however, it has to be concluded that Carden's behaviour was not a vital ingredient, except that he was not the man to take a stand against the whole conception.

As for the Admiralty, it bears repeating that the advice they gave to Churchill and Carden was of a very low intellectual calibre. No thought had been given to technical questions that were beyond the competence of any civilian (or second-rate admiral) to divine. Perhaps Churchill's War Group was pleased to have a proposed plan by the First Lord of the Admiralty that did not risk the Grand Fleet and endorsed it for that reason. On the other hand, Churchill and most of the War Council knew that some naval authorities (including Fisher) had reservations about the scheme and went ahead nevertheless. The strangeness in the whole discussion, however, is that while the naval attack was being prepared and carried out, these same people were engaged in furious debates about the need for troops to support the attack they had all agreed could be tackled by ships alone. It is to these debates that we must now turn.

CHAPTER 5

No Going Back

At the very moment the first shells from the bombarding fleet were hurtling towards the Turkish forts, opinion in London about the wisdom of the naval endeavour was wavering. Fisher, of course, had not wavered. He was still trying to undermine the naval attack by any means possible. On 19 February he informed Hankey (but not Churchill) that enemy submarines were to be expected at any moment in the eastern Mediterranean and might render naval operations untenable. There was an urgent need for immediate military action.[1] Lloyd George seemed to agree. Ever mindful of his preferred area of operations, the Balkans, he wrote a memorandum for the Cabinet warning that unless a large force was on hand to occupy the Gallipoli Peninsula, the prospect of bringing in to the side of the Triple Entente the 1½ million troops of Bulgaria, Greece and Rumania was remote.[2] Churchill was also moving towards the need for troops. He stated that over 100,000 men could be concentrated near the Dardanelles. These would consist of 29 Division and a Territorial division from Britain, the Royal Naval Division which was on its way to the area, the Anzacs from Egypt and a French division which he assumed would be sent. This force could occupy Constantinople after it had surrendered to the fleet and then 'compel' the surrender of all European Turkey. The force could then join with Lloyd George's Balkan Army and advance on Austria–Hungary.[3]

The tenor of this discussion did not please the Secretary of State for War, Lord Kitchener, who expressed bemusement at the increasingly insistent demands for troops, especially from those who had earlier been proponents of a purely naval attack. Had they not assured him that the fleet alone would sway the policy of the Balkan states? On 24 February when the War Council reconvened, he testily asked Churchill whether he 'now contemplated a land attack', because if the naval attack succeeded for what purpose were 100,000 troops including Regulars required?[4] Would not the Anzacs and the Royal Naval Division (RND) suffice for a 'cruise in the Sea of Marmora'? These questions put Churchill on the spot. It was he who had assured the War Council that Turkey could be defeated without the use of troops; that had been one of the plan's great selling points. Yet here he was before the same body arguing for the use of substantial numbers of soldiers. His only reply to Kitchener was that if the naval attack was temporarily held up by mines, 'some local military operation' might be required. This was disingenuous. Any military operation to assist the clearing of the mines would require nothing less than the occupation of the entire southern section of the Peninsula—hardly a 'local' matter. It would need at least the 100,000 troops mentioned by Churchill and perhaps more. This would make the operation second in size only to the Western Front.

At this point Hankey entered the debate by circulating to members the Committee of Imperial Defence paper of 1906 which had tended to the view that neither a land attack nor a combined operation at Gallipoli was likely to succeed against Turkey. This might have suggested that Hankey was against any extraneous operation in the Mediterranean. But he appended to the 1906 document a note of his own which stated that since 1906 'a great many of the factors have changed, particularly [in] the development of naval guns and gunnery, so that its conclusions cannot be regarded as entirely applicable to modern conditions'. What the War Council made of this mish-mash of opinion was precisely nothing. They proceeded as if Hankey had not spoken. The only direct conclusion reached by the War Council regarding troops was to instruct General William Birdwood (commander-in-chief, Anzac forces) to contact Admiral Carden and obtain his thoughts on what military assistance he might require.

But the War Council of 24 February did something else, although no one present seemed to notice. Early in the meeting Churchill had made the statement that 'we were now absolutely committed to seeing through the attack on the Dardanelles'. This was remarkable. One of the fundamental premises of the naval attack was that it could be broken off if success was not forthcoming. Yet later in the meeting Kitchener backed Churchill's view. In the course of the discussion over troops he said, 'if the fleet would not get through the Straits unaided, the army ought to see the business through. The effect of a defeat in the Orient would be very serious. There could be no going back.'

These statements indicated a major change in attitude on the part of the First Lord of the Admiralty and the Secretary of State for War. The proposal initially put to the War Council had been for a minor naval attack that could be easily terminated should it prove too costly. Between them, Churchill and Kitchener had signalled a potentially much greater commitment. If the naval attack failed, additional resources, indeed an entire army, would be provided to ensure success. It is a matter for some wonder that no member of the Council saw fit to query this shift in position.

However, Kitchener's somewhat surprising attitude should not conceal the significant differences that remained between him and Churchill. This was evident in their continuing tussle over the 29 Division. Kitchener remained adamant that Regulars were not needed to support a naval attack. They would only be provided if the navy had definitely failed. Churchill clearly wanted them on hand immediately to assist the navy, but would not admit directly that he now envisaged a land attack. This lack of frankness on Churchill's part obscured the need for any serious debate on the issue. So on 26 February when the War Council reconvened to discuss the use of troops, nothing came of it. Churchill restated his position. Kitchener restated his. The 29 Division would remain in Britain until the result of the naval attack became clear.[5]

Oddly, during this period a mood swept through Britain's decision makers that the naval attack might indeed succeed. What caused this euphoria is difficult to identify. It was hardly justified by the actions of the bombarding squadron. Certainly the outer forts had fallen (though not by bombardment, but this perhaps had not been made altogether clear by Carden). And the operations had produced a favourable effect in some of the Balkan states which Britain was trying to attract to the Triple Entente.[6] Venizelos, the Greek Prime Minister, even offered three divisions for operations around Constantinople, but the Russians were not altogether happy with this proposal (they wanted the Ottoman capital for themselves), and neither was the Greek king, Constantine I, who was pro-German, had considerable constitutional power and had not been consulted by

Venizelos. The Greek offer, like others in the past, soon disappeared into the mists of the Aegean.[7]

At the Admiralty the new feeling of optimism was recorded by Richmond's wife in her diary. She noted that Churchill was behaving as though the operation 'was all his own idea' and went on to say that Richmond was 'enchanted at the success of the Bombardment up to now' (an interesting insight into the adherents that the prospect of success can attract).[8] Apparently Richmond had asked to be sent out to Carden in some capacity but had been told by Oliver that 'it wd be all over before he cd get there'.[9]

Sir Frederick Hamilton, the Second Sea Lord, who was later to tell the Dardanelles Commission that he had always been opposed to the naval attack, offered the following on 1 March: 'We have knocked out the 5 forts at the entrance [and] there is no difficulty in dealing with the other forts . . . then all is plain sailing as the Bosphorus forts all face North so that we can attack them in rear . . . it will be a great thing taking Constantinople and opening the Black Sea.'[10]

Even Fisher, with his warnings of German submarines and his recent comment to Admiral Sir David Beatty that 'Diplomacy and the Cabinet have forced upon us the Dardanelles business. So damnable in taking away the Queen Elizabeth',[11] could now inform Jellicoe, 'We seem to be getting on nicely in the Dardanelles.'[12]

The mood soon spread to the War Council. Hankey, who was now acting more as a strategic adviser to this body than as its Secretary, wrote a detailed paper entitled 'After the Dardanelles: The Next Steps', which discussed what peace terms might be offered to Turkey when the inevitable day of its surrender arrived.[13]

The question of peace terms was taken up with alacrity by the Council on 3 March. Constantinople was immediately conceded to the Russians, apparently without a thought of how the Balkan states might view the prospect of having a Great Power in occupation of the most important strategic position in the Middle East.[14]

From this point the meeting diverted down some very bizarre byways. Churchill stated that Britain should demand as a minimum the surrender of all of Turkey in Europe. He then made the startling suggestion that the Turkish army ought to be hired as mercenaries.[15] He was assured by Lloyd George, however (on the basis of what intelligence we cannot be sure), that the Turks had always fought badly as mercenaries, so no more was heard of that.

The attention (such as it was) of the War Council then turned to Bulgaria. All considered it vital that this backward Balkan state with its ox-drawn artillery should be brought in on the side of the Entente. An inconclusive discussion followed on the best methods to achieve this. Asquith brought proceedings to an end by stating that 'it was by no means improbable that Bulgaria was already on the move'. Kitchener agreed with him. That seemed to solve the Bulgarian question.

The Danube then appeared on the agenda, apparently because it was a potential route of approach into southern Austria and Germany. Churchill (surprisingly it might be thought) deprecated a large force of British troops being deployed along this route. It was for the Balkan states to provide these forces, he said. The proper strategy for Britain was 'an advance in the north through Holland and the Baltic. This might become feasible later on with our new monitors [shallow draft ships with heavy guns that could bombard shore defences]. The "operation" in the East should be regarded as merely an interlude.'

It was possibly fortunate that the War Council ended at that moment. Of all Churchill's utterances about the Dardanelles during this period, this has some claim to being the most gnomic. First he had argued for the attack by ships alone. Then he became a passionate advocate of a large force with a Regular army component being available to 'reap the fruits' of the naval attack, one of which presumably was to head a coalition of Balkan states to attack Austria-Hungary and Germany from the rear. Now he was saying that as far as the British were concerned all this was a mere interlude, intended to kick-start a Balkan coalition but nothing more. Britain must then get back to the northern (or western) theatre and 'operate' (there is a desperate vagueness here) through Holland or the Baltic.

Perhaps, however, it is possible to find some kind of consistent line through this maze. Churchill was an advocate of the naval attack because it was one of the few operations put forward by him that won at least some support from his naval advisers. Then, as naval opinion wavered he became an advocate of a military force, either to help the navy through by occupying the Peninsula or to force the Turks into a rapid surrender. Either way Regular troops were essential, for only a force with Regulars (so Churchill thought) could make short work of Turkish forces on the Peninsula, impress the Turks with the seriousness of British intentions and press the Balkan states into joining a British-sponsored (rather than led) coalition against the Central Powers. So the Regulars were essential to get the business done quickly. Then Churchill could get back to his northern schemes, which incidentally he thought would meet with no opposition from his admirals because he would have been proved right about the Dardanelles.

For a brief moment, however, even the importance of Regular troops receded. The day after the War Council of 3 March, Churchill informed Kitchener that the navy expected to be in the Marmara in two weeks and that he wished 'to make it clear that naval operations in the Dardanelles cannot be delayed for troop movements'.[16] This was pretty rich coming from one who had berated Kitchener for holding back 29 Division, but the War Minister let it pass.

In any case it was becoming obvious that the naval attack had not quite wrought the diplomatic revolution in the Balkans that the War Council had assumed on 3 March. The British ambassador in Sofia, Sir Henry Bax-Ironside, informed Grey that so far from being on the march, the Bulgarian Cabinet had not been shaken by operations at the Dardanelles. They remained neutral but pro-German. Rumania would also remain neutral but pro-Entente. Carden's operations had not changed the stance of these Balkan states by even a scintilla. Then a rumour broke that Britain and France had indeed promised Constantinople to the Russians. There was immediate talk of a Bulgarian-Rumanian-Greek alliance to *oppose* this move.[17] Allied policy in the Dardanelles was starting to create as many problems as it was meant to solve.

The reactions of the Balkans threw a douche of cold water over the optimism in London. Carden's feeble operations inside the Straits in the first week of March threw another. As we have seen, the fall of the outer forts was followed by precisely nothing. Over the next week no forts were destroyed, no mobile howitzers put out of action, no mines swept. This lack of progress was being watched with alarm by some military observers on the spot. Birdwood, following the instructions of the War Council, had been to see Carden. On 5 March he told Kitchener that he doubted whether the navy could force the passage unassisted by troops.[18] General Sir John Maxwell, GOC (General Officer Commanding) Egypt, told Kitchener that he agreed with Birdwood's appreciation and urged the War Minister to prepare a strong force to land on the Peninsula.[19]

By this time confidence within the fleet was waning. De Robeck, Carden's second in command, had reached the conclusion that the forts could be dominated for short periods but not destroyed. Should this prove to be the case, even if the battleships could enter the Marmara, they could not rely on unarmoured ships running the gauntlet of unsubdued guns to sustain them. He concluded:

> Strong military co operation is considered essential in order to clear at least one side of the straits of the enemy and their movable batteries. I am not prepared to suggest the proper place for landing or to indicate the method the military should employ but I would point out from my almost daily observations that the enemy are continuously making new entrenchments and improving their position at the southern end of the straits and a landing at Morto Bay and Seddul Bahr with a view to attacking the ridge of which Achi Baba is the commanding point would be extremely costly.[20]

De Robeck was clearly suggesting that there would be no naval progress without military co-operation. But by emphasizing the strength of the Turkish defences and the high casualties that would be incurred in subduing them, was he suggesting that the whole affair be abandoned? We will never know because his paper was never discussed by the War Council. One thing, however, is certain. De Robeck considered that purely naval operations had no chance of success.

Carden had also reached the conclusion that most of the guns would have to be destroyed by strong landing parties. He was not, however, willing to tackle Churchill head-on about the matter, so his hesitations were hedged around with technical problems being experienced by the ships' guns and the (supposed) shortages of ammunition.[21]

Meanwhile, back in London, Churchill was becoming agitated at the lack of progress by the fleet, and it was around this time that he ordered Carden to make a full-scale attack on the forts. Other political figures were more concerned at parcelling up the Turkish Empire. Asquith called a special War Council on 10 March to which the opposition leader, Andrew Bonar Law, and the leader of the Conservative Party in the House of Lords, Lord Lansdowne, were invited. The Conservatives were asked whether their party would support the cession of Constantinople to the Russians. They said it would. Should the Entente win the war, Russia would from then on control the Straits—a circumstance that British foreign policy had strived for a hundred years to prevent.[22]

Kitchener was not impressed by these flights of fancy. He too had been monitoring the progress (or the lack of it) by the fleet. And he may have been moved by the warnings of his military colleagues, Birdwood and

Maxwell. Suddenly he announced that the 29 Division would after all be available for duties in the east. His ostensible reason was the increased security of the Western Front, but in truth nothing much had changed in that area since the beginning of February. He now opined that he could find about 130,000 troops for operations 'against Constantinople'—Naval Brigade 11,000, Anzacs 34,000, 29 Division 18,000, French Division 18,000 and 48,000 Russian troops. The Russian forces were largely a chimera but even without them this was a considerable force. No one at the War Council now asked for what purpose the troops would be used or why the navy now needed men in such numbers. For whatever reason, an army of at least 80,000 (and perhaps close to 130,000 if the Russians came in) was being assembled for operations at the Dardanelles.[23]

To command such a force it was considered that the services of a senior general were required. That man would not be Birdwood as he had fondly imagined and as his experience in the area might logically have dictated. Sir Ian Hamilton, Kitchener's Chief of Staff in the South African War, 1899–1902, and in 1915 in charge of Eastern Command in Britain, was sent out instead—a man who it can reliably be said knew little of the Dardanelles, the Turkish army or of modern war. Certainly Hamilton was not aided by Kitchener in his preparation for command. On 12 March he was taken to see the War Minister, who presented him with his new post and with a Greek plan for an unopposed landing on the Gallipoli Peninsula. Later he received a large-scale map of the area and a 1912 hand-book of the Turkish army. These were his only guides. He left for the Dardanelles on the 14th with a few officers dug out from the War Office. Their destroyer was called HMS *Foresight*.[24]

Hamilton had been instructed that the operation was still a naval one and that he was only to intervene after all naval expedients had been exhausted. However, he had also been instructed by Kitchener that 'having entered on the project of forcing the Straits, there can be no idea of aban-doning the scheme'.[25] Clearly, then, Kitchener was still hoping that the naval attack would succeed and that his army and its underprepared commander would play only a secondary role.

Indeed, the War Council was still strongly under the impression of an impending naval victory. Nothing else can explain their total disregard of an important paper by Hankey sent to Asquith on 16 March. In the paper Hankey (who had changed remarkably from the optimist of early March) asked the War Council to pause and consider what it was that they had decided. He reminded the Council that they had initially embarked on a naval-only operation but were now facing the possibility that it might require troops to see it through. He warned them that surprise had now been lost, the Turks had increased their defensive works on the Peninsula and that he considered any military operation would now be 'of the most formidable nature'. He urged the Council to 'cross-examine' the naval and military authorities on such matters as the sufficiency of troops, administrative arrangements for an opposed landing, the amount of heavy artillery available to the army, the suitability of naval gunfire in supporting infantry, ammunition supply and communications on the Peninsula. He concluded 'unless details such as these, and there are probably others, are fully thought out before the landing takes place, it is conceivable that a serious disaster may occur'.[26]

There is no evidence that anyone on the War Council reacted to this paper. It is not even clear that Asquith distributed it to them, although no doubt Hankey conveyed the gist of it to at least some of them. Possibly, their lack of response reflected a confidence in Kitchener that such details would be settled before any major military undertaking commenced. As we will see, sadly for the British troops, this was not the case. Almost none of the matters mentioned by Hankey were considered either by the General Staff in London or by Hamilton and the local commanders.

Hamilton arrived at the Dardanelles just in time to witness the disastrous attack of 18 March. He noted de Robeck's willingness to 'have another go' but that was not at all his own view. He told Kitchener:

> I am being most reluctantly driven to the conclusion that the Straits are not likely to be forced by battleships . . . and that, if my troops are to take part, it will not take the subsidiary form anticipated [and that] it must be a deliberate and progressive military operation carried out at full strength so as to open a passage for the Navy.[27]

Hamilton's staff agreed with him. One of them noted that opinion was unanimous that the 'navy cant [sic] do it alone'.[28] Remembering the views of Birdwood and Maxwell, it is hardly surprising that Kitchener telegraphed back to Hamilton: 'You know my views—that the passage of the Dardanelles must be forced, and that if large military operations on the Gallipoli Peninsula by your troops are necessary to clear the way, these operations must be undertaken'.[29]

Naval opinion was virtually now unanimous that the army should land. De Robeck asked Wemyss (in charge of the base at Lemnos) for his opinion and was told that combined action was essential. That was also the view of de Robeck's own staff and of the captains of some of the ships.[30] Only Roger Keyes, the commander of the destroyer force, dissented. He wanted to reorganize his ships as minesweepers and renew the assault on the Narrows. But even he realized that this would take several weeks and that nothing could be done until the beginning of April at the earliest.[31]

Back in London, the War Council did not seem to realize that they had a crisis on their hands. At Churchill's request, they authorized another naval attack but then got back to discussing 'The Partition of Turkey in Asia'.[32]

The crisis came soon enough. Having received authorization for the recommencement of naval operations, Churchill sat back to await de Robeck's new plan. It never came. On 23 March (the delay came about because yet again a gale was blowing in the Dardanelles) de Robeck, Hamilton and their respective staffs attended a meeting on the *Queen Elizabeth*. At that meeting de Robeck decided to abandon the naval attack and prepare to support a military landing. Given the weight of opinion held by the naval and military authorities, this was hardly a surprising decision. It might have represented a change from the admiral's initial response to the events of 18 March, but that probably was no more than bravado. With a third of his fleet sunk, a third badly damaged, with no dreadnought to tackle the *Goeben* and with a general willing to land a large force of troops, there was an inevitability about the whole affair.

Churchill, however, was shocked. He immediately drafted a telegram to de Robeck from the Admiralty War Group ordering him to resume the attack.[33] The War Group finally rebelled. They insisted that the admiral on the spot was in the best position to judge. Churchill insisted that at least a letter be sent to de Robeck pointing out the dangers of a land operation. Fisher threatened to resign if it was sent. Churchill agreed to modify it, which he did in some haste and in the end sent virtually the same letter that Fisher had tried to veto. Fisher protested again but the matter was ended by de Robeck's reply, which arrived on 27 March:[34]

The original approved plan for forcing the Dardanelles by ships was drawn up on the assumption that gunfire alone was capable of destroying forts. This assumption has been conclusively proved to be wrong. . . . The utmost that can be expected of ships is to dominate the forts to such an extent that gun crews cannot fight the guns . . . . To destroy forts therefore it is necessary to land demolishing parties.[35]

He concluded by saying that the only way to do this was to capture the Peninsula. Churchill was forced to accept this. He was now opposed by all military and naval opinion at the Dardanelles, and by his own Admiralty group in London. He meekly telegraphed back: 'the reasons you give make it clear that a combined operation is now indispensable. Time also has passed, the troops are available & the date is not distant.'[36]

Why Churchill fought so hard for the renewal of the naval attack is not clear. If he had been inclined to wait, the military force that he had been pleading for, including the 29 Division, would be available to land and assist the fleet. Churchill's lack of interest in this option is puzzling. Perhaps he was driven by sheer impetuosity. Perhaps he had been swayed by a naval intelligence report that suggested that the Turkish forts were almost out of ammunition. Perhaps it was merely a matter of not wanting to admit that his first idea had been wrong and that the navy could not force the Straits unaided. Perhaps too he felt that failure at the Dardanelles would fatally weaken his case for operations in northern waters ('Holland and the Baltic'), to which he had recently said that operations against Turkey were merely a preliminary.

What no one, including Churchill, paused to reflect on was that a decision had now been taken to invade the Gallipoli Peninsula with a force of about 80,000 men. Only Hankey had suggested that this number would prove inadequate, and his objections had been swept aside. Even he did not suggest that a decision be postponed until a plan had been drawn up; or that such a plan be considered by the General Staff in London before being approved. There is no evidence that any of these vital questions were considered. The War Council, last seen annexing large slabs of Asia Minor, did not reconvene to consider whether there should be a military landing. Kitchener had spoken and as far as they were concerned that seemed to be good enough. So the military operation was approved by default. There was no discussion, no plan and no political authorization. This was in fact a worse situation than preceded the naval operation, when at least the War Council had a chance to debate the Carden plan, however sketchy it was.

Who was responsible for this state of affairs? Asquith, as Prime Minister, must bear an overall responsibility, though hardly anyone assigns him any blame. Yet there is no evidence that he circulated Hankey's damning assessment of the military option to any member of the War Council, surely a major omission. As Prime Minister his veto must have ended the operation, but given his distance from military affairs it is almost inconceivable that he would have exercised it in the face of Kitchener's determination to go ahead.

This brings us to the War Minister. Kitchener must carry a great deal of the responsibility. It was his decision, in Lloyd George's phrase, to 'pull the navy's chestnuts out of the fire', and the operation could only have gone ahead with his approval.

Churchill's responsibility is great but of a lesser order than Kitchener's. Certainly the First Lord of the Admiralty was the originator of the naval attack, although even here the poverty of naval advice he received must be borne in mind. Yet when he lost faith in the naval plan he not only refused to halt it but strove mightily to ensure that troops would be on hand to bale the navy out. By never stating his concerns directly, he lost whatever chance there was to convert the naval attack into a proper combined operation. As a body, the War Council has escaped entirely the censure of historians. However, they were the chief decision-making body on all matters relating to the central direction of the war.[37] There is little evidence to suggest that any of them opposed the naval attack or, when that failed, the subsequent decision to land an army. What is remarkable is that although they were aware that Kitchener was bent on a military operation, none of them sought a meeting to thrash out the issues. Indeed, they spent too much time in parcelling up the Turkish Empire and not enough time on how that end was to be attained, or whether as an end it was worth attaining. As a vehicle for the higher direction of the war they could not provide a counterweight for the optimism of a Churchill, the arrogance of a Kitchener or the insouciance of an Asquith, because in general they were of the same cast of mind. If the political leadership in Britain could be said to be on a learning curve about the conduct of a major war, in early 1915 they were still hovering around its point of origin.

CHAPTER 6

The Military Plan

Kitchener's instructions to Hamilton were to prepare an operation for the invasion of the Gallipoli Peninsula. In drawing up his plan Hamilton had to consider three main factors: the geography of the Peninsula and whether troops could be manoeuvred across it; the size and position of the Turkish force ranged against him; and whether the force available to him (about 80,000 men) was sufficient to overcome both geography and enemy.

The geography of the Peninsula would prove a key factor in the campaign. From the extreme north around Bulair to the extreme south around Cape Helles the Peninsula is approximately 50 miles long. Its width varies greatly. At Bulair there is a thin neck of land between the Gulf of Saros and the Sea of Marmara which is just 3½ miles wide. From there the Peninsula gradually broadens. At the town of Gallipoli, which gives the area its name, it is 10 miles wide. Just a few miles further south it reaches its greatest width—12 miles—between Suvla Bay on the Aegean side and the Straits. From that point there is a slight tuck at the Narrows and a gradual tapering until Cape Helles is reached. In all, the area of the Peninsula is no more than 400 square miles, about the same extent as Greater London in 1914. Across this tiny area range five series of hills and mountains.

The first of these is in the north around the Bulair isthmus where steep hills slope down to the very shoreline of the Gulf of Saros. Adding to the natural defences posed by the terrain were three defensive lines constructed

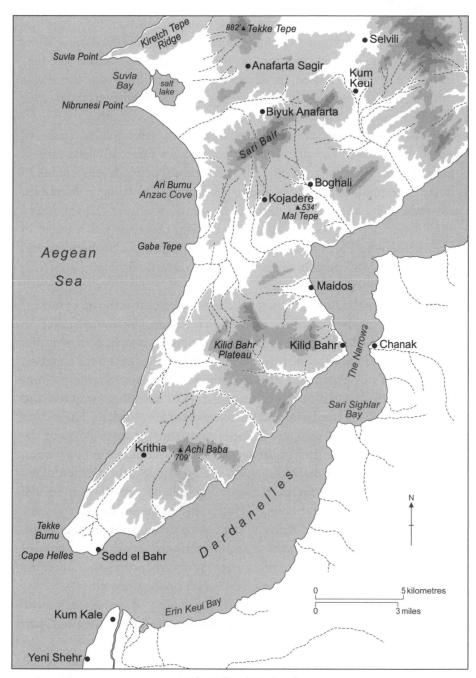

4 The Gallipoli Peninsula

across the narrow neck (first built during the Crimean War, 1853–6, by the British and French) and subsequently strengthened by the Turks. There were a few small landing beaches but they were all overlooked by the hills and the lines of defences. In all respects, the terrain made the Bulair isthmus very favourable to the defence and a most unpromising area for Hamilton's military operations.

Further south lies the Suvla Plain and its semicircular chain of surrounding hills. The plain is dominated by a huge salt lake, dry in midsummer but at the time the Gallipoli plan was being developed, full of water. The plain generally provides good going for troop movements. However, there are several gullies hidden from view from the sea and in 1915 it was covered with vegetation that could make the going tough in places. The whole area is overlooked by the Anafarta Ridge, between 550 and 670 feet high, which, moreover, had a number of serviceable approach roads from the Turkish side.

Just south of the Anafarta Ridge and connected to it is the most precipitous feature on the Peninsula, the Sari Bair Ridge. The highest point on the ridge, Koja Chemen Tepe, some 971 feet above sea level, is to be found in the north. From there the ridge runs roughly south-west until it ends in a spur north of Gaba Tepe. Other prominent features on the ridge (from north to south) are Hill Q and Chunuk Bair (870 feet), Battleship Hill and Baby 700. Between this ridge and the sea are two lower ridges. The second is almost as tangled as Sari Bair. It slopes away from the main ridge at Baby 700, has as its main feature a relatively large flat area known as 400 Plateau and ends just south of Brighton Beach. The first ridge is the smallest of the three but the closest to the sea. It is only 3 miles long, starting to the north of Baby 700 and ending at Plugge's Plateau just to the south of Ari Burnu. These ridges between Sari Bair and the sea make the going most difficult. Even the lower ridges are tangled and precipitous, divided by a series of tortuous ravines. In 1915 the whole area was covered with gorse and other small shrubs, difficult to penetrate even when unencumbered.[1]

To the east of Sari Bair there are more ridges, not as dominating, but still formidable military obstacles and only ending just short of the Kilid Bahr Plateau.

There are several beaches on the coast, the first a small confined site just south of Ari Burnu, later known as Anzac Cove. Further south is Brighton Beach, much longer and gently sloping but being directly opposite the second ridge, a difficult area from which to deploy troops.

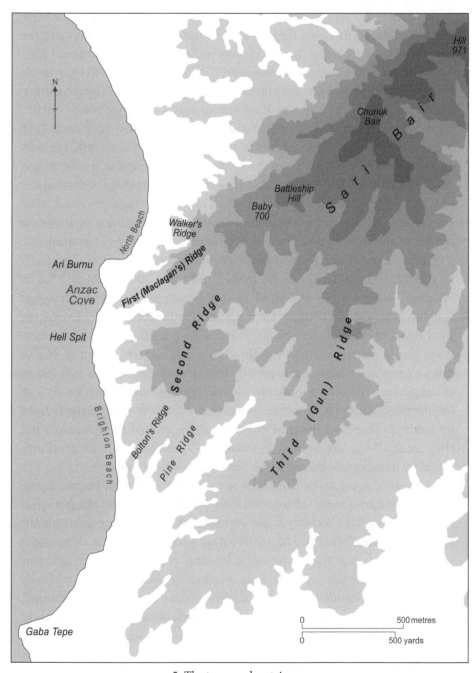

5 The topography at Anzac

South of Gaba Tepe and quite close to the Narrows forts, there are some good beaches. In this area there is a break in the mountain chain and the ground is reasonably flat. In 1915 it was under orchard cultivation.

Inland from this area stands the Kilid Bahr Plateau. This is the key to the Narrows defences and securing it was therefore essential to Hamilton's ultimate objective. It juts across the Peninsula in a great rectangle 600 to 700 feet high. Defences were being prepared around its perimeter in March 1915 because it covered the approaches to the Narrows from the south, the west and the northwest. Except from the southwest, the ground falls very steeply from the edge of the Plateau and it would have provided a formidable obstacle to approaching troops. It is worth noting that the most precipitous edge of the plateau lies directly inland from Gaba Tepe, posing an immense barrier to any troops landed on the central section of the Aegean coast.

From the toe of the Peninsula the ground appears to slope very gently to the top of Achi Baba, a cone-shaped hill some 700 feet high. This is, however, deceptive. The ground is deeply intersected by ravines and nullahs (deep ditches) which form natural fortifications. Achi Baba itself provided a useful observation site for directing artillery fire and its rearward slopes offered many areas for concealing batteries of guns. It also gives a panoramic view of any activity to the south. Seddelbahr fort can be distinguished and any troop movements, whether hostile or friendly, can be identified with ease. There is, however, no view over the Narrows from its summit. There are beaches at the southern end of the Peninsula but they are small, the largest being just some 400 yards in width. All are dominated by hillocks just inland or by Seddelbahr village and fort.

The Asiatic shore, from Kum Kale to the Narrows around Nagara Point, is dominated by a series of wooded hills which rise to form steeper spurs further inland. This country is also intersected by a number of rivers, the most formidable being the Menedere near ancient Troy. The shoreline is generally steep but there are some landing places, especially near the entrance of the Straits at Kum Kale. Further up the Straits the minefield batteries were provided with ample concealment by folds in the ground. Moreover, the land on the Asiatic side is overlooked from the Peninsula, making troop movements hard to conceal. And there was also the problem that any troops landed there would have presented an open right flank to the Turkish forces in Anatolia.[2]

So much for the geography and defences of the Peninsula. What of the size and location of the forces that the British expected to encounter? On mobilization, the Turkish army was about 500,000 strong.[3] However, it was already fighting on three fronts. Early in the war the Turks had threatened the Suez Canal and then invaded the Russian Caucasus. They also had to counter the British Indian Army which had invaded the province of Mesopotamia and was moving on the strategic oilfields near Basra. Nevertheless, the Gallipoli Peninsula was of such obvious strategic importance to the Turks that even given these commitments it was hardly likely to be neglected. At the beginning of the war just the garrison troops for the forts were actually on the Peninsula, although there were three divisions nearby. After the bombardment of the outer forts in November 1914, the 9 Division (III Corps) was immediately moved to Chanak on the Asiatic side. Soon after that two more divisions of III Corps (7 and 19) were moved to the town of Gallipoli, giving three divisions totalling around 30,000 men on or in the near vicinity of the Peninsula. It is notable that III Corps was one of the best in the Turkish army, having survived the Balkan Wars (1912–13) intact.[4]

The naval attack on 19 February 1915 ensured that the Turkish garrison on Gallipoli would be further reinforced. By 18 March the Turks had decided to form a new Fifth Army of two army corps (six divisions) under the command of General Liman von Sanders, former head of the German military mission to Turkey. The landing places on the Peninsula would still be guarded by III Corps with its 7 and 9 divisions. The 19 Division would be in central reserve, able to send troops to the southern or northern areas as required. The 5 Division and a cavalry brigade were kept further back in Army Reserve close to the vulnerable area of Bulair. The XV Corps was placed on the Asiatic shore with the 3 and 11 divisions disposed near the main beaches. By the time of the Allied landings, the Turks had about 40,000 infantry and 100 artillery pieces on the Peninsula or nearby. On the Asiatic side there were 20,000 infantry with 50 guns.[5] In addition, the mobile batteries of the Straits defences could be called upon. These consisted of 30 howitzers and mortars on the European side and 28 similar pieces across the Straits. All could be used to support the infantry, providing they were not required to ward off an attack by the British fleet.

The quality of the Turkish force varied greatly but many of the infantry had served in the Balkan Wars and had therefore more battle experience than most of the Allied troops that would oppose them. For support most companies were supposed to be supplied with four machine guns (either Hotchkiss or Maxim), but in fact the number of these guns was limited and few companies had their full complement.[6] The artillery of the Turkish army was a hodgepodge of equipment ranging from quite modern German pieces to some that dated back to the 1890s. A typical regiment might have 22 modern and 24 older pieces which could throw shells varying from 88 pounds in weight to 10 pounds.[7] Needless to say the older types were of doubtful accuracy and the shell weights of the lighter pieces were quite useless against any form of entrenchments.

Exactly who situated these forces around the Gallipoli Peninsula has been a matter of some controversy. Older sources claim that they were specifically placed by Liman von Sanders.[8] Recent authorities have suggested that von Sanders merely confirmed what had been arranged by lower-order Turkish commanders before he arrived.[9] In any case the troops defending the Peninsula were placed along the coast in small outpost screens, well dug in with wire, in positions that overlooked the most obvious landing beaches.[10] There was a central reserve (19 Division) which could intervene as required, and the 5 Division was held back by von Sanders to protect the isthmus at Bulair. The Fifth Army commander also identified the beaches around Cape Helles, and Kum Kale on the Asiatic side, as other likely positions for Allied landings.[11]

The Turkish dispositions demonstrated strengths and weaknesses. Most of the coastline from Gaba Tepe to Morto Bay was covered by a thin screen of troops. North of Gaba Tepe, 5 Division covered Bulair, and the few troops in the Sari Bair region could be strengthened from the central reserve, which could also provide counterattack units for other areas on the Peninsula. However, the screening garrisons on the coast were very small and there was every chance that if they were overwhelmed by the landing forces, counterattacks would not be mounted in time or in sufficient strength to force the invaders back to the sea.

* * *

What did Hamilton know of the topography of the Peninsula? He had at his disposal a 1908 sheet taken from a general survey of Turkey. The historians of mapping at Gallipoli have noted 'it gave a general picture of the theatre but very little detail and was useless for artillery work'.[12] It is clear from a glance at the map that it showed such features as the tortuous area inland from Anzac, the formidable contours of the Kilid Bahr Plateau and gave at least some idea of the contours around Cape Helles. What it did not show was enough contour detail to allow the artillery to use it with confidence. But that was the case on the Western Front as well in early 1915.

So Hamilton had his 1908 map and the advantage of making several reconnaissances along the Aegean coast of the Peninsula by ship. From the ship he could certainly identify the commanding heights of the Peninsula, those inland and to the north of Gaba Tepe, the formidable country near Bulair and such prominent features as Achi Baba in the south. He also identified at Helles 'a complete system of trenches and entanglements, supported by guns in concealed positions, covering landing places at southern extremity of Peninsula'.[13] Hamilton was then under few illusions about the difficulty of the ground and he was quite well informed about the strength of the Gallipoli garrison, most British estimates suggesting the Turks had about 50,000 troops at hand.[14]

With these difficulties in mind Hamilton sought advice from some of his senior commanders. Their replies make interesting reading.

General Maxwell was commander-in-chief in Egypt, and although not directly involved in the Gallipoli operation gave Hamilton the benefit of his experience in the Middle East. He advised a landing on the Asiatic coast and told him that he would be wise to ignore the Peninsula altogether because its confined spaces gave 'no liberty of Manoeuvre, you are cramped & very liable to be held up and have a sort of miniature Flanders to fight'.[15]

Closer to the action was General Archibald Paris, the commander of Churchill's naval contingent and the only high authority to have seen service on the Western Front. Paris deprecated the whole affair, stating that landing anywhere on the Peninsula would be 'hazardous in the extreme under present conditions', and he noted that however many troops the Turks had on the Peninsula, there were a further 250,000 'within striking distance'.[16] Paris seemed to be about to conclude that the operation should be abandoned but then went on to speculate that there were reasonable landing places north and south of Gaba Tepe, and that with the aid of the fleet an unopposed landing might be secured at Helles. If such a landing was made, however, he stressed the need for rapid movement inland as the further the troops penetrated the less efficacious the fire support from the ships would be.[17] There was much food for thought in Paris's memorandum but it pointed in no clear direction. No reply to Paris from Hamilton has been discovered.

Two members of Hamilton's staff also tendered their opinions. The first was Colonel Cecil Aspinall, Hamilton's operations officer. He suggested that the most favourable landing place 'will be at the S W extremity of the peninsula, where the fleet can cover the landing and the eventual advance from both flanks and from the rear'.[18] He was much more sanguine than Paris about the assistance naval gunfire could give to troops advancing well inland. However, Aspinall did recognize that the beaches around Cape Helles were very small, and he therefore suggested a second landing between Gaba Tepe and Fisherman's Hut to advance directly on the Kilid Bahr Plateau. At the same time a feint landing at Bulair should also be made to distract the Turkish defence.[19]

General Walter Braithwaite was Hamilton's Chief of Staff. He came to much the same conclusions as Aspinall. He considered Bulair too heavily defended and Suvla at an awkward angle to any line of advance on Kilid Bahr. The Asiatic shore could be ruled out because it could be attacked from its open flank; naval co-operation would be at a discount; the country was particularly difficult and the chief defences at the Narrows were on the European side. The best beaches for landing were to the south of Gaba Tepe but they had been prepared for defence, including underwater obstacles, and were open to enemy artillery on the Kilid Bahr Plateau to which the ships could only reply by indirect fire. As had Aspinall, he recommended a landing just north of Gaba Tepe because of its proximity to the Narrows, and at Cape Helles because of the support that could be offered by the guns of the ships. He also recommended a feint attack at Bulair.[20]

The two men who were actually to command the landing forces were General Birdwood (Anzac contingent) and General Aylmer Hunter-Weston (29 Division). Birdwood had been sent by Kitchener as an observer to the Dardanelles in February, and had arrived at the conclusion that a cautious advance from Helles would be the best plan. He opposed any landing at Bulair because of the strong defences but made no other suggestions.[21] Later, he changed his mind and suggested (as had Maxwell) that the main landing be made on the Asiatic shore. He thought it would be unopposed and that the army could work up towards the Narrows in conjunction with the navy, and that there would be no difficulty in dominating the Gallipoli Peninsula even though the ground there (the Kilid Bahr Plateau) was higher.[22]

Perhaps the most remarkable appreciation came from Hunter-Weston, who was later to receive opprobrium as one of the most brutal and incompetent commanders of the First World War. He began with a burst of optimism, stating that if successful the operation would have an effect out of all proportion to the numbers engaged. There his optimism ceased. He went on to state that since the outbreak of war the Turks had been given ample time to convert the Peninsula into 'an entrenched camp'. All the landing places were protected by trenches and machine-gun nests, and in some cases the beaches had been wired. Suvla and Helles provided the best opportunities to effect a landing, but any force at Suvla would be vulnerable to attack from the north. Consequently they would have to leave a large covering force to deal with this threat and this would mean that the remaining troops would be too weak to attack the strongly defended Kilid Bahr Plateau. Helles was his preferred alternative but the narrowness of the Peninsula at the cape gave little scope for manoeuvre. This was pretty dispiriting stuff from Hunter-Weston. But it was about to get worse. He concluded:

> Throughout the war none of the combatants has been successful in breaking quickly through even indifferent entrenchments. The usual result has been stalemate. Success has only been obtained after long and careful preparation and the expenditure of an enormous amount of High Explosive Gun ammunition . . .. We [the army] are now very short of gun ammunition and particularly short of High Explosive Shell. There appears therefore every prospect of getting held up on an entrenched line across the Peninsula, in front of the Turkish Kilid Bahr plateau trenches—a second Crimea . . ..
>
> The information available goes to show that if this Expedition had been carefully and secretly prepared in England, France and Egypt, and the naval and military details of organization, equipment and disembarkation carefully worked out by the General Staff and the Naval War Staff, and if no bombardment or other warning had been given . . . the capture of the Gallipoli Peninsula and the forcing of the Dardanelles would have been a perfectly feasible operation and would almost certainly [have] been successful. . . . But if the views expressed here in this paper be sound there is not, in present circumstances, a reasonable chance of success. . . . The return of the Expedition when it has gone so far will cause discontent, much talk, and some laughter; will confirm Roumania and Greece in the wisdom of their neutrality, and will impair the power of our valuable friend M. Venizelos. It will be a heavy blow to all of us soldiers, and will need great strength and courage on the part of the Commander and the Government. But it will not do irreparable harm to our cause, whereas to attempt a landing and fail to secure a passage through the Dardanelles would be a disaster to the Empire.[23]

Here then was an interesting collection of opinion for Hamilton to digest: Maxwell had spoken of a miniature Flanders; Paris of the prospect of fighting much of the Turkish army; there was confusion from Birdwood; and black pessimism from Hunter-Weston ('a second Crimea'). Only the members of Hamilton's staff (Aspinall and Braithwaite) had sounded any kind of positive note. And even Braithwaite had advised Kitchener's secretary (Fitzgerald) that the operation would be 'a real big job. This place has been properly fortified; it is really a huge entrenched camp, and we have got to land certainly under rifle fire, probably under howitzer fire, and find entrenchments barring our way almost directly we . . . land.'[24]

Braithwaite and Aspinall, however, were privy to Hamilton's thinking in a way that the other commanders were not. They knew that there was never a possibility that Hamilton would recommend the operation be abandoned. The only questions exercising Hamilton's mind were about where to land and when. Accordingly, most of the negative advice proffered by his commanders, though it contained much wisdom, was ignored.

The factors underlying Hamilton's position are not difficult to discern. The first is the authority structure of the British (and most other) armies in this period. Kitchener, as Secretary of State for War, had appointed Hamilton with the observation that 'having entered on the project of forcing the Straits there can be no idea of abandoning the scheme'.[25] Asked later by the Dardanelles Commission whether he regarded this instruction as a 'peremptory' order to capture the Peninsula, Hamilton replied that he did—a not unreasonable interpretation of Kitchener's statement.[26] And Hamilton was not the type to stand up to Kitchener. After all he had been the great man's staff officer in the South African War and was in the habit of taking orders from him. Moreover, he was of a sunny disposition. So on receiving Hunter-Weston's despondent appreciation he immediately dashed off a letter to Kitchener complaining of the fact that he had to 'struggle with all my might against this pessimism'.[27] And he was later to write wearily to the War Minister about the 'extraordinary perspicacity' with which his senior generals were identifying the difficulties in an attack upon the Peninsula.[28] Finally, Hamilton was 61 and had been plucked from Central Command in England, hardly the most prestigious of posts. This was clearly his last chance to command troops in the field.

Hamilton therefore developed his plan. In essence it was a slight variant on the Aspinall/Braithwaite schemes. There would be two feints to disguise the main thrust of the attack. The first would be at Bulair in the north,

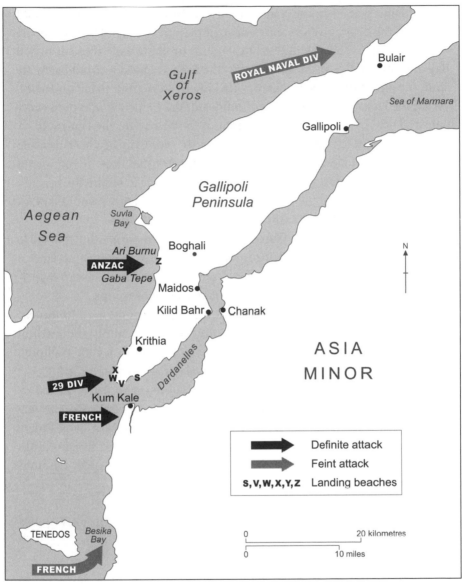

6 The military plan

where some warships and elements of the Royal Naval Division would cruise off the coast, give the appearance of preparing to land but eventually withdraw. The second would be in the south on the Asiatic shore at Besika Bay and Kum Kale. At the latter point, the French Division would actually land, the intention being to distract Turkish artillery from firing on Helles. When the Helles landings were consolidated, the French would then evacuate and take up a position on the right of the British on the Peninsula.

The main attack would take place on the very tip of the Peninsula around Cape Helles. After a bombardment by the fleet, a reinforced brigade of 29 Division would land as a covering force to secure the beaches and advance inland to the Achi Baba Ridge. The main force would land as soon as it became clear that the covering force was ashore.

At the second landing at Gaba Tepe, after a bombardment of the ridge from that promontory to Nibrunesi Point, the Anzacs would land a covering force of one brigade. It would seize the position noted in map 7, which would protect the landing of the main body of troops.[29]

This was the extent of Hamilton's plan, and apart from some administrative detail such as ship to shore communication, water supply and medical arrangements, it was also the extent of his operation order for Gallipoli. Not even the landing beaches at Helles or Gaba Tepe were specified.

Some more detail was spelled out in two subsequent orders issued by Braithwaite to the corps commanders in the following weeks. To Hunter-Weston at Helles, he restated the objective as being the Achi Baba Ridge. He then added some necessary details. There would be five landings around Cape Helles at beaches S, V, W, X, Y (see map 6). The landings would be carried out in four stages:

(1) A bombardment of Helles during which the 2,000 troops at Y would land.
(2) Landing of 2,900 troops at S, V, W and X.
(3) Landing of 2,000 troops from a converted collier, the *River Clyde*, at V Beach.
(4) Landing of the remaining covering force at V, W and X.

Braithwaite then proceeded to detail the four stages by which the Helles contingent would reach the Achi Baba ridge. The first objective would consist of a fairly straight line across the Peninsula, capturing those features that dominated it—Hills 114, 138 and 141, and the village of Seddelbahr.

The second objective involved a considerable advance by the troops at W and X to link up with the troops at Y beach, but a quite small advance on the right to the southern edge of Morto Bay. The third stage would again involve a considerable move by the left to capture Yazy Tepe, a hill to the north-east of Krithia, the village itself and features to the east of it. The whole manoeuvre in its final stage would involve a small move on the right to reach the force landed at S Beach. From that position the Achi Baba Ridge would be attacked, mainly by those forces on the right—which were still a considerable distance from it.

Braithwaite had at least filled in some of the details omitted by Hamilton in his sketchy operations orders. However, some of Braithwaite's ideas were decidedly peculiar. The first objective was unexceptional, but the second left his force with a position diagonally across the Peninsula and his third with an even sharper diagonal. Both of these positions would have laid them open to flanking attack by Turkish forces moving along the Dardanelles side of the Peninsula. But the real oddity was that the force at Y was to be left unutilized until the day after the landing and the force at S until the day after that. In short, about a third of the covering force would take no part in the action until the battle was three days old.

As for the Anzac landing, Braithwaite added little to Hamilton's outline. He told Birdwood that the covering brigade was first required to capture 'the hill in Squares 224, 237 and 238 (Sari Bair on War Office map)'. Whether the possession of the very 'crest of the mountain' was necessary to secure the position was left to Birdwood's discretion. The main force was given as its final objective the storming of Mal Tepe. Braithwaite considered this feature to be the key to the ridge which ran across the Peninsula to Maidos and its capture would, at least by implication, cut communications between the southern and northern Turkish forces on the Peninsula.[30]

These orders, even added together, had one overwhelming quality: they were desperately vague. The final objectives for Hamilton's force—the Kilid Bahr Plateau and then the Narrows' defences—were nowhere stated. Perhaps it was made obvious verbally to Hunter-Weston and Birdwood that they were to proceed on to these features after the ones specified in the orders (Achi Baba Ridge and Mal Tepe) had been secured. Perhaps Hamilton considered the final objectives were so obvious that they did not require restating in his orders. It is more likely, however, that this omission is just one example of the lack of precision in the effusions that emanated from GHQ.

The instructions given for the attack at Helles provide further illustration of the lack of clarity. From the numbers of troops to be landed it could be *implied* that V Beach was to be the key point in the operation, followed by W where the next largest number would land. But this was never explicitly stated by GHQ. Also left unclear was the role of the substantial flanking forces on S, X and Y beaches. This was decidedly peculiar. As the orders stood, the strongest landings were to take place in front of the strongest Turkish defences at V and W beaches. These defences (underwater obstacles, wired trenches, the fort and village at Seddelbahr which could both conceal considerable numbers of troops) were revealed to Hamilton and Braithwaite in their offshore reconnaissances. In this circumstance it would have been prudent to develop a contingency plan in case of failure at these points. The flank landings at S, X and Y could have provided just such a plan as at these three points the British would be landing behind the fortifications at V and W. A simple pincer movement could have taken these positions from the rear. Yet no such orders were issued. The considerable forces landed on the northern, western and eastern flanks were merely instructed to await progress from the south. Here was a failure of imagination of the high command which would cost their troops dearly.

The orders issued to Birdwood were in some ways even less precise than those for Helles. Hunter-Weston's objective, the Achi Baba Ridge, was at least clear. For Birdwood's covering force, the objectives were lamentably unclear. What was the 'hill' referred to in Squares 224, 237 and 238? The country in this area contained many hills. Presumably it was the high ground of the second and third ridges that was meant, but this was not explicit. Also, what was the 'crest of the mountain' noted by Braithwaite? Was it Chunuk Bair which was in the squares mentioned, or Koja Chemen Tepe which was actually the highest point on the ridge but was north of square 228? For Birdwood's main force, Mal Tepe was at least a specific objective but what exactly was implied by the instruction to 'storm' it? Was it heavily defended? Should it be captured rapidly? The covering force might be expected to thwart counterattacks from the north, but what of any coming from the south? And what was Birdwood's force to do when it had captured Mal Tepe, sit and wait for 29 Division, or actually advance on the Kilid Bahr Plateau?

No specific details on any of these matters were issued by GHQ. As we will see, some were provided by the corps commanders, who in the process altered in some significant ways those orders received from above. If anyone at GHQ noticed this they did not comment, and indeed it is difficult to see what else Hunter-Weston and Birdwood could have done in the absence of more detailed instructions from the commander-in-chief.

* * *

While Hamilton's orders may have lacked precision, during the period in which he was developing his plan he at least exuded confidence. He was scathing about the doubters such as Hunter-Weston, whom he considered saw only difficulties. There is nothing in his extensive correspondence with Kitchener that would have led an observer to conclude that the commander of the Mediterranean Expeditionary Force doubted his ability with 80,000 men to overthrow the Turkish Empire. Problems were brushed aside, the Turkish opposition derided, the fighting qualities of his own troops lauded.

Then, ten days before the battle doubts began to creep in. On 15 March, for the first time Hamilton asked Kitchener for reinforcements—an Indian brigade stationed in Egypt. He then told the War Minister that the area south of Krithia was not devoid of Turkish troops, as they had both assumed, but contained a 'large number of men tucked away in the folds of the ground there, not to speak of several field batteries'. Finally, after describing for Kitchener in some detail the formidable wire entanglements at Helles he noted that experiments with naval gunfire on these positions had produced no 'visible effect whatever'. He concluded that 'I fear an enormous expenditure of ammunition will be necessary to smash these wire entanglements; and we have not got it.'[31]

It is hard to know exactly what Hamilton was trying to communicate to Kitchener with these observations. He might have been hoping that Kitchener would call the whole operation off. More likely, he was just putting the case for more resources. Possibly he was just warning him that the operation was not going to be a pushover and that losses were to be expected even if a landing could be effected.

There was one bizarre coda to all this. On the night before the landing Hamilton wrote out some instructions entitled 'Suggested Action In The Event Of The 29th Division, or the Australians Failing To Establish Themselves Ashore'. This could be taken as a sign of last-minute nervousness or merely a prudent contingency plan. But it is the plan itself, not the fact that it was drafted, that warrants attention, for this was not just a scheme for re-embarkation. It was a design to shift the whole focus of the operation from the Gallipoli Peninsula to mainland Turkey. To avoid the impression of a defeat the Gallipoli operation would be converted into a 'feint' and the force immediately transported to Enos on the mainland shore of European Turkey. Once established ashore it was 'to prepare for an advance against the Turkish army'.[32] Hamilton did not go into detail about how his force of 80,000 was to overcome the dozen or so Turkish divisions (about 150,000 troops) that stood between it and the Turkish capital, or the diplomatic effect of landing an Anglo-French force virtually on the Bulgarian border. It hardly needs stating that this outlandish scheme had not received the sanction of any political or military authority in Britain. Nor would such approval have been given had it been sought. The main importance of this episode is that it demonstrates what in the end Hamilton thought he could accomplish in the Middle East with a small, undertrained and untested force.

CHAPTER 7

Bodies Everywhere
The Helles Landings

As noted earlier, Hamilton's orders to his corps commanders for the landing lacked both precision and detail, but Hunter-Weston was at least told where he was to land and which troops had been assigned to the particular beaches. The seven and a quarter battalions that made up the covering force would be disposed as follows:

2¼ battalions at Y Beach
1 battalion at X Beach
1 battalion at W Beach
2¼ battalions at V Beach
¾ battalion at S Beach

Then from the main force an additional 2 battalions would disembark at X and form the divisional reserve, 1 would land at W and the remaining 2 at V to reinforce what seemed to be (but was never specified) the pivotal point of the British attack.[1]

Hunter-Weston also inserted some necessary details himself. It was at last specified that the ultimate objective of his force was to capture the Kilid Bahr Plateau from the south. And he had divided the intermediate objective (the capture of the Achi Baba ridge line) into five distinct phases, although he had not included a timetable showing when he expected each objective to be reached.[2]

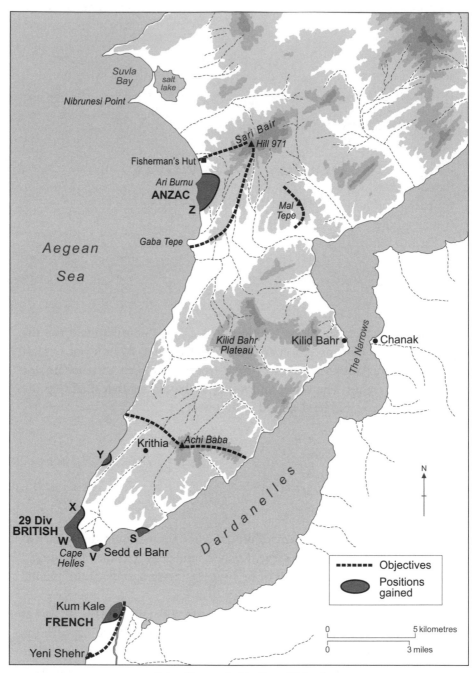

7 Landings and objectives, 25 April

What was still left desperately vague was the role to be played by the flanking forces at S and Y beaches. In Hunter-Weston's orders the only mention of the force at Y was that when phase 2 was reached by the more southern formations they would 'join hands with the forces landing at Y Beach'.[3] The force commander was apparently also told verbally by Hunter-Weston to capture a field gun just inland and to the right of the landing.[4] Those at S were given no instructions at all, but the area in which they would land was designated to be the right of the line for phase 3 of the advance on Achi Baba. There was a strong implication in this that the flanking forces were to land and merely await the arrival of the main force from the south, to which they would provide a reinforcement of fresh troops to give impetus to further advances.

Various expedients were adopted to transfer the men from the larger warships and cargo vessels to the shore. At S Beach the troops would transfer to lifeboats which would be towed by trawlers until the water became too shallow for the larger craft. The men would then row themselves ashore. At V, W and X beaches the troops would disembark from battleships and a trawler in 18 tows. Trawlers would then take them close inshore and naval ratings would row them for the last 50 yards or so. At V Beach, as soon as the first tows hit the beach the *River Clyde* with its 2,000 troops was to be run aground and its battalions reinforce those already ashore. At Y Beach, trawlers were to convey the troops almost directly ashore 'till they felt the bottom' in the words of the operation order. Then the landing parties were to storm up the cliffs (there was virtually no stretch of beach in this area) and await events.[5]

Covering fire from the warships was to be provided for all the landings except Y Beach, where surprise and the lack of evidence of any enemy troops were considered sufficient to see the men safely ashore. On all other beaches the bombardment of the Turkish defences in the first instance was to last half an hour. As the troops approached the shore it would lift onto 'the first objective of naval fire', the Turkish artillery,[6] which would be located some miles from the beaches. So as the troops closed with the enemy they would have no supporting gunfire.

Shortage of ammunition remained a persistent problem. The ultimate purpose of military operations on the Peninsula was to get the fleet through to overawe Constantinople. The naval command had no desire to reach their destination with depleted magazines. Accordingly they limited the number of shells available to support the army. Where the heaviest shells were concerned only 20 rounds per gun *as a maximum* were allocated. Limits (if more generous) were placed on all other calibres and it was firmly stated that 'this allowance should not be exceeded without urgent military necessity'.[7] There is no evidence to suggest that anyone in the naval command considered what might happen if military operations failed for lack of fire support, or pondered the utility of having magazines bulging with shells if the minefields, their supporting guns and the forts remained in Turkish hands.

Staff liaison received very lackadaisical treatment in the orders. Hamilton and his staff would cruise between the five Helles beaches and Anzac on the *Queen Elizabeth*. Hunter-Weston and the 29 Division staff would cruise off Helles on the *Euryalis*. How the two groups were to communicate was not specified.

* * *

While Hamilton's plans were being drawn up, preparations for the military landing were proceeding. The main base from which the troops would be embarked for the Peninsula was the Greek island of Lemnos, acquired by the British in murky circumstances in February. Since then a senior naval officer (Admiral Wemyss) had been appointed to 'govern' the island.

The base was soon in crisis. The 29 Division had embarked from Britain on 10 March. When the transports carrying the force arrived at Lemnos, two problems became apparent; first, the way the ships had been packed put paid to any rapid disembarkation on hostile beaches; and second, Mudros harbour was quite unsuitable as an area in which to repack the ships. The 29 Division therefore was dispatched to Alexandria in Egypt, which had the necessary port infrastructure for handling cargo on a large scale. While this delay has been much criticized for denying the British the advantages of a late March or early April landing, these criticisms have no substance. Transports could only be 'tactically' packed for a landing once Hamilton's plan had been made and the order of landing established. This aspect of the plan was not finalized until mid-April, and as the military operation was only authorized by Kitchener on 23 March it is difficult to see how any plans could have been finalized earlier. Moreover, the criticism overlooks the weather. For troops to be supported ashore with a regular supply of munitions and food, periods of relatively calm seas were required. In the Mediterranean, such periods are not to be found with any regularity before late April and early May.[8] Indeed, a major storm on

21 April delayed the landings from the 23rd to the 25th. In the light of all this, sustained operations on the Gallipoli Peninsula probably started as early as was prudent.

From early April attention refocused on Lemnos. On 10 April Hamilton and his staff arrived, and shortly after that the troops of 29 Division and the Anzac Corps. The troops practised embarking and were given lessons by the navy on how to handle small boats. By 20 April all was ready and the units began boarding their assigned ships.

The armada supporting the landing was a formidable one. There were 22 heavy warships, including one from the Russian Imperial Navy, more than 20 destroyers, and an associated group of small craft such as trawlers. The troops and their equipment were placed in 67 transports, the numbers on a ship varying from 250 to 2,300. In all, over 60,000 troops would be transported to the Peninsula. They consisted of the following:

29 Division	17,649
Anzac Corps	18,124
RND	9,907
French	16,762
Total	62,442

On board one of the ships steaming out of Mudros was a company commander in the Royal Munster Fusiliers, Captain G.W. Geddes. His destination was V Beach at Helles, where he would land from the *River Clyde*:

After three weeks at Mudros, during which time we practised landing from our Transport into ships boats—in full marching order—by the aid of a pilots rope ladder, we left at 5.30 p.m. on April 23rd for the great adventure.

A perfect evening, as we steamed stealthily out on H.M.H.T. 'Caledonia', an incident memorable for its solemnity and one might say grandeur. Men-of-war, transports and ships of every sort. All the crews cheering us on our way, and those with bands playing us a farewell. . . .

We arrived at Rabbit Island early the following morning, the wind had got up, and in consequences, the sea. Wild rumours were prevalent that the elements might force a postponement. However at 4.30 we transship to an ex-channel steamer and went on board the River Clyde, which we had previously inspected in Mudros harbour . . .. In the early hours of the 25th we sailed from Rabbit Island. Dawn broke on April 25th, a beautiful morning and not a breath of wind and a slight haze which rapidly disappeared.[9]

We will return to Captain Geddes in due course.

As the *River Clyde* was approaching the Peninsula the first troops in the south were already ashore. These were the under-instructed men at S and Y beaches.

At S Beach just 750 men from the South Wales Borderers were to land. They were late. The beach is on the eastern fringe of Morto Bay and therefore well inside the Straits. Apparently no allowance had been made for the Dardanelles current, which slowed the ships, or for the detours that had to be made to avoid the French minesweepers operating in the same area.[10] In the event the landing did not occur until 7.30 a.m., an hour after the scheduled time. The beaches and the ground inland were deluged with shells from the navy. Disregarding the 20-round limit on the use of heavy shells, the *Lord Nelson* and *Cornwallis* fired over 200 heavy rounds and over 2,000 rounds of 12-pounder shell.[11] As it happened they found few targets because the Turks had not anticipated a landing inside the Straits. Just one platoon of enemy soldiers armed only with rifles faced the British, with one more on the British left in the central area of Morto Bay.[12] The British landed without difficulty, charged a Turkish trench capturing 15 soldiers and proceeded to the high ground overlooking De Tott's Battery.[13] However, the platoon of Turks to their right then opened fire and caused some 50 casualties before being forced to withdraw.[14] By 8.30 a.m. the British position was secure with its right on De Tott's and its centre and left on a ridge 400 yards to the north-west.

And there, sans orders and sans purpose, the troops stayed. Their War Diary recorded that until 9.00 a.m. they 'watched the landing at Seddelbahr (V Beach), this did not appear to be a success, we could see the troops trying to work up through the ruined village but without success'. At 10.00 a.m. 'troops observed moving from X beach, moving East. This attack however appeared to be diverted towards Seddelbahr. From this fact we gathered that the landing at Seddelbahr has failed & we were quite isolated.'[15]

In retrospect, it seems strange that these men observed the V Beach disaster yet, although they were only a mile away, did not intervene by

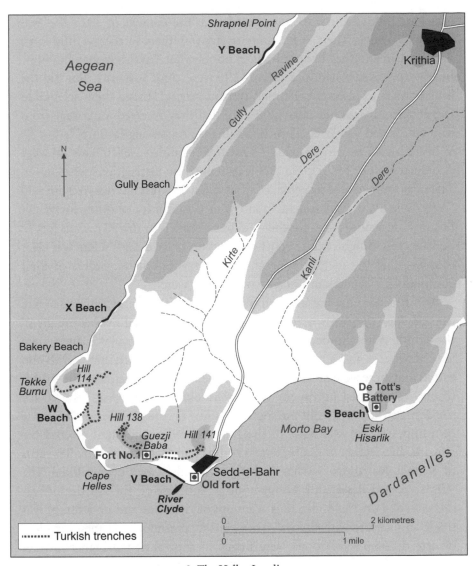

Aegean
Sea

Shrapnel Point

Y Beach

Gully
Ravine
Dere
Dere

Krithia

N

Gully Beach

Kirte

Kanli

X Beach

Bakery Beach

Hill
114

Tekke
Burnu

W
Beach

Hill 138

De Tott's
Battery

S Beach

Eski
Hisarlik

Morto Bay

Guezji
Baba

Hill 141

Fort No.1

Cape
Helles

V Beach

Sedd-el-Bahr
Old fort

River
Clyde

Dardanelles

------- Turkish trenches

0   2 kilometres

0   1 mile

8 The Helles Landing

attacking Seddelbahr from the rear. But in the context of 1915 this was asking too much. Their orders were to stay put, there were now only some 700 of them and they had no intelligence of what Turkish troops might be nearby (a prisoner had told them 2,000 were close at hand). Nor did the high command intervene. Hunter-Weston, having landed them seemed to forget them. It was not until 2.00 p.m. that they received a message from him which said 'On W & Y beach landing is progressing favourably but on V beach attack is held up by wire. Australians doing well.'[16] This message contained no call for help. In fact it contained no instructions whatsoever. The next message was received a day later. On 26 April Hunter-Weston said 'Well done SWB. Can you maintain your position for another fortyeight hours. I am sending you another 4 days supplies plus the 50 rations lost in boats to you tonight. Send report of situation twice a day.'[17] Here was clear evidence that the men at S Beach were carrying out the orders of their commander by remaining exactly where they were.

At Y Beach events started even more satisfactorily than at S Beach. Here the 1 KOSB (King's Own Scottish Borderers), reinforced by a company of the South Wales Borderers and two companies of Royal Marines, were landed between 4.45 a.m. and 5.15 a.m.[18] The men stormed up the cliffs and found that there were no enemy troops to be seen. By 7.00 a.m. all the British troops had formed up on the cliffs overlooking Y Beach and waited for the expected advance from the south. Nothing eventuated. Sometime in the morning, Colonel Matthews of the Marines and his adjutant crossed the considerable feature of Gully Ravine and reconnoitered to within 500 yards of Krithia. No troops—either friendly or hostile—were encountered. The village seemed deserted.[19] About noon a company of Turkish troops was seen moving on Helles but they were out of rifle shot and no attempt was made to interfere with them.[20] Then, in the afternoon, Matthews made a bizarre decision. His troops were firmly in control of the higher ground just inland from the cliffs but he decided that this position might obstruct 86 Brigade's advance from the south. So despite the fact that 86 Brigade was nowhere to be seen, he pulled his men back to their original position at 'the crest of the Cliff'.[21] It was now 3.00 p.m. The troops had been ashore for at least eight hours, had seen few Turks and had done nothing. Matthews ordered them to entrench.

Meanwhile the Turks were on the move. They had received definite intelligence of the landing at Y Beach at 9.30 a.m. The commander of the 26 Battalion (9 Turkish Division), which was defending the southern tip of the Peninsula, had already committed most of his reserves to V and W beaches. He had just one company left. He ordered this force to move on Y Beach and he instructed two batteries of field artillery south of Krithia to direct fire onto the area. He also informed Colonel Sami Bey, the commander of the 9 Division, that he was in urgent need of support.[22] The detachments sent by Sami were a reinforced battalion (1/25) and a machine-gun section from his central reserve near Seraphim Farm on the Kilid Bahr Plateau. They were sent forward with orders to attack from the north and throw the invaders into the sea.[23]

After some delay these orders bore fruit. At around 4.00 p.m. Matthews' men came under artillery fire. Then about an hour later the counter-attack from the north (between Gully Ravine and the sea) commenced. Immediately Matthews found himself in a precarious position. Despite his orders, the troops were not properly entrenched. The ground was hard and matted with plant roots. The heavy entrenching tools that were needed had inexplicably been left on the beach. Over a period of ten hours no one had thought to fetch them. Now it was too late. The Turkish attack was fierce and backed by machine-gun fire, from which the British had little protection. Nevertheless, with the help of the heavy guns of the *Sapphire* it was driven off. The Turks learnt a lesson from this. They would make no more attacks in daylight. At about 11.00 p.m. two more companies of Turkish troops arrived. From that point until daybreak they launched a series of attacks against the British positions. The fleet was helpless to give any support. Nevertheless the British held on. When day broke the carnage of the night was revealed. The Turks had lost 50 per cent of their strength and had momentarily retired. The British had suffered over 700 casualties, about 30 per cent of their force, and were much shaken.[24]

What happened next is controversial. During the night some troops (most of them wounded) drifted back towards the beach. In the morning they signalled the navy to take them off. The navy responded. But many taken from the beach were unwounded stragglers, traumatized by their night-time ordeal. In this way what amounted to a general evacuation of the right flank of the British position commenced. All this went unnoticed by Matthews because at the time it was taking place (7.00 a.m.) he had once more been attacked by the Turks. This effort broke the British line and the Turks almost penetrated to the edge of the cliff before the situation was restored by a bayonet charge. The Turks then retired. They had in fact shot their bolt. They had been attacking a larger force now for some fourteen hours, were exhausted and had suffered many casualties. They would make no more attempts to displace the British.

None of this mattered because the British were in the process of displacing themselves. After the attack Matthews finally discovered that his right flank had re-embarked. He had already sent a message to GHQ that the situation was desperate and that he required immediate reinforcement. He received no reply. Looking over to the beach he saw that an embarkation of yet more troops was continuing. He decided to let it continue. In a few hours Y Beach was deserted.[25] The British would not reach this position again until June.

Much has been made of the fiasco at Y Beach. It has been argued that if the beachhead had remained in place or if Hamilton had diverted troops from V to Y much of the slaughter on the southern beaches could have been avoided and the tip of the Peninsula could have been in British hands by 26 April.[26] This is a mixture of fantasy and hindsight. The troops at Y Beach had been given no orders to advance across the Peninsula, were new to battle, had no intelligence of the number of Turks south of Krithia and were unaware of the check at W and V beaches. Besides, Matthews, who had shown himself almost devoid of initiative, would have stayed in command even had he been reinforced. The fact stayed that if the higher command had wished these troops to play a more active role on the 25th, they should have given them orders to that effect. In 1915 even a purposeful commander would have been reluctant to disobey orders and strike out into the unknown. As for the evacuation, it mattered little. As events were to prove, there would be no prospect of imminent succour from the south. The bridgehead, had it remained, would have been isolated and, as the enemy mustered their reserves, subject to increasingly heavy Turkish counterattack. Much depleted, because of the high level of casualties, the end result can hardly have been in doubt. Inevitably, there must have been an evacuation of some kind, perhaps carried out in more difficult conditions than those on the 26th.

Meanwhile another successful flank landing had been made on the tiny strip of sand that was X Beach. The covering force (2 Royal Fusiliers) were told that they were to move to the south and capture Hill 114. They were then to secure the flank to the north-east of the beach, the implication being that this would secure the left flank of the entire advance once the troops from W and V came up from the south. Once again there were no contingency plans. The force at X Beach had no orders to assist if matters at the tip of the Peninsula did not go well. The divisional reserve of two battalions (1 Borders, 1 Royal Inniskilling Fusiliers) who were also to be landed at X Beach later in the morning were given no orders at all. Presumably they were to be at the disposal of the divisional commander and to be used as circumstances dictated, but this was nowhere specified.[27]

The landing of the covering force at X Beach passed almost without incident. The *Implacable* came so close inshore that an anchor slung from its bows grounded. The ship then deluged the beach with fire.[28] This was too much for the 9 or 12 Turks in the area, so the battalion landed without loss.[29] What happened next is not easy to piece together. It is clear that by the time the covering force formed up and began moving up the slopes of Hill 114 (about 8.00 a.m.), the Turks were reacting. The Royal Fusiliers were attacked by a force of probably one and a half companies. One company seems to have been the 9/26 from the central battalion reserve south of Krithia. The other detachment of about 100 men was almost certainly sent from the 12th Company overlooking W Beach.[30] The ferocity of their attack drove the Fusiliers back. On the right, however, there was a gap in the Turkish line, and assisted by a force from W (of which more later) the British pushed through and gained the summit. The view was remarkable. The whole southern tip of the Peninsula as far as S Beach could be observed, including hills 138 and 141 which were the objectives of the troops at W and V respectively. The Fusiliers were not immediately in a position to take advantage of this situation, even had they been given permission to do so. They were overextended, making their firing line very thin, and they were required to move men to the north-west of Hill 114 to keep the left flank safe.[31] However, by 9.00 a.m. the divisional reserve had begun to land. Some companies of the 1 Borders were ordered up from the beach to strengthen the Fusiliers' line, which they did, driving back another Turkish counterattack in the process.[32] Early in the afternoon a company of the other reserve battalion (Royal Inniskilling Fusiliers) was also sent forward and secured a position from about 1,000 yards north-east to 500 yards south-east of X Beach.[33] In these positions the whole force dug in and awaited developments.

The import of this episode needs to be appreciated. The Turks, even though spread so thinly at the southern tip of the Peninsula, had reacted against the landing at X with speed and determination for good reason. By capturing Hill 114 the British had outflanked the entire Turkish position at Helles. They were behind the defences at Hill 138, Guezji Baba and

Hill 141, as well as Seddelbahr village and fort—all the defences holding up their compatriots at W and V. They also had on hand, in the firing line and on the beach in reserve, 2,500 men, about three times more than all Turkish forces south of Krithia. It is clear from Turkish accounts that they regarded this as the key landing at Helles on 25 April, and feared that as a result they might have to withdraw to a second line further up the Peninsula.[34] In moving their men away from W Beach (which as we will see was to have wide ramifications), they were not to know that the British force at X Beach had no further objectives than Hill 114, that their purpose was not to sweep down from the rear over the two or three Turkish companies holding up the advance at W and V but to remain in situ until those forces drew level with them. Poor maps, which did not indicate before the battle that Hill 114 was the key to Hill 138 and points south, were partly responsible for this situation. But it was also true that Hamilton and Hunter-Weston had failed to provide a contingency plan in case of success.

While the opportunities or non-opportunities were going begging at X, great events were unfolding at V and W. At V Beach the landing place and the Turkish defences were truly formidable. They have been described thus:

> [V Beach] west of Seddel Bahr consisted of a strip of about 500 yards of sandy beach flanked on the east by Seddel Bahr village with the walls of the old fort running right down to the sea and on the west by the steep cliffs rising up to the lighthouse on Cape Helles. Within a few yards of the beach there was a line of steep sandy bank, cut by nullahs at intervals, and beyond this the ground rose in the form of an amphitheatre of terraced cultivation to the crest on which stood the old castle. Three lines of wire entanglement stretched right across, the lowest being about 25 yards from the beach. Machine guns and pom-poms had been concealed in the walls of the old fort and the cliffs to sweep the beach on both sides and Turkish infantry were entrenched and well concealed all round as well as in the village and the old fort, the approach to which was barred by the highest of the wire entanglements. The whole beach was commanded by both sides and in front.[35]

The plan to capture these formidable defences was to land the Dublin Fusiliers from tows and then ground the *River Clyde* with the remainder of the Dublins, the Munster Fusiliers and two companies of Hampshires on board. The plan went wrong from the beginning. It was obvious when the fleet arrived off Tekke Burnu that the tows for V Beach were making slow-going against the current and would not arrive on schedule at 5.30 a.m. Then at 6.40 a.m. a staff officer from 29 Division on the *Euryalis* off W Beach noted that the *River Clyde* had just steamed past and was not making much progress either.[36] In the event the tows with the Dublins and the *River Clyde* arrived at V Beach simultaneously at 7.00 a.m., one and a half hours late. Did this matter? To some extent it did. The plan for covering fire from the navy at V Beach was distinctly odd. Notwithstanding the importance of the landing in Hamilton's overall plan, just one ship (*Albion*) was directed to fire on the beach defences in the first instance. Despite indifferent light, which made it difficult to distinguish particular objects on shore, *Albion* opened fire at 5.04 a.m. As no boats were seen approaching, it ceased fire 20 minutes later. An awkward pause ensued. Around 6.00 a.m. fire was again commenced on the trenches close to the old fort but a ship off Y Beach (*Sapphire*) reported that some of these shells were falling among British troops on the cliffs there, so at 6.25 a.m. fire was halted again.[37] This was a sorry farce. *Albion*, one of the most ancient of the pre-dreadnoughts with just 4 woefully inaccurate heavy guns, had fired on V Beach for just 40 minutes during a period in which no troops were in sight. In fact during the entire day *Albion*, perhaps keeping the need to conserve ammunition to the forefront, fired just 12 shells from its main 12-inch armament, at a time when it had a large target in the shape of the Seddelbahr castle clearly visible.[38] Another ship (*Cornwallis*) was supposed to join the bombardment after its duties at S Beach had been completed but, as we have seen, that landing was delayed until 7.30 a.m. Then, for reasons that have never been satisfactorily explained, *Cornwallis* tarried off S and did not arrive at V until well after 9.00 a.m. Whether any of this mattered, given the inaccuracy of the fire of the pre-dreadnoughts and the difficulty they had in seeing small targets because of the dust and smoke produced from their first shots, is doubtful. But the troops deserved a decent fire support plan and they did not receive one.

The first to land at V Beach were the Dublin Fusiliers from the tows. They were met with a devastating fire from machine guns and riflemen in the trenches, the fort and the castle.[39] Few survived the first minute. Most did not even leave the boats, which 'drifted helplessly away with every man in them killed'.[40] Others were wounded and drowned. A few ran for the 'steep sandy bank' mentioned earlier and gained some protection there. On the extreme right two platoons which had been landed at the Camber, directly in front of Seddelbahr village, got ashore safely. A few of these managed to penetrate into the village where they were overwhelmed by the defenders. Most were pinned down on the beach, unable to move.[41]

Meanwhile the sally ports cut into the sides of the *River Clyde* were prised or forced (one jammed) open. The scene that greeted troops on the ship was devastating. They could see the dead Dublins and they could also see that there was no clear path to the beach. A steam pinnace was supposed to tow some lighters to the shore and place planks over them for the debouching troops. But the steam vessel had broken down and there was nothing between the troops and dry land. At this point Commander Unwin of the *Clyde* took matters into his own hands, connected the lighters himself and dragged them to within a few yards of the shore.[42] The troops then rushed towards the beaches.

One of the first to exit from the left sally port was Captain Geddes and his company of Munsters:

Off we went the men cheering and dashed ashore with Z Company. We got it like anything, man after man behind me was shot down but they never wavered. Lieut. Watts who was wounded in five places and lying on the gangway cheered the men on with cries of 'Follow the Captain'.

Captain French of the Dublins told me afterwards that he counted the first 48 men to follow me, and they all fell. I think no finer episode could be found of the men's bravery and discipline than this—of leaving the safety of the River Clyde to go to what was practically certain death.

Leaving the Clyde I dashed down the gangway and already found the Lighters holding the dead and wounded from the leading platoons of Z Company.

I stopped on the second lighter and looked around to find myself alone, and yelled to the men following out of the Clyde to come on, but it was difficult getting across the lighters. I then jumped into the sea and had to swim some dozen strokes to get ashore. There is no doubt that men were drowned owing chiefly, I think, to the great weight they were carrying—a full pack, 250 rounds of ammunition, and 3 days rations—I know I felt it. All the officers were equipped and dressed like the men.

There was a small rocky spit jutting into the sea which was absolutely taped down by the Turks and few, if any, survived who attempted to land there.

We all made, Dublins and all, for a sheltered ledge on the shore which gave us cover. Here we shook ourselves out, and tried to appreciate the situation, rather a sorry one. I estimated that I had lost about 70% of my company [probably about 140 men], . . .

Seeing that Sed-El-Bahr and the beach to our right was unoccupied, and fearing the Turks might come down I called for volunteers to make a dash for it, and make good the right of the beach. The men responded gallantly. Picking Sergt. Ryan and 6 men we had a go for it. Three out of the men were killed, one other and myself wounded. However we got across and later picked up 14 stragglers from the Company of the Dublins who had landed at [the Camber] . . . .

I reported to Colonel Tizard by semaphore from the shore that I could do nothing, as I had no men left. He told me to go for my objective Fort No.1 but it could not be done.[43]

Indeed, it could not. Nor could the 200 souls that remained from the covering force, scattered under their ledges, wounded, traumatized, exhausted, do anything but stay where they were. About 9.00 a.m. the bridge of lighters was joined to the shore, but the first company to make use of it suffered the same fate as the others. Common sense then prevailed on the *Clyde* and further landings were halted. The 1,000 men to embark would wait until nightfall. The main effort of the 29 Division had failed.

The Turkish force that had caused this carnage consisted in the first instance of just one company (10) of the 3/26 Battalion. Their own circumstances were far from happy. Their historian speaks of the 'hellish' fire they endured from the ships and from machine guns mounted in the bow of the *River Clyde*. Their losses were severe and at first their repeated calls for reinforcements were ignored. Finally around 8.30 a.m. 11 Company was released from reserve and joined them in Seddelbahr.[44] They arrived just in time to catch some units of the British main force diverted by Hunter-Weston to V Beach. These troops (2 companies of Hampshires and 500 Worcesters) by and large met the same fate as their predecessors. Their commanding officer was killed and most soon became casualties. Quick thinking from troops on the beached *Clyde* saved two companies which were safely diverted inside it.[45] But the force on the beach was still little more than 200 strong.

Why did the command send this force into the maelstrom at V Beach? Unbelievably, Hunter-Weston, although he was offshore in *Euryalis* at W Beach, only a short distance from V, seemed to have no idea of what was happening in front of Seddelbahr. Certainly, a message from an unknown but particularly ill-informed source at 7.30 a.m. had told him that 'troops from collier appear to be getting ashore well'.[46] Then at 7.50 a.m. a message from the *Lord Nelson* unhelpfully added that British troops could be seen in Seddelbahr village.[47] Probably the *Lord Nelson* had spotted the remnants of the force landed on the Camber, but the fact is that Hunter-Weston made no attempt to see for himself the situation at V Beach, though his ship could have arrived there in just a few minutes. Hamilton did arrive off Seddelbahr about 8.00 a.m. and could see that all was not well. The *Queen Elizabeth* promptly fired a few 15-inch shells and some from its 6-inch armament in the general direction of Seddelbahr. The *Cornwallis*, which had also finally arrived, added to this fire.[48] These shells may well have stopped any Turkish thought of a counterattack against the 200 troops huddled on the beach. Hamilton also informed Hunter-Weston that no progress was possible at V and troops that were still to land there should be diverted to W.[49] For the moment nothing further of note happened at V. The 1,200 remained in the *River Clyde*; the 200 on the beach. Night was eagerly awaited.

Meanwhile, the landing at W Beach, where the additional troops were to be diverted, had not started promisingly either. W Beach was the second main landing point for the 29 Division at Helles. The 1 Lancashire Fusiliers, who were to make the initial assault, were to assist the forces from X in securing Hill 114, capture Hill 138 which overlooked Seddelbahr and advance north on Achi Baba in conjunction with the other units of the division.

The situation facing the British at W was hardly favourable to the achievement of such objectives. The spoon-shaped beach was only some 200 yards across. It was protected by trenches and wire and on each flank was overlooked by cliffs. A major problem was that the cliffs might act as the sides of a funnel and direct the landing force into the centre which was well covered by Turkish machine-gun and rifle fire. The attackers, however, would have weight of numbers on their side. Protecting W Beach was just one company (12) of Turkish infantry, some 200 men facing an entire battalion which would be reinforced as the morning went by with units from two additional battalions.[50]

A staff officer from 29 Division on the *Euryalis* observed the opening phase of the landing:

Went up on deck about 5 am in the dim light of dawn. Found a dead calm sea, and the ship just moving. Gallipoli was just visible in the dim morning mists and the Lancashire Fusiliers already seated in the tows of cutters and pinnaces alongside. All was deadly still and silent, the engines of our ship hardly made a sound. One couldn't help pitying the men sitting there in their boats, feeling as nervous as one feels before a polo match [!!]. It was indeed a hush before the storm. There lay the Peninsula with not a sign of life on it . . . at 5.30 am we all went on to the Bridge and the Bombardment began.[51]

The fire of the ships at W Beach was hardly more effective than that at V. Again just one ship (*Swiftsure*) had been assigned to the beach for covering fire, with occasional help from Hunter-Weston's floating head-quarters, the *Euryalis*. Once more the Dardanelles current delayed the tows (had no one in the navy over the last six weeks taken note of the strength of current?), so that by the time the tows were nearing the beach (6.00 a.m.) the bombardment had ceased. In any case in the bad light all targets on the beach had been missed and fire had soon moved to battery positions 4,000 to 8,000 yards distant from W and then on to Achi Baba.[52]

Our staff officer, who was not at all convinced that the bombardment had been effective, again takes up the story.

The Lancashire Fusiliers had left the ship in 6 tows, each tow consisting of a pinnace with 6 cutters. These were now approaching the shore . . ..

The boats were now close to the shore, 'W Beach'. This was a short stretch of sandy beach about 200 yards long and 10 yards wide, cliffs on each side, those on the left climbable, those on the right precipitous with a track accessible beneath them. The beach itself was covered with barbed wire down to the water's edge and beneath it. The exits to the beach were sandy undulations with a solitary tree and a hut, and two nullah beds leading up to a neck whence the ground dipped over to the main wooded Krithia Valley. On the right the ground sloped up to Hill 138, where the Turks had a redoubt and much barbed wire was visible. There were Turkish trenches everywhere.

The boats disappeared in the smoke of the bombardment. Suddenly a heavy rifle fire broke out and we heard the dreaded rattle of machine gun fire. We felt that all was up and feared disaster. Such a thing as the possibility of a landing effected against heavy machine gun fire never entered one's head.[53]

Why this man, who was the Intelligence Officer for the entire division, thought the Turks would not possess machine guns (they had two at W Beach) is a mystery. But he was correct in fearing disaster. The tows came under heavy fire some hundreds of yards from the beach, and there were many killed and wounded aboard when they touched bottom. When the survivors landed they were met with a deadly crossfire from both cliffs and from the trenches to their front. Various attempts were made to force a passage through the wire but all failed. The initial attack had broken down at the water's edge. Then the Brigade Major (T. Frankland), coming ashore with a fresh tow, managed to divert the attack to the left and the men disembarked under the cover of the cliff. A few men followed Frankland up the path to the top where a brief bayonet fight ensued, Frankland killing either two, four or six Turks 'with a rifle taken from a private soldier'. More men followed and Frankland (who was a paragon of initiative) directed them against the southern slopes of Hill 114 where they were eventually to join with the troops from X Beach. Frankland, who had succeeded to the command of 86 Brigade as Brigadier. Hare had been wounded, then decided to move towards the right where brigade headquarters was to be set up and Hill 138 attacked. He collected some 100 men and set out along the cliffs toward the hill. Although he was unaware of it, this movement was assisted by a break in the line created by the diversion of a Turkish unit to counter the British attack from X Beach on Hill 114.[54] This had opened a gap in the defences at W Beach through which Frankland and his men proceeded. The group then split into two parties. The first tried to break through the wire protecting Hill 138 but were driven back by Turkish fire. The second, led by Frankland, headed for the lighthouse. Here they found themselves entangled in the wire and trench defences of yet another hill— Guezji Baba—which came as a complete surprise to the British because it was not marked on any of their maps. The party was too small to attack Guezji Baba but Frankland managed to set up a signalling station from where he got in touch with the *River Clyde* and could at last pass the true state of affairs back to Hunter-Weston. Frankland then decided to see the situation at V Beach for himself but he was held up by wire entanglements and shot down as he tried to struggle free.[55]

The 86 Brigade was now leaderless, but back at the beach help was arriving. Most of the 4 Worcester Battalion and the 1 Essex had been diverted by Hunter-Weston from V to W, not because he had any knowledge of the situation at V but because his entire attention was directed on W and he had been made aware that a considerable crisis was looming there. These troops landed between 10.00 a.m. and 1.00 p.m. (the sources are vague on this point) and gradually moved towards Hill 138. The first attempt by the 1 Essex to capture it failed. Shortly after 2.00 p.m. the Worcesters moved up and a combined attack on Hill 138 succeeded, the 40 or 50 Turkish defenders retreating on Guezji Baba. Leaving a garrison on Hill 138, British troops then attacked and carried Guezji Baba.[56] The hills to the west of V Beach were in British hands.

The defence of these two hills was an epic of Turkish tenacity. They were only ever defended by a few platoons from 10 Company, reinforced by a few men from the reserve. Yet it took the best part of three British battalions some seven hours to capture them. Certainly the British were hampered by the lack of accurate covering fire; there was no artillery and the ships' guns were useless. But the defending force led by an intrepid sergeant, Enizeli Yahya, fought with skill and endurance in holding on for so long against such odds.[57]

It was now late afternoon and despite their tenacity the Turks were in a precarious position. Three of the four hills at Helles were in British hands. The enclave around Seddelbahr was all that remained to them. Moreover, the British had over 1,000 relatively fresh troops on the *River Clyde* who could be landed under the cover of darkness. Had the Turks possessed any local reserves, late afternoon was the time to use them. But in fact there were none—all had been expended in delaying but not stopping the 29 Division.

The remainder of the story can be quickly told. During the night the troops from the *River Clyde* were safely disembarked. They even managed to make a forward movement at night and establish a foothold in the village.[58] The Turks mustered a few men from a reserve battalion (2/25) but dispersed them in penny-packet night attacks on Hill 138 and the British troops in Seddelbahr. This time the British were too strong. They had machine guns on the heights and near the old fort. All Turkish efforts to dislodge them failed.[59]

In the morning of 26 April the attention of the British force turned to Seddelbahr village. Following the customary ineffectual bombardment by the ships, an attack went in. After a period of confused street fighting, numbers told and the Turks were driven out. Hill 141 was the next objective. A frantic Turkish appeal for reinforcements went unanswered and just after 2.00 p.m. their last stronghold on the tip of the Peninsula fell. Shortly afterwards the command went out for the Turks to withdraw up the Peninsula and establish a new line of defence. Helles was in the hands of the 29 Division.[60]

How is the battle at Helles to be summed up? The capture of the tip of the Peninsula cost the British about 3,800 casualties, about 20 per cent of the infantry strength of the 29 Division. Turkish casualties are difficult to estimate. The 3/26 lost 50 per cent casualties and there is no reason to think that the other forces engaged piecemeal as reserves lost any less. If this estimate is correct the Turks lost about 800 to 1,000 casualties.[61]

So the Turks won the battle of the casualties but the British were still able to establish themselves ashore. Why was this? The simple answer is weight of numbers. If we count just X, W and V beaches, the British had about 4,000 men ashore by 8.00 a.m., 9,500 by 10.00 and about 17,000 by dawn on 26 April. The Turks could not match this build up. Just over 700 of their men faced the first landings and by the end of the day they had hardly more than 2,500 deployed against the southern beaches and probably no more than 3,500 by dawn the next day. With this disparity the result was not in doubt.

What of the way the battle itself was conducted? Possibly the greatest Turkish mistake was in the distribution of their forces. At the landings just half the 3/26 Battalion was deployed near the beaches and the other half kept back in reserve. This led to the situation where they were spread too thinly to cover all the landing places. The landing at Y Beach might always have come as a surprise to the Turks, but Hill 114 was an obvious British target and yet had no defenders. The attempt to provide them opened a gap in the Turkish line which eventually allowed Hill 138 and Guezji Baba to be captured and the whole Turkish position in the south to be outflanked. Had more of the battalion been deployed closer to the beaches, the Turks might have been able to mount some counterattacks that could have seriously threatened the small British toeholds.

As for the British, even taking the inexperience of the troops and commanders into consideration, the overall impression is one of lack of initiative and dash. Frankland stands out as such a beacon because his type was so rare. The more common approach was exhibited by Matthews at Y Beach and the various commanders at X Beach. At X Beach, despite all the excuses that can be summoned to explain the lack of action there, it still does not seem to be beyond the wit of a local commander to have summed up the situation and acted accordingly. S and Y beaches were only lost opportunities in theory; it was at X Beach that the real possibilities of the day went begging.

The higher command cast a baleful light on the battle. Hamilton's plan contained the germ of a good idea (the flank landings), but this opportunity was missed because he seemed determined to hit the Turks where they were strongest, at W and V beaches. On the day of battle Hamilton did not consider it his job to interfere with Hunter-Weston, which would have been sound if Hunter-Weston had had any grip on the battle. Unfortunately for the British this was far from being the case. Hunter-Weston's attention and his person remained anchored off W Beach for most of the day. He was out of contact with S and Y, neglected X and seemed determined to avoid any knowledge of V. He failed to receive most messages sent to him and took no steps to gather information for himself. His one positive move (to shift troops from V to W Beach) had nothing to do with the situation at V and only succeeded because the Turkish defence was stretched too thinly. For one who had been so perceptive before the event, his actions on the first day of battle are puzzling in the extreme. At any event, the British were ashore. There were lessons aplenty to be derived from 25 April. Would Hamilton and Hunter-Weston apply them to their next endeavour?

CHAPTER 8

A Perfect Hail of Bullets
Landing and Consolidation at Anzac

While preparations were being made for the Anzac landing, Birdwood mulled over the plan given to him by Hamilton and Braithwaite. The GHQ plan had called for the seizure of a large part of the Sari Bair Ridge to protect a later advance across the Peninsula to Mal Tepe. There were aspects of this operation that concerned Birdwood. What would his force do when it arrived at Mal Tepe? What size force would be available for this operation after the occupation of the ridge?

As the day of battle approached there were more worries for the Anzac commander. Intelligence from reconnaissance voyages near the coast and from aircraft had revealed that there were guns on the southern extremity of the third ridge, and more guns and troop concentrations in the cultivated area of Peren Ovasi south-east of Gaba Tepe.[1] These revelations, in Birdwood's opinion, opened the prospect that his force could be immediately counter-attacked from two directions—down the ridge from the north, the obvious direction, but now up the ridge from the south as well.

To meet this threat Birdwood changed the plan. While not relinquishing any objectives along the ridge to his north, he extended the front to meet the danger from the south. He considered the capture of Gun Ridge would block any move made by Turkish troops from Peren Ovasi, so he ordered it be taken as a first priority by the covering force. Only when Gun Ridge was secure should this force turn its attention to the heights of Sari Bair to the north.[2]

All this had major implications for the operation. Adding Gun Ridge extended the objective by 1,500 yards and spread the force terribly thin. A ridge line now some 5 miles long would need to be captured before any advance across the Peninsula could commence. And in giving the southern objectives priority Birdwood was running the risk that the high ground to his north, which dominated the whole Anzac position, might be seized by the enemy while his men were concentrating on the lower ground further south.

This change of plan has largely gone unremarked by commentators. At the time it also seems to have gone unremarked by Hamilton and Braithwaite. Indeed, there is no evidence to suggest that Birdwood discussed the changes with them and certainly no evidence that they grasped the implications of the changes if he did.

There were other puzzling aspects to the planning of the Anzac operations. While there were now two plans, one brought forth by GHQ and one by Birdwood, neither had specified exactly where the force should land.

Hamilton's orders to the Anzac Corps regarding landing sites were characteristic of the terrible imprecision that was such a feature of the higher command at Gallipoli. All Hamilton said was that the force should land somewhere between Nibrunesi Point and Gaba Tepe. This was useless as a guide because it covered a stretch of coast 6 miles long.

Braithwaite, Chief of Staff to Hamilton, refined his chief's instruction by narrowing the landing point to between Fisherman's Hut and Gaba Tepe. But this was still a distance of 3 miles so there was still no precise direction.

Admiral Cecil Thursby, the naval officer in charge of the Anzac landing, added a little more precision, presumably after consultation with Birdwood. He fixed the right flank of the landing 'about one mile north of Gaba Tepe' and stated that the landings would extend northwards from that point for '8 cables' (a cable was 200 yards).[3] In other words the initial landing would take place over a distance of about 1,600 yards with its right 'about' 1 mile north of Gaba Tepe.

Yet if Thursby's intended landing zone had been developed in conjunction with Birdwood, the corps commander seemed to pay it very little attention. In his own orders, written after Thursby's, Birdwood merely stated that the landing would be 'North of Gaba Tepe'.[4] Even in his order to the covering force that would undertake the initial landing, Birdwood merely spoke of the 'Gaba Tepe—Fisherman's Hut landing place'.[5] Nor did the orders to the covering force itself (3 Brigade) shed any light on the matter; there was no mention whatsoever in their orders about where the men were to land.[6]

The only other attempt to define the landing place came from Thursby on the very eve of battle. At 7.05 p.m. on 24 April, Thursby altered the position of the right flank of the landing from 'about one mile north of Gaba Tepe' to 'about 800 yards north of Gaba Tepe',[7] shifting the landing area about half a mile to the south. It is not difficult to speculate about the reason for this change. It was exactly in line with Birdwood's new objectives on Gun Ridge, all of which lay directly opposite the area where Thursby was now suggesting the force should land. This would seem conclusive as an explanation, were it not for the fact that neither Birdwood nor Thursby made any further mention of this last-minute change. In his first communication to Hamilton after the landing, Birdwood indicated that he had aimed for a point 1 mile north of Gaba Tepe.[8] This was also his position under cross-examination at the Dardanelles Inquiry, as it was Thursby's.[9] Under these circumstances it is doubtful whether the change to the south was ever implemented.

What can be made of all of this? It appears that the main priority for military and naval commanders was to land the Anzac force somewhere between Gaba Tepe and Fisherman's Hut. Not one instruction given by any authority for the landing place is much more precise than this. Even Thursby only specified that the southern flank should be about a mile north of Gaba Tepe. It appears that the exact landing point for the Anzacs was not seen as a high priority by the planners. Certainly they did not want to land too close to Gaba Tepe with its artillery and machine guns. Nor did they want to land to the north of Fisherman's Hut because that was too far from the main ridge and too distant from the desired line of advance across the Peninsula. Any point in between those locations would be sufficient (providing the landing was made on a broad enough front) to allow troops to divert right or left to the ridges that were their objectives. And as there were thought to be few Turkish defenders in the immediate area, the deployment after the landing was not seen as a major difficulty.

* * *

The Anzac troops would be landed in four waves somewhere north of Gaba Tepe. The initial wave would consist of just 1,500 men from 3 Brigade. They would be transferred to 3 battleships at Lemnos and brought to within 5 miles of the coastline where they would be transferred to 12 tows of rowing boats. These tows would then be attached to steam pinnaces which would bring them to within rowing distance of shore where they would land at around 4.30 a.m. The second wave would land just after the first. They would be on seven destroyers which would disembark their 2,500 troops in the same manner as the battleships.[10] These 4,000 troops would make up the covering force and it was their task to seize the heights from Gun Ridge in the south to Chunuk Bair in the north.

The third wave would comprise the remainder of 1 Australian Division (2 and 1 Brigades). They would be disembarked from transports by the boats that had landed the covering force.[11] The 2 Brigade was given specific orders to reinforce the northern flank on the heights beyond Battleship Hill.[12] The 1 Brigade was to remain in reserve.

Two brigades (NZ Brigade, 4 Australian Brigade) of the New Zealand and Australian Division (NZ & A) would land in the fourth wave. This force would land sometime during the afternoon of 25 April. It was never made clear what its task would be. If 1 Australian Division had secured the heights, it might have provided the force that was to proceed across the Peninsula to Mal Tepe. Birdwood's orders, however, indicate that he thought this movement would not take place for some time. The NZ & A Division is perhaps best thought of as an additional reserve which could be thrown in as events on the day dictated.[13]

In the late evening of 24 April the Anzac force left Mudros on Lemnos and steamed north-east towards the Gallipoli Peninsula. The story is taken up by the War Diary of the Anzac Corps, which was on the battleship HMS *Queen*:

1.am.	Attending ships stopped—Boats swung out. Flat calm.
1.35.am.	Moon 5 fingers above horizon dead astern and above Mudros island. Troops began disembarking. Destroyers began to close up. Embarkation absolutely silent on Queen.
2.35.	Tows from battleships reported all ready—destroyers all close up.
2.53.	Proceeded due east under steam.
3.30.	Battleships stopped—orders to tows to 'Go ahead and land'.
4.00.	Signal made to destroyers to come on.
4.5.	First streak of dawn.
4.30.	Firing heard on the beach.[14]

An officer of 10 Battalion in one of the tows continues:

Towed to within 50 yards of shore by steam boats . . . one sound was heard escape—the splash of the oars. We thought that our landing was to be effected quite unopposed, but when our boats were within about 30 yards of the beach a rifle was fired from the hill in front of us above the beach right in front of where we were heading for. Almost immediately heavy rifle & machine gun fire was opened up on us. We had to row for another 15 yards or so before we reached water shallow enough to get out of the boats. This was at about 4.15am—We got out of the boats in to about 3ft of water & landed on a stony bottom. The stones were round & slimy & many officers & men slipped on them & fell in to the water, but all bravely & silently made all haste towards the beach under a perfect hail of bullets. Many men fixed their bayonets before reaching the shore. I ordered men to lay down, fix bayonets & remove packs. This was done in a couple of minutes. The men of 9th, 10 & 11 Bns were all mixed up on the beach, but there was no time to reorganize so I ordered *all* to advance. The men sprang to their feet at once & with a cheer charged up the hill held by the Turks & drove them off, following up the success by firing on the quickly retreating foe.[15]

So the Australians were ashore. But where were they? After they had left the battleships most of the tows had bunched together and some had even proceeded across the paths of the others. Most deposited their men in a small cove (later known as Anzac Cove) just south of Ari Burnu. Others had drifted north of the cove and dropped their troops into the next small bay.[16] The Anzac landing place has been the subject of much discussion over the years. It has been said that the battleships anchored too far north and that the subsequent problems sprang from this mistake. Others have claimed that the current flowing off the Aegean coast of the Peninsula carried the men to the north. Another theory is that the midshipmen in the directing tows lost direction in the dark and drifted north. A variation on this theory states that the tows which crossed the path of the others had realized the mistake and were trying to land as far to the south as they could.[17]

Probably all this controversy is as misdirected as its protagonists claim the Anzacs were. The landing took place well within the Fisherman's Hut–Gaba Tepe parameters which were all that the higher commanders seemed concerned about. As for the bunching of the tows, this could have taken place for any number of reasons, but crowding together for security, or loss of direction in the dark, would seem sufficient explanation for some minor mistakes off an unknown and hostile coast in the dark.

In any case the initial landing was not as chaotic as it has sometimes been portrayed. There had certainly been some casualties, especially in those boats to the north of Ari Burnu, where a machine gun had opened fire from around Fisherman's Hut.[18] Others had been drowned by the weight of their packs as they slipped into the water. More had succumbed to the fire of the 200 or so Turkish riflemen who were in the immediate vicinity of Anzac Cove.[19] Certainly the bunching of the tows had caused an intermixture of men from the 9, 10 and 11 Battalions. But when they proceeded to climb Ari Burnu they found themselves on a small, triangular, flat area (Plugge's Plateau) where some reorganization took place. Given the urgency of the situation (it had been emphasized at all levels that speed was essential to gain the inland ridges), the mixture of units and the fact that it was still grey dawn, the sorting of men into battalions could only have been rudimentary. Nevertheless, officers could still generally send men from 9 and 10 Battalions to the south for the advance on Gun Ridge, and men from 11 Battalion to advance up the ridge towards Battleship Hill and beyond.[20]

At this moment help, in the form of the second wave, started arriving. Here there was not the bunching of tows that had occurred earlier. It was now light and the individual tows and the coastline could be seen. As a result the second wave landed on a broad front of about 1,500 yards with its assault battalions deposited in the correct order (9 and 10 Battalion with some companies of 12 to the south, 11 and the bulk of 12 Battalion to the north). Thus at around 4.45 a.m. the 4,000 men from the covering force were ashore and the front of advance had broadened from a few hundred yards to 2,000.[21]

It was at this point that the absurdly ambitious nature of the plan started to manifest itself. As groups of men set out for their objectives, the country swallowed them up. A dense, gorse-like bush covered the slopes, making them difficult to penetrate and concealing the rugged nature of the country the men had to cross. For example, the troops deploying northwards seemed, from Plugge's Plateau, to have rather a straightforward climb up to the heights called Russell's Top and Baby 700. What was not evident from Plugge's was that Russell's Top was joined to Baby 700 by only a narrow path between two steep gullies, while Baby 700 was separated from Plugge's by a winding, razorback ridge. Moreover, it was not difficult, even in daylight, for a column of advancing men to be diverted down different valleys or depressions without realizing that their compatriots were no longer in front of them. In other areas, such as near a feature called the Sphinx, the slopes were so precipitate that much time had to be expended in finding a climbable path. Most importantly of all, although on the map the distance, say, from Battleship Hill to the southern extremity of Gun Ridge was no more than 5,000 yards as the crow flies, the distance at least quadrupled if the hilly and tortuous nature of the terrain was taken into account.

In short, 4,000 troops deploying in such country, over such distances, would soon find themselves split into small groups, hardly able to form anything like a continuous firing line and incapable of maintaining a continuous presence on the ridge because of its great length.

So very quickly it became appropriate to identify groups of about 50 to 100 men and call them not by their battalion numbers or company letters but by the name of the officer (of whatever rank) who led them. Thus between 5.00 a.m. and 7.00 a.m. advancing on Russell's Top and Baby 700 there was Tulloch, Margetts and Lalor's group (to mention only the most prominent), while to the south advancing on 400 Plateau and Gun Ridge there was Salisbury, Loutit and Ryder's group.[22]

Such groups of men could hardly hold extensive sections of the main ridge or maintain themselves against concerted counterattacks. But help was on the way. At 6.00 a.m. the 2 and 1 Brigades began to arrive in Anzac Cove. Disembarking these troops was a slower process than had been imagined. Many of the boats returning from landing the covering force were packed with wounded who had to be dealt with before the boats were available for a second run into the beach. Moreover, guns on Gaba Tepe were starting to burst shrapnel shells over the landing area. Nevertheless, by 7.30 a.m. the reinforcements were coming ashore in large numbers.[23] The first troops to be deployed were from 2 Brigade. They had specific orders. The 5 and 7 Battalions were to move to the north, occupy Battleship Hill and Baby 700 and act as a guard for the northern flank. The other battalions were to act as ammunition carriers and constitute the brigade reserve.[24]

In the event, this order hardly survived the landing of the brigade. Colonel Sinclair Maclagan, the commander of the covering force, found himself faced with a considerable dilemma. His orders from Birdwood were to secure the southern flank and advance on Gun Ridge as a first priority to safeguard the force from counterattack by the strong forces said to be south of Gaba Tepe. Yet the small groups he sent (from 9 and 10 Battalions) to that area were hardly sufficient for the task. The small groups from 11 and

12 Battalions sent to the northern flank to secure the high ground were also hardly strong enough to withstand an onslaught by the Turks. At around 9.00 a.m. the commander of 2 Brigade, Colonel James M'Cay, arrived at Maclagan's headquarters. Maclagan immediately asked him to redirect the 2 Brigade to the right to secure the southern flank. M'Cay demurred and pointed to his orders. Maclagan no doubt pointed to Birdwood's orders and eventually he prevailed. The 2 Brigade would not go to the high ground to the north but to the south to assist the 9 and 10 Battalions.[25] A few minutes earlier Maclagan had made another decision. He ordered 3 Brigade to abandon any attempt to reach Gun Ridge that day. He could see 2,000 or so Turks massing on it and deemed his whole right flank was in danger of being driven in. His men must withdraw all groups in advance of the second ridge and dig in on that line.[26]

What Maclagan was witnessing was the arrival of the first Turkish reserves on the battlefield. The Turkish 9 and 19 Divisions had their head-quarters near Maidos on the Peninsula's eastern coast, and became aware of the landings at Ari Burnu within 30 minutes of the Anzac force reaching the beach. The first to respond was Sami Bey, the commander of 9 Division. At 5.00 a.m. he ordered two battalions of the 27 Regiment and a machine-gun company to advance on Gun Ridge.[27] He also passed on the news of the landing to the 19 Division and its commander, Lieutenant-Colonel Mustapha Kemal. Kemal's response was not as immediate as legend would have it. For three hours he tried to contact higher authorities to obtain definite orders. At 8.00 a.m. he gave up and took the initiative himself. The best regiment under his hand was the 57th. He directed it to Hill 971, the highest point of the Sari Bair range. And he did more. He accompanied his troops with the intention of personally directing the battle.[28] Although they did not know it, the Anzac forces were now in real danger. Approximately 5,000 Turks were making for the beachhead and they would arrive first at the most vulnerable points of the line, the southern and northern flanks.

Meanwhile the battalions of 2 Brigade (and some from 1 Brigade as well) were moving to the right. But when they reached 400 Plateau they did not dig in; that aspect of the orders did not reach them. Instead they immediately attacked across it. Initially they gained ground because there were only stragglers ahead. But soon they encountered units of the 27 Regiment which had reached the area around 10.30 a.m. Opposition suddenly became much more intense and they were driven back. For the remainder of the day a see-saw battle took place across the plateau. The exact course of particular events in this period is obscure. Casualties certainly mounted, reserves were sucked into the fight. At dusk neither side could claim the plateau as theirs.[29]

Despite the inconclusive nature of the conflict, at least the southern flank held. To the north it was a different story. Between 9 and 10 a.m. a Turkish counterattack, delivered by the scattered platoons that had opposed the landing, drove the Australians off Baby 700. Maclagan saw this event from his command post, but he had now committed most of his reserves. The best he could do was order to the heights some companies from 1 Brigade which were still nearby. These forces achieved some success. They regained Baby 700 and advanced on Battleship Hill. In conjunction with General William Bridges and Birdwood, a decision was then taken to send the NZ & A brigades to the north to bolster that flank. The problem was that most of these troops had not yet arrived. In what must be regarded as a major administrative bungle, no troops at all arrived at Anzac between midday and 6.00 p.m. The only units available were the Auckland Battalion and two companies of the Canterbury Battalion on a warship which carried the NZ & A commander, General Alexander Godley. They had disembarked around noon and were now ordered to proceed to Baby 700.[30] It was too late. Between 2.30 p.m and 4.00 p.m Turkish artillery fire increased on the Australian left. At 4.30 p.m. a concerted counterattack was delivered by Kemal's 57 Regiment.[31] The small groups of Australians gave way. Battleship Hill and Baby 700 were lost. They would never be regained.

The question now was: could the northern flank hold at all? It was known that some parties of Turks had penetrated to Russell's Top and were in fact between the Anzac forces and the beach. Reinforcements were desperately needed. Had not the transportation arrangements fallen into almost total disarray, these would have been available in numbers. The remainder of the NZ Brigade and the 4 Australian Brigade had arrived off Anzac Cove around 5.00 p.m. Yet the only troops disembarked immediately were some companies of the Wellington Battalion and the 16 Battalion.[32] Others such as 15 Battalion had two companies ready to be disembarked from destroyers at 4.50 p.m. But because of the disorganization on the beach they were not landed until 10.30 p.m. In the meantime the destroyers came under shell fire and casualties resulted.[33] The landing of 14 Battalion was even more disorganized:

Arrived off Kaba Tepe at Landing place about 5 P.M. About 6 P.M. lighters commenced to come along side with wounded. Men of 14th Bn moved from troop decks to make room for the wounded who continued to come aboard all night; many of our men working all night assisting them aboard. About midnight 3 officers and 90 men disembarked under Captain Wright and reported to H.Q. N.Z.& A Division. These were given orders to entrench themselves and act as a reserve.[34]

The bulk of the battalion (25 officers and 810 men) were not disembarked until 1.30 p.m. on 26 April.[35]

In this way only driblets of reinforcements could be sent to the endangered northern flank. But although the officers on the beach did not know it, these would prove sufficient. The Turks, on 25 April anyway, had shot their bolt. Several factors contributed to this. As night fell they were forced to halt their artillery fire for fear of hitting their own men. Also, as the Anzacs knew to their cost, the difficult terrain broke up formations and made large-scale, concerted operations almost impossible, especially in the dark. Also like the Anzacs, the Turkish troops were tired. They had marched considerable distances and engaged in heavy fighting for many hours. Finally, one of Kemal's regiments designated for a counterattack at 400 Plateau had collapsed. The 77 Regiment had come under heavy naval fire and had been attacked by the forces of first 3 and then 2 Brigade on the plateau. They were mainly men from the Arabian Peninsula who, it might be imagined, felt no desperate need to lay down their lives for the Turkish Empire. In the words of the *Turkish Staff History:*

They [the 77 Regiment] had hidden themselves in the dense heath and upon the intensive bombardment of the English battleships they fled the battleground. In fact [many of these troops] had fought against the English bravely [but] the darkness of the night, the unending bombardment of the fleet, irregular formation of the terrain had increased the dispersion of the troops. Control was lost; everything was out of control.[36]

Meanwhile, it was not only the Turks who were losing control on the night of the 25th. As darkness descended, troops from various sections of the Anzac line who had become separated from their units began to drift back towards the beach. There was only ever a trickle of these men, but the commanders on the spot had no sure knowledge of the situation on all sections of the front or whether the drift back might not open gaps in the line or become a flood. Maclagan was also aware that there were gaps which the meagre late-afternoon reinforcements could not fill. Of particular worry were the positions just short of the second ridge around Pope's Hill and Bloody Angle. These positions left open the possibility of a Turkish counterattack down Monash Valley, which could bring the enemy perilously close to the beach.

Other clear heads such as Cyril Brudenell White, Chief of Staff to General Bridges, realized that the original plan lay in ruins. Any reinforcements would now have to be employed to shore up the existing perimeter. There would be no advance across the Peninsula to places such as Mal Tepe because there were no troops available. In these circumstances might not the best way to help the 29 Division be an evacuation and a redeployment at Helles?[37]

In this atmosphere a hurried meeting was called at Bridges' headquarters, a hollowed-out scoop of sand in a hill near the beach. Maclagan, perhaps because he was in closer touch with the troops, thought nothing could stop a Turkish attack from the north. Godley was also pessimistic. Brigadier Harold Walker, Chief of Staff to Birdwood, was more sanguine. Bridges, who had exercised little influence on the battle so far, now had to decide. What he decided was to ask Birdwood. Bridges' news came as a considerable surprise to the Anzac commander. He had been ashore around 3.00 p.m. and although he had been told that the line was not yet secure, he had left thinking that 'the situation was not such as to cause great alarm'.[38] The Corps War Diary continues:

> Later both of the Divisional generals [Bridges and Godley] represented that GOCs presence was necessary on shore. He landed again at 8 p.m. A long conference was held at which the necessity and possibility of re-embarkation was discussed. The GOC decided that we must hold on.[39]

In fact the GOC made no such decision. Like Bridges he decided to pass the matter up the chain of command. After the meeting at Bridges' HQ, Birdwood scribbled a note, almost certainly meant for Hamilton but not addressed to anyone. It read:

> Both my divisional generals and brigadiers have represented to me that they fear their men are thoroughly demoralised by shrapnel fire to which they have been subjected all day after exhaustion and gallant

work in morning. Numbers have dribbled back from the firing line and cannot be collected in difficult country. Even New Zealand Brigade which has only recently been engaged lost heavily and is to some extent demoralized. If troops are subjected to shellfire again to-morrow morning there is likely to be a fiasco, as I have no fresh troops with which to replace those in firing line. I know my representation is most serious, but if we are to re-embark it must be done at once.[40]

The unaddressed message eventually reached Thursby at 11.00 p.m. As a precautionary measure he immediately sent a message to all ships ordering them to lower all boats and prepare to send them in to the beach. At this moment the *Queen Elizabeth*, with Hamilton aboard, arrived off Gaba Tepe. Thursby took the message across by launch, Hamilton was woken and an impromptu conference called with Braithwaite, de Robeck, Keyes and two senior officers from Anzac, including Cunliffe Owen the artillery commander. Hamilton read Birdwood's message and asked for opinions. The decisive replies came from Thursby and Keyes. Neither commander considered a night evacuation a feasible operation. That decided it. Hamilton sat down and addressed what he hoped was a morale-boosting message to Birdwood. In brief, he told him that an evacuation would take two days, and that 'there is nothing for it but to dig yourself right in and stick it out'.[41]

There is little doubt that this was the correct decision. Naval opinion had to carry the day on the matter of evacuation. A night operation would have been extremely hazardous, the position of many groups in the firing line was not known with any certainty and a general order to retreat to the beach might have caused panic resulting in a shambles.

It seems certain that Birdwood and his senior commanders (Walker was an exception) momentarily lost their nerve. The objective situation was not nearly as dire as described in his note. The line was holding; there was no sign of a major attack from the Turks; the force (as against some individuals in it) was not demoralized. But it was dark, the circumstances of the conference were hardly conducive to clear thinking and the sight of stragglers on the beach must have been unnerving. Later Birdwood tried to deny that he favoured evacuation, writing to Hamilton that he had only sent the message for the information of the commander-in-chief.[42] There is no need to take this seriously. The use of words such as 'demoralized' and 'fiasco' reveals clearly enough the state of Birdwood's thinking. As time went on all concerned tried to distance themselves from the decision to

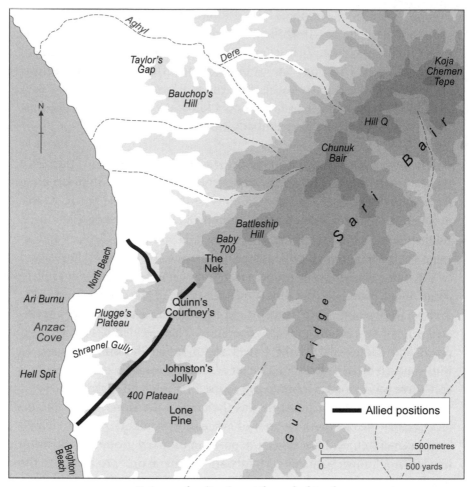

9 Anzac: the situation at the end of April

call for an evacuation. There is no need to take any of that seriously either.[43] The fact is that Hamilton, under naval advice that no other course of action was possible, held his nerve when few others did.

So ended the first day at Anzac. None of the objectives had been achieved. The troops were just short of the second ridge and a considerable distance short of the third ridge. All the high ground was in the possession of the Turks. As for the force that was to advance on Mal Tepe, it had been consumed in shoring up the firing line. There could be no cross-Peninsula movement unless reinforcements arrived in numbers. Even had such troops been available, it might have been a very difficult task keeping them supplied as they advanced away from the crowded and disorganized 'base' at Anzac Cove. Moreover, Turkish reinforcements had already arrived on the battlefield and more could be expected in the days to come. Any future operations would have to take that unpalatable fact into account.

What had gone wrong? In essence there was little more that the troops could have done to convert the landing into something more substantial. It was the plan and the Turks that had thwarted the endeavour. It really was absurdly ambitious to expect a force of one and two-thirds divisions to occupy the precipitous slopes of the third ridge and stage an advance across a Peninsula that would have been open to counterattack from north and south. Birdwood's tampering with the plan only made things worse because it added another mile to the length of ridge that had to be captured.

Maclagan has come in for much criticism for diverting the 2 Brigade south to the area of Gun Ridge instead of allowing it to carry out its original instructions to seize the high ground around Battleship Hill. It should be clear by now that Maclagan was not changing the plan; he was attempting to carry out Birdwood's instructions. Perhaps it should have been obvious to Maclagan that the high ground to the north, which dominated the Anzac position, was intrinsically more important to his force than was Gun Ridge. However, at the time he made the decision he could see the first of the Turkish counterattacks massing on Gun Ridge, and he was one of a whole raft of officers on Gallipoli whose every instinct was to follow orders. Had 2 Brigade moved north to the left flank, what would have happened? It is difficult to speculate but it seems reasonable to suppose that Baby 700 could have been held. On the other hand, this might have come at the expense of losing 400 Plateau to the Turkish 27 Brigade, who almost captured it despite the presence of 2 Brigade. What seems clear is that these small adjustments in the Anzac perimeter on

25 April would not, in the overall scheme of things, have counted for much. The troops were a long way from their real objectives—Hill 971, Chunuk Bair and Mal Tepe—and it is doubtful whether the actions of any local commander could have got them much closer.

The myth that the force was landed in the wrong place and that this fatal dislocation to the plan caused it to fail should be put to rest. The force did not miss the parameters which were all that were given to delineate the landing area, and the confusion caused by the bunching of the tows only affected the first wave of 1,500 men. The others landed more or less in their designated positions and if there was confusion, it was no more than might be expected after a night landing on a hostile coast.

Another myth that should be set aside is that the terrain alone stopped the Anzacs achieving their objectives. The difficulty of conducting military operations in the rugged country faced by the troops should certainly not be minimized. However, it was the celerity with which the Turkish command propelled reserves towards the battlefield and the tenacity with which those who met the landing continued to fight that turned the tables. The initial group slowed the Anzac advance for long enough to allow the Turkish reserves to deny the Anzacs not only the third ridge but the second as well. It was the enemy and the plan, not the chosen place of landing and the subsequent terrain, that denied the Anzacs their objectives on the first day.

* * *

But if the Anzacs were relieved to have avoided an evacuation, the Turks were not inclined to let them consolidate their toehold on the Peninsula in peace. Consequently, in the days that followed the landing, a number of counterattacks were ordered against the Anzac positions. On 27 April the Turks attacked three times, once in broad daylight and twice at night. On 1 May they attacked again. These operations had three factors in common: they were uncoordinated; they lacked consistent artillery support; and they all failed with heavy casualties. The fire from the ships (particularly important on 27 April) and machine-gun and rifle fire proved sufficient to deny the Turks any real gains.

On the Allied side Hamilton had forbidden all offensive efforts at Anzac while the Helles battles were in progress.[44] The only way forward then for the moment was by raiding, in order to straighten the line or otherwise improve a position. Nowhere was this more necessary than on the right of Monash Gully where three posts—Quinn's, Courtney's and Steele's—clung to its lower slopes. The Turkish trenches overlooked these precarious positions and were just 40 yards away. On the 15 May it was determined by the command that 15 Battalion would capture some trenches near Quinn's Post. The scheme was well thought out. It was to be a night attack with two assaulting parties, each consisting of 30 men and each designated to capture a particular section of enemy trench. When these trenches were in Australian hands, two digging parties of 20 men would be sent forward to improve the alignment of the trenches and help fight off any Turkish counter move. An additional 10 men were allotted to each assaulting column to bring in the wounded. Guides, who knew the area well, were also supplied to each column. Yet the scheme failed disastrously. The Turkish defenders were waiting with rifle fire, grenades and machine guns. The right column gained the enemy trench despite suffering heavy casualties. However, when the left column attacked it was wiped out by concentrated machine-gun fire. This isolated the rightward party which was forced to withdraw. The follow-up troops never left their trenches. Of the 60 who attacked, 25 were killed and 21 wounded—a casualty rate of 77 per cent.[45] If this small raid demonstrated anything, it was that gaining ground at Anzac was going to be a slow and costly affair.

Yet this logic had not penetrated the Turkish political or military command. Nor did it recommend itself to the local Turkish leaders. So at a meeting on 11 May, the Turkish Minister of War Enver Pasha, von Sanders and the divisional commanders decided on a concerted attack along the whole line to eliminate the Anzac bridgehead.[46] The attack was to be made by elements of four divisions—Kemal's 19 Division in the north, the 5 Division and two new formations, 2 and 16 Divisions in the centre. The 77 (Arabian) Regiment would also attack in the south.[47] The operation was set for the early hours of the morning of 19 May and was meant to catch the Anzac forces by surprise.

The timing and circumstances of this operation were hardly optimal. The Turks were aware from 6 May that considerable forces from Anzac had been diverted to Helles. Yet by the time of the attack the two brigades had returned, and although reduced in numbers, formed a useful reserve to those in the firing line. Moreover, the Anzac artillery position had improved. There were now 43 guns supporting the force, an inconsiderable number by Western Front standards but an improvement from the early days of the landing. Moreover, the Turkish artillery support was feeble. At their disposal were just six batteries of mountain guns (useless against well-dug trenches), four batteries of field guns and one howitzer battery 'without much ammunition'.[48] Overall, then, the Turks had fewer and less appropriate guns than the defenders.

Neither did the Turkish operation come as a surprise. In the days before the battle, aerial reconnaissance had noted concentrations of Turkish troops moving towards the Anzac perimeter.[49] As a result one of the front-line battalions noted:

> The previous evening information was received that Turkish reinforcements . . . [were nearby]—and to be on the alert for a night attack also orders for all troops to stand to arms at 3 am. . . . Thus under cover of darkness trenches were repaired, rifles cleaned and a reserve of ammunition and spare rifles sent up to our trenches.[50]

So just 30 minutes before the Turkish attack their enemies were alert and well-munitioned.

The main Turkish effort was made early in the morning of 19 May in the centre of the Anzac line. At Courtney's, the 14 Battalion experienced it thus:

> A heavy fire was opened on Quinn's Post on our left and Walker's Position on our right from midnight until about 3.30 am. Then it increased in volume both in front of our trenches and on the flanks. This was immediately followed by a determined charge on the part of the enemy who threw many bombs. Our men reserved their fire until the enemy advanced when they at once poured in a heavy fire. Two companies were then holding the trenches and another was sent up as support. A very heavy fire was kept up until daylight when the enemy commenced to retire to their own trenches. During the retirement heavy losses were inflicted on the enemy by our rifles and machine guns. Our artillery opened fire at daybreak and the enemy replied with shrapnel on our trenches without much damage. About 8 am. the attack was renewed but gradually faded out, and our troops took opportunity during the lull to clean up our trenches and repair the damage done.[51]

Thus did three companies of troops help repel the attack of an entire division. The Australian casualties were 11 killed and 70 wounded. They had fired 23,000 rounds of rifle and machine-gun bullets.[52]

To the south of 14 Battalion, opposite Owen's Gully, stood 3 Battalion:

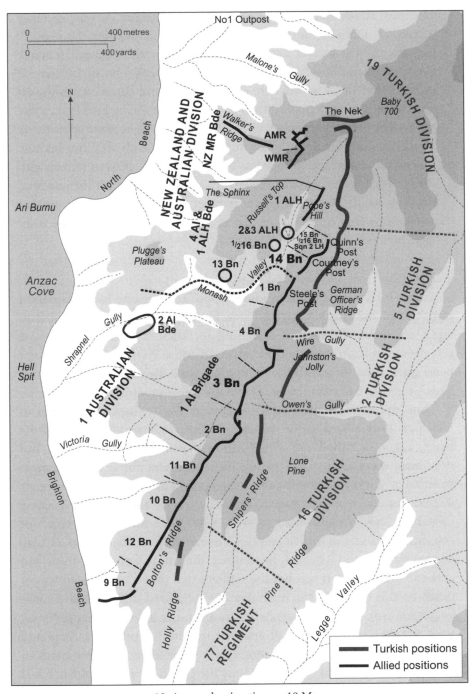

10 Anzac: the situation on 19 May

The main attack on our position developed at 2.45am. We were specially warned by Div Hdqrs to expect an attack in force during the night & were standing to arms at 2.45 am when the main attack began. The attack extended along the whole front of the Army Corps. The Turks attacked in successive lines, which were close together and came on with great determination. They pushed right forward to our Firing Line & . . . a few [got] right on the parapet. As they got closer the light was improving & as soon as we were able to distinguish them clearly our fire became very deadly, so much so that the Turks were compelled to retreat with very heavy loss. As soon as the enemy commenced to retreat our men [positioned] themselves along the parapet and it was from this time that our losses were heaviest as the enemy's retreat was covered by fire from their trenches & hill in rear.[53]

The battalion lost 14 killed and 31 wounded.

And so it was along the whole line. Opposite Johnson's Jolly 4 Battalion noticed that the attackers seemed 'bewildered' and wandered from left to right across the front as if searching for their objective. These were certainly men from the newly introduced Turkish 2 Division who had not been given time to familiarize themselves with the intricate terrain over which they were to manoeuvre. They were killed in large numbers.[54]

Thus, the great Turkish attack collapsed. An attempt to restart it at 5.00 p.m. only added to the carnage. On just four small sections of the front (2, 3, 4, 14 Battalions) a few Turks managed to reach the parapet, but they were soon dealt with. In all, the battle was the greatest disaster suffered by Turkey during the entire Gallipoli campaign. Of the 30,000 or 42,000 Turkish troops engaged (estimates vary), about 10,000 became casualties.[55] Of these probably about 3,500 were killed. The stench of rotting bodies was in fact so bad that an armistice was agreed on 24 May so that they could be buried. In contrast, the Anzac forces lost 160 killed and 468 wounded.[56] It was not the artillery that proved the instrument of death on this occasion; the Australian gunners fired just 143 heavy shells and 2,800 from their field artillery. However, the infantry fired no fewer than 948,000 rounds of small-arms ammunition from their rifles and machine guns. This hail of fire would have stopped any infantry attack in the open.[57] May 19 was not the last time the Turkish forces would attack at Gallipoli but never again would they do so as part of a major operation.

CHAPTER 9

The Killing Fields of Krithia

How did the Turkish command react to Hamilton's operation on that first day? Von Sanders was aware from early on 25 April that a major attack was underway. Reports from the Gulf of Saros, Kum Kale, Ari Burnu and Helles all indicated that hostile squadrons of ships had gathered, and that landings in at least some of these localities were commencing. Von Sanders made a few rapid decisions. Ari Burnu was in hand with the 19 Turkish Division moving towards the area. The landing on the Asiatic coast he regarded as merely a diversion and was prepared to let the commander of XV Corps deal with it.

One aspect of the deception plan had a greater effect. Von Sanders' attention focused on the narrow isthmus of Bulair, which was now reported to have a squadron of British ships close offshore. He therefore ordered 7 Division, whose headquarters were at Gallipoli, towards Bulair, gathered a group of staff officers and rode to a narrow ridge overlooking the isthmus to see for himself. While he was there, Essad Pasha, commander of III Corps, arrived with the news that although the situation at Anzac Cove was under control, a dangerous situation seemed to be developing at Helles. Von Sanders immediately dispatched Essad south to take command while he continued to worry about Bulair. The British fleet was certainly close inshore, but no attempt to land was being made and the thought that this was merely a feint operation began to dawn on von Sanders. Then Essad's first report from Helles arrived. The 9 Division was being hard pressed and substantial reinforcements were urgently required. This was a crucial moment for von Sanders. It was slowly being revealed to him that there were two main landings—one at Helles and the other (probably) at Anzac Cove. He there-fore rode to the headquarters of 7 Division and changed its orders. It was now to embark two battalions that evening on transports in Gallipoli harbour and send them to Helles. In addition, three battalions of 5 Division were also ordered through the Dardanelles to reinforce the southern area. Later a report arrived from Mustapha Kemal (19 Division) that the advance from Anzac Cove had been halted. At this the commander of the Fifth Army retired for the night well satisfied that the situation was in hand.

The morning confirmed his view that he was faced only with landings at Helles and Anzac, so he dispatched the remainder of the 5 and 7 Divisions to those two areas respectively, and ordered the 11 Division from the Asiatic coast to Chanak where it could be ferried to the Peninsula. He informed the government in Constantinople that he required the 15 and 16 Divisions from the capital and the 12 Division from Smyrna. In addi-tion, despite the tension on the Turkish-Bulgarian border, the garrison at Adrianople was stripped of some of its troops and most of its guns for deployment on the Peninsula.[1]

A lack of suitable vessels meant a delay for those units earmarked for Helles and it was not until the early morning of 26 April that they arrived at Maidos. Nevertheless by the 27th two fresh battalions from 7 Division (20 Regiment) were in the line south-west of Krithia, while to their left the line was held by the remnants of the Helles garrison and a fresh battalion from the Broussa Gendarmerie.[2] In addition two battalions, one from 9 Division and one from 5 Division, were in reserve. In all the Turks had 6,000 men south of Krithia, at least half of them fresh.

The British deception plans had worked to some extent. The Bulair demonstration had kept von Sanders guessing for most of 25 April and kept the 7 Division away from Helles for 24 hours. The French at Kum Kale had not deflected von Sanders but had kept the batteries in that area from firing across the Straits at 29 Division. But the fact was that no fewer than six divi-sions (5, 7, 11, 12, 15, 16) were heading towards the Peninsula. On the other side, Hamilton could expect no reinforcements of this magnitude. In these early days the perennial problem of the Gallipoli campaign began to assert itself. The Turks could reinforce faster by land than Hamilton could by sea. The immediate question then was: could Hamilton strike before these large elements of the Turkish army appeared on the battlefield?

*   *   *

The British command certainly tried. Hunter-Weston, who had predicted disaster before the landings, was very pleased to have his troops firmly ashore. So was Hamilton. He stated after the war that he regarded the achievement of landing as an end in itself and had given little thought as to what should happen next.[3] Nevertheless, even the most aggressive of commanders would have found an immediate advance from Helles a challenging proposition. Seddelbahr was only to fall on the afternoon of 26 April. Most troops, including those who had not been in heavy combat, were tired, having had little sleep since the 23rd. The beaches, to some extent because of their small size, were a chaos of stores, ammunition, food and equipment of all kinds. The schedule for landing the 29 Division and all its accoutrements was supposed to be 60 hours. The time actually taken was 10 days despite excellent weather.[4] So two days after the landing, on the 27th, there were few artillery pieces ashore and no pack mules to carry ammunition or food and water forward. Indeed, at times as many as half the men were out of the firing line and engaged in making roads and carrying stores.[5] Moreover, it was proving difficult to land the French who were to take over the right of the line from the British. Delays on the beaches meant that they did not land until the evening of the 26th.[6]

All this meant that no military operations could be contemplated before 28 April. So, on the 27th the British and the French were forced to confine themselves to a forward march to the positions from which the attack would be launched. At 4.00 p.m. the movement commenced. In lines of platoons the men eased forward to a line that stretched from Morto Bay on the right (where the French took over from the South Wales Borderers) to Gully Beach on the left. There was no opposition. It was clear that the Turks had withdrawn to a new defensive line. What was not clear was where it was.[7] Nor was the exact position of their own troops clear to the British command. The 87 Brigade was more or less on its start line but the line of 88 Brigade to its right was far from regular. Its left battalion was well behind the 87th, facing north but separated from its centre unit which faced due east. Finally the right battalion was facing north but hundreds of yards ahead. When the whistle blew at 8.00 a.m., 88 Brigade would start from three different locations and two different directions.

Hunter-Weston's plan for an attack all along the line on 28 April would be anything but a straightforward affair. On the left 87 Brigade would have the easiest task. It was merely required to advance 5 miles and occupy Hill 472 to

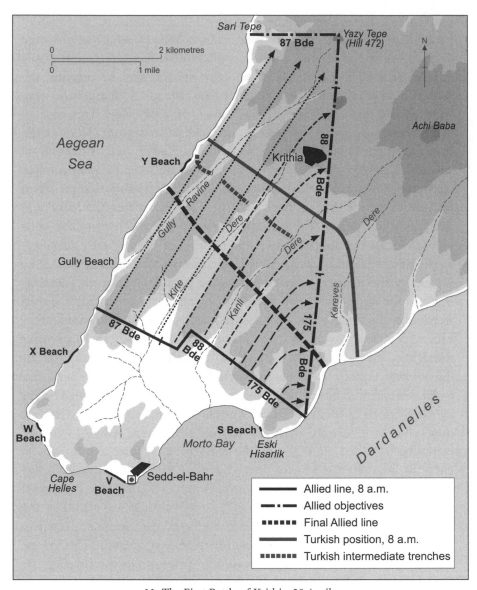

11 The First Battle of Krithia, 28 April

the north of Krithia. On its right the 88 Brigade and the French (175 Brigade) were to execute an enormous 90-degree turn to the right so that they would finish facing east instead of north. In the process they would capture Krithia.[8]

It is not clear that all the troops understood this plan. The orders total no more than a small paragraph and are littered with map references which would have taken considerable thought to interpret. Moreover, the orders were only issued at 2.00 a.m. on 28 April, just six hours before the start time. In addition, because of the heavy casualties, many officers were occupying levels of command that were new to them. As the British official history noted: 'All three brigades were in charge of inexperienced brigadiers. Only one of the three brigade-majors was left alive, and of the twelve original battalion commanders only three remained on duty.'[9] The French coped with the convoluted orders by ignoring them. On the day of battle they would implement a quite different plan.

There were other problems. Just 28 guns had been unloaded onto the beaches but there was only ammunition for 20 of them. So the divisional attack would go in supported by 14×18 pounders, 4×4.5-inch howitzers and some mountain guns. On the Western Front at this time a divisional attack might expect the support of some 200 guns which would include some heavy (6-inch and above) howitzers. Moreover, if the troops did manage an advance they would rapidly run out of what fire support there was, because there were no horses or mules to pull the guns and ammunition forward. Of course the navy would provide fire support as well, but experience suggested that this would be of limited use in an infantry attack. Exacerbating the whole situation for the operators of both land-based and ship-based guns was the fact that neither gunners nor sailors knew where the main Turkish line of resistance was. Nor were patrols sent out to locate it.

One final point must be made about the First Battle of Krithia. It was not a trench warfare battle. Both the British and Turks had dug a few trenches at various points across the Peninsula but they were still operating mainly in open country. None the less this gave the defence an advantage. The Turks could use folds in the ground to conceal machine guns while the British and French were advancing in upright skirmishing lines as they might have done at Waterloo.

* * *

The Allied attack commenced at 8.00 a.m. on 28 April. It was a complete fiasco. By the end of the day all the troops were occupying the original start line. The 29 Division had suffered 2,000 casualties, the French 1,000.

Many factors contributed to this debacle. The most important were a lack of coordination in launching the attack, the tiredness of the troops, lack of ammunition and fire support, loss of control by the high command and the lack of fresh reserves.

As far as coordination was concerned, almost all battalions, instead of advancing as a unified body, found themselves alone without protection on either flank. For example, on the left of the attack, 87 Brigade was forced to divide its battalions on either side of Gully Ravine. This feature, which the high command considered a small, dry watercourse, was in fact a ravine with sides up to 100 feet high and 200 yards wide. The rightward battalion therefore had no protection on its left. As it happened, it had none on its right either because the awkwardly placed 88 Brigade was starting from well to its rear. The attack by the rightward battalion was stopped by enfilade fire within minutes.[10] Things were no better in the centre or the right of the Peninsula where each battalion of 88 Brigade attacked alone and there was no coordination with the French, who changed Hunter-Weston's plan for a more sensible arrangement but neglected to tell 88 Brigade what they were doing.[11] In sum, of the six battalions that made the initial attack, not one went forward with a neighbouring battalion.

During the attack the exhaustion of the troops became only too evident. The Border Regiment of 87 Brigade, attacking between the sea and Gully Ravine, got forward some 500 yards but then ran into a Turkish trench which contained a machine gun. They charged the trench on two occasions but this effort proved too much and they started to drift backwards, some even moving down the cliffs to the beach to gain some respite.[12] This action was one of the few in the campaign where the intervention of the navy played a part. A 15-inch shrapnel shell from the *Queen Elizabeth* caught a group of Turks in the open, killing 49 and bringing their attack to a halt.[13]

The movements of 88 Brigade are difficult to reconstruct because of the brevity of entries in their war diaries, but the brigade diary noted that the men 'started tired'.[14] Moreover, they had no idea where the Turks were actually located. For 800 yards the advance of 88 Brigade was unopposed. Then a withering fire was opened on them from enemy troops who could not be seen. Soon the losses and exhaustion took their toll and the 88 Brigade's plod towards Krithia came to a halt.[15]

In any case the advance in this area had no chance. The men ran out of ammunition. Their frequent requests for bullets did not go unnoticed by the staff but there was no means of carrying supplies forward.[16]

Of all the accounts we have of this battle not one mentions the artillery. Fire from the 20 guns was too feeble and dispersed to rate a single comment. This was hardly the fault of the gunners who had no idea where the Turks were and, during the course of the battle, no idea where their own men were either.

The lack of fresh reserves was a persistent problem. In the 88 Brigade area the much-worn 86 Brigade was pressed into service. But when it was called forward two of its battalions were diverted to the right to secure the junction with the French and played no real role in the attack. The remaining two consisted of the remnants of the Lancashire Fusiliers and the Royal Fusiliers. Remarkably, considering that they had to carry their reserves of ammunition into battle, small parties of these exhausted men reached a small wood just short of Krithia. But they were unsupported and an order to reorganize their much-mixed units resulted in an unintended retreat which eventually saw them back on their start line.[17]

The 87 Brigade attempted to solve the reserve problem by novel means. They appropriated some companies of the Royal Naval Division who were carrying materiel from the boats to the beach. At 4.00 p.m., when the brigade's attack was in dire trouble, the command deployed these units. But at the same time a staff officer from 29 Division headquarters ordered them back to the beach.[18] They set off 'at the double' leading to the belief that a general retreat had been ordered. Back came the remainder of the brigade. They too finished where they had started.[19]

The command exercised little control over any of this. Hunter-Weston was still at sea (in all meanings of the phrase) when the battle started. He then moved to Hill 138 where according to one observer he had a 'front row, dress circle' view.[20] What use he made of it is harder to determine, except to send out liaison officers who had no knowledge of the local situation or whose interventions (anyway in the case of 87 Brigade) were hardly helpful.

* * *

On the Turkish side, the failure of the Allies at the First Battle of Krithia seemed to represent an opportunity. Casualties had been high, ground gained nil. Perhaps now was the time to throw the invaders back into the sea. That certainly was the view of Enver in Constantinople. On 30 April he gave a peremptory order to this effect to von Sanders. The German commander was of like mind. He too thought that the time was ripe for a counterattack in the south.[21] His hopes were based on the fact that fresh regiments from the 7, 9 and 11 Divisions had arrived on the Peninsula. Moreover, although he may not have been aware of the state of the Allies in great detail, he must have known that the recent battle had weakened them. In fact 29 Division could muster only 7,000 men, the French considerably less. In addition there were four weak battalions of the Royal Naval Division at Helles (probably no more than 2,400 men), and although an Indian brigade had disembarked from Egypt it was not yet in a state to be deployed. Nor had the artillery position markedly improved: just 28 guns were deployed at Cape Helles.[22]

Nevertheless, von Sanders was concerned about the effect of Allied artillery and the fire from the ships on troops attacking in the open. This was a particular threat at Helles because the main lines of resistance were some 1,800 yards apart. He therefore ordered his commanders to carry out a night attack on 1–2 May.[23]

Any night attack is fraught with difficulty. There is the problem of maintaining cohesion and direction in the dark, and the difficulty of fire support once the troops have gone over the top. On the positive side, such an attack might cause confusion to the defenders, nullify their fire support and perhaps start a panic. As the Allied line was only some 1,500 yards from the beaches, this might be sufficient to turn confusion into a rout. The whole affair was essentially a gambler's throw based on the premise that a confused attack would overwhelm a confused defence.

The greatest danger faced by the Turks was that they would be discovered traversing the expanse of ground between the two armies. To avoid this they adopted two stratagems: they timed their advance so that it coincided with the darkest hours before moonrise and they removed the bullets from the soldiers' rifles to prevent accidental shots. The attack in the first instance would be by bayonet alone.[24]

To an extent these expedients succeeded. An artillery bombardment opened on the Allied line at 10.00 p.m., but when the 9,000 Turkish infantry attacked, most of the Allied front-line troops were taken by surprise.

For the British the greatest danger came in the centre, which was held only by the much-reduced Dublin and Munster Fusiliers. The enemy infiltrated down Krithia Nullah which bisected the front in this area. In short order the Turks reached the British support trenches and then brigade headquarters at Grey Tree Farm. But as was becoming usual in these encounters, while the front troops were overrun, the reserves behind them were intact. A counterattack by the remaining elements of the 86 and 88 Brigades caught the Turks in the open and drove them back.[25] The British position was restored. On the left, the Turks made no incursions.

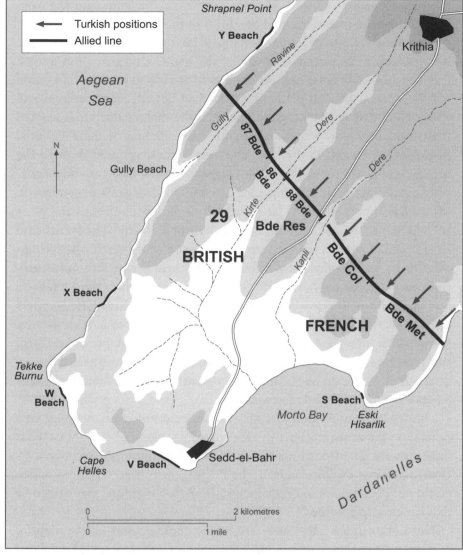

12 The Turkish night attack, 1–2 May

Between the coast and the right of Gully Ravine machine-gun fire from well-entrenched troops stopped the Turks in their tracks.[26]

The most serious situation developed on the centre right. Here the heaviest and most sustained attack of the night was carried out against the French, who because of their late arrival at Helles and their immediate involvement in the First Battle of Krithia had not adequately entrenched. Fierce hand-to-hand fighting took place in the shallow ditch that marked their front line. This was too much for one battalion of the 4 Colonial Regiment which fled to the rear. The Turks quickly poured through the breach, leading the remainder of the brigade to follow their comrades backwards. A desperate situation resulted. Some Turkish units penetrated to Morto Bay, others almost as far as Seddelbahr. Important command posts such as Sniper's Wood and Zimmerman's Farm also fell.[27] The French and British artillery were now in imminent danger of being overrun. But groups of gunners seized rifles, moved forward and held the Turks until British reserves (4 Worcesters) arrived.[28] These men immediately fixed bayonets and charged the Turks, who, with no protecting trenches or fire support and in unknown country in the dark, hastily disappeared in the direction from which they had come. Once the situation had been stabilized, the French reserves went into action. The 6 Colonial Regiment counterattacked at 5.00 a.m. on 2 May and reoccupied their original positions. So shortly afterwards did the 4 Colonial.[29]

Hunter-Weston decided that this was an excellent moment to inflict a reverse on the retreating enemy. He ordered an attack all along the line. It failed utterly. The troops were tired, short of ammunition and dazed by their nighttime exploits. Indeed, the 86 Brigade was so shattered that it could not obey orders and remained stationary. No ground was gained by this lamentable episode.[30]

Not to be outdone, the Turks attempted another foray on the night of 3–4 May. This attack was made by troops of the Turkish 15 Division straight after a 20-mile march. Predictably it failed, the troops being reduced to a 'disheveled and wretched' condition.[31] The Turkish divisional commander had certainly had enough. One more night attack, he announced, and he would resign.[32]

* * *

What now could be done by the British command? Casualties in the 29 Division were over 4,500, leaving just 6,000 worn-down troops to carry on. The French had suffered casualties in like proportion. General A. D'Amade, commander-in-chief of the French Forces, had at least made a move to rectify this situation by asking for reinforcements. Hamilton had not. This puzzled Kitchener who complained to Maxwell in Egypt that the territorial division (42) could be sent to Hamilton '*if he wants them*'.[33] Perhaps stirred into action by the French, Hamilton wrote to Kitchener: 'May I have a call on the East Lancashire Territorial Division in case I should need them? . . . You may be perfectly sure that I shall not call up a man unless I really need him.'[34]

* * *

This was a communication at which Hamilton would excel—uncomplaining, determined to make the best of what he had, and at the same time mealy-mouthed and highly detrimental to his army.

In the event, shipping could be found for just one brigade from the East Lancashire Division. So for the next push, which Hamilton no less than Hunter-Weston was determined to make 'in a couple of days', there would be only one brigade of fresh troops available. Bizarrely, the other reserves would consist of two brigades of Anzacs (New Zealand Brigade and 2 Australian Brigade). Apparently on 3 May Birdwood had informed Hamilton that the position at Anzac had 'stabilised'. Hamilton took this to mean that Birdwood was taking a sanguine view of his situation and that any reserves he had (the two brigades just mentioned) were available for service elsewhere. The two brigades, which had been through some of the toughest fighting in the north, were diverted to Helles. No protest was forthcoming from Birdwood, although he must have looked on the disappearance of his only reserves with trepidation.

At the same time that reinforcements were slowly proceeding towards the Peninsula, Hunter-Weston was ensuring that when they arrived they would be scandalously misused. The First Battle of Krithia had broken down through an over-elaborate battle plan, a lack of artillery, a lack of information on where exactly the Turkish line was and a lack of fresh reserves. Yet these elements still featured in the next plan to emanate from the commander of the 29 Division.

To read Hunter-Weston's battle plan is to enter a world of textual analysis, where intricate movements need to be deconstructed and a welter of map references need to be related to actual places on the ground. However, where his orders for the First Battle of Krithia took up less than half a page, those for the second battle went on over many pages. It would seem a reasonable supposition that busy officers did not have the time, patience or the skills in deconstruction to make much sense of any of it.

Once again the attack would pivot on the right. In that sector the French would advance some 750 yards and capture Kereves Dere Ravine. When that position had been secured (but not before), the British centre would execute an intricate 90-degree right turn, capture Krithia from the west and continue until Achi Baba was taken. Meanwhile the French on the right and the British on the Aegean coast would advance straight ahead. The final objective was a line across the Peninsula just to the north of Achi Baba.

So difficult were these manoeuvres that there was a real danger that the troops executing the turning movement and those proceeding straight ahead would gradually diverge creating a potentially dangerous gap, and then collide as they approached the final objective. In the first instance, then, a considerable percentage of the attacking forces had to be held back in order to fill potential gaps.[35] So the complexity of the plan actually reduced the already weakened force available for the initial attack.

As for artillery, the numbers had certainly increased since the previous battle. There were now 105 guns ashore, of which 6 were heavy howitzers and 6 heavy guns.[36] But not all of these could take part in the battle because of a shortage of ammunition for some types and the fact that the man or mule power necessary to drag them forward was not yet available. Frustratingly, we do not know exactly how many guns took part in the opening bombardment on 6 May, but 75 would seem to be a reasonable estimate.

But in the circumstances that prevailed at Helles an increase of guns from 20 to 75 did not represent an enormous accretion of strength. The location of the main line of Turkish resistance was still a mystery to all on the British side, as was the location of the skirmishers and machine guns that were known to have been placed some distance in front of it. The task facing the gunners was therefore impossible. All they could do was fire in the general direction of the Turks and hope that some of their shells found targets. And they would only be able to do this for 30 minutes, because by then shells would be running low and the position of any British units that had managed to advance would be unknown.

The reserves have already been mentioned. Their disposition was unorthodox. The freshest troops (125 Brigade, 42 Division) were placed on the extreme left facing Gully Ravine. In the first instance this meant that they would have the shortest distance to travel to reach their first objective. Perhaps Hunter-Weston considered that as they had only reached the Peninsula on 5 May and had been given no chance to reconnoitre, a straightforward task was called for. The two Anzac brigades, which made

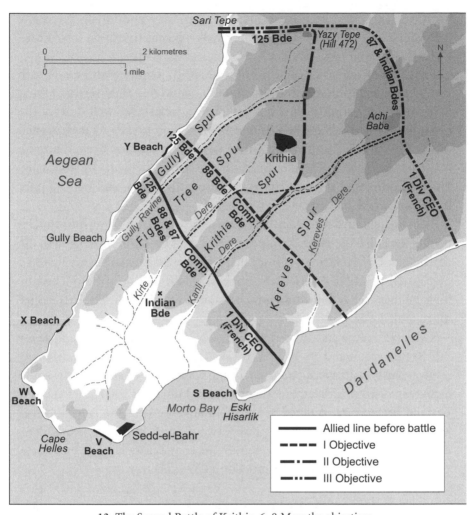

13 The Second Battle of Krithia, 6–8 May: the objectives

up most of the so-called Composite Division, were not initially given any role in the battle at all. Probably they were present to exploit any break-through achieved by the others.

In the event there was to be no breakthrough. On the right, the French reached the start line 40 minutes late, thus depriving themselves of what meagre artillery support was on offer. Their attack stalled well short of the pivot point on which the whole operation was to turn.[37] As it happened this was of little moment as the British were in no position to capitalize on a French advance.[38] Their entire line was being held up by concealed machine guns well short of the Turkish front position, and by 3.00 p.m. the whole attack had ground to a halt.[39]

The orders issued for 7 May listed the same objectives as for the 6th. The results were also the same. Artillery support was even more feeble than the day before. The French now found that they were facing an enemy that had dug a well-positioned series of trenches, which had been untouched by their gunners. They gained no ground; nor did the British. The battle once more fizzled out.

Two days' failure and all common sense seemingly made it imperative for the British command to call off the battle. The troops were exhausted, artillery shells were scarce. A rethink of the whole state of affairs in the south seemed in order. Instead, there were no second thoughts. On 8 May the New Zealand Brigade was ordered to make an advance over the bare slopes of Krithia Spur, the 87 Brigade to press forward on its left. There would be a 20-minute preliminary bombardment.[40] The New Zealanders had no chance. The commander of the 12 (Nelson) Company explains why:

> About 9 o'clock Colonel Brown called up his company commanders and gave a short verbal order, 'The battalion will attack from the front-line trenches at 10.30 am precisely, 12th Company will lead.' Then he smiled and added, 'And I am sorry gentlemen, that I cannot give you any further information'. It was indeed a meagre order. Usually they give the sector from which to attack, the point to attack, amount of artillery support to be expected, and the co-operation of other troops. We knew nothing, not even how far it was to the front line.[41]

In these circumstances it was remarkable that the men gained a few hundred yards. But then they were hit by machine-gun fire that rendered Fir Tree Knoll, over which they were attempting to advance, 'untenable'.[42] At

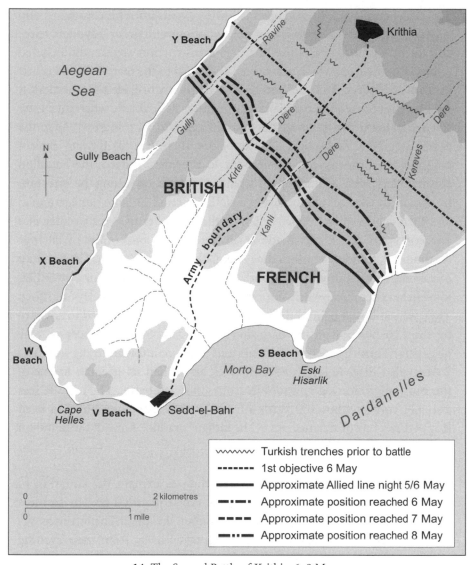

14 The Second Battle of Krithia, 6–8 May

4.00 p.m. Hamilton, who had been following events from his command ship *Arcadian,* decided for reasons that are still obscure to order 'bayonets fixed' and an attack along the entire line.[43] This instruction apparently included 2 Australian Brigade which was some 1,000 yards to the rear of the firing line in front of Krithia. An order was hastily written by brigade headquarters at 5.05 p.m. It reached the battalion commanders at 5.20 a.m. when they were startled to learn that their advance would begin in 10 minutes.[44] As in the case of the New Zealanders the day before, there was no time to explain anything to company commanders or to the men. Indeed, the battalion commanders were also unsure of what to do. One, on asking the direction he should attack was told to start in a NNE direction until he came to a road and then 'change direction left'.[45] Under these conditions it is a wonder that any concerted attack was made at all. Yet at 5.30 p.m. units of all four Australian battalions set off in the general direction of Krithia. They at once came under heavy shrapnel fire and after some time stopped for a 'breather' in trenches occupied by British units involved in the previous days' fighting. They were still well behind their own front line. They continued to advance by short rushes but on the bare slopes of Krithia Spur they became easy targets for Turkish machine-gunners and were soon forced to dig in.[46] The 2 Australian Brigade lost 1,000 casualties, about half its strength in one of the most misconceived episodes in a misconceived battle. The brigade had also not come within 100 yards of the Turkish front line but had been stopped by a line of skirmishers.[47] The indignant tone of one of the battalion commanders can be heard in his report:

> I might state that I was not allowed time to explain the situation to Platoon commanders or sergeants, and consequently I had to do most of the explaining during the advance under shrapnel. The advance was too rushed at the start, the men being taken away from their evening meal with the greatest haste.[48]

Here ended for the moment the attempt to capture the Kilid Bahr Plateau from the south. Reinforcements and ammunition would be needed before another attempt could be made. But as the attackers had found, the Turks had already begun digging lines of trenches. Was the 'second Crimea' predicted by Hunter-Weston before the battle about to become a reality?

1 Lord Kitchener, Secretary of State for War and the real instigator of the military operation, at Gallipoli in November 1915, where he reluctantly came to the conclusion that the operation was doomed.

2 Anzac Cove, 11.00 a.m., 25 April. The scene belies the myth that this was a great killing ground on the first day of the campaign. At this time the troops had moved inland and reinforcements were yet to arrive.

3 Two Sikhs (on the left) and two Ghurkas (on the right) pose at Helles. The Indian Brigade took part in some of the most desperate fighting at Gallipoli – at Helles in April and May and at Anzac in August.

4 Tortuous country to the north of Anzac perimeter across which thousands of troops were required to manoeuvre during the August offensive.

5 Australian troops advancing from Plugge's Plateau, 25 April.

6 Shells exploding supposedly over the Turkish line during the Second Battle of Krithia, 6 May. In fact, the British gunners had no idea where the Turkish trenches were and were thus able to give little support to the attacking troops.

7 Senegalese troops. Part of the French contingent at Gallipoli was from the French colonies.

8 Aghyl Gere where so many units lost their way during the August attack. Note the scattered bones.

9 British troops moving towards Helles pass the battleship *Implacable*, 25 April 1915.

10 General Aylmer Hunter-Weston at Helles. His conduct of the landing and the three battles of Krithia left much to be desired. During his later battles he seemed to hit upon a formula for success but was then invalided back to Britain and these small achievements were largely forgotten.

11 General Sir Ian Hamilton (left) and General William Birdwood inspecting the Royal Naval Division.

12 Enter the French. Wine barrels being towed to a ship for transport to the Gallipoli Peninsula.

13 The base at Suvla Bay during the first phase of construction. The purpose of the Suvla Bay operation was to establish a base for all troops in the northern theatre of Gallipoli.

14 Vice-Admiral John de Robeck (left) on Imbros. De Robeck brought more vigour to the naval attack than Carden but with no more success. His refusal to continue the operation after 18 months incurred the wrath of Winston Churchill.

15 Power and Futility. The *Queen Elizabeth* at the Dardanelles. The 15-inch guns of the most modern battleship in the world proved ineffective against the Turkish forts.

16 British troops at Ghurka Bluff, near Gully Ravine, an area that saw some of the most intense fighting at Helles.

17 The landing at X Beach represented a chance not taken by 29 Division at Helles. Note the narrowness of the beaches at the tip of the Peninsula.

18 General Otto Liman von Sanders, Commander of the 5th Turkish Army. His performance during the Gallipoli campaign was solid but he has perhaps been given credit for the Turkish defence that more properly belongs to the Turkish soldiers.

19 Column of French troops at Helles. The French contribution to the Gallipoli operation has largely been forgotten, yet they suffered as many casualties as the Australians.

20 The 9 Australian Battalion on their way to the Gallipoli Peninsula. They landed opposite 400 Plateau and took part in the desperate fighting in that area on 25 April.

21 The *River Clyde* and part of the British base at Cape Helles just before the evacuation.

22 A Turkish gun, well protected by the surrounding earth works. Guns such as this proved difficult targets for the British fleet.

23 Chanak (Canakkale) under British naval fire. The results appear devastating but few of the large forts in this area were put out of operation.

24 Turkish officers on the heights of Sari Bair overlooking the Anzac positions.

CHAPTER 10

Last Throw in the South

After the failed Turkish offensive on 19 May, Anzac descended into stalemate. This did not mean that the front became passive. Constant raiding, tunnelling and shelling kept troops occupied and on edge. But for the moment there would be no large-scale attacks attempted by either side.

Once more the action shifted to Helles. There the Turks had not been idle. They had dug trenches and trench systems that began to approximate those on the Western Front. This did not go unnoticed by the British command. Just after the conclusion of the Second Battle of Krithia, Braithwaite noted:

> Owing to the numerous and well planned entrenchments now held by the enemy in the vicinity of Achi Baba and also at Kaba Tepe, the operations in the immediate future will approximate more to semi-siege warfare than to open operations in the field. Further progress must now be made by continuous and systematic attacks on certain portions of the hostile line rather than by a general action involving the advance of the whole line at once.[1]

There was much sense in this. At Helles the British had just 78 artillery pieces of which only 4 were heavy howitzers. The French too were short of heavy artillery. In all, the Allies had around 145 guns, to use against the

Turks' 7,000 to 8,000 yards of trench.[2] To make a comparison with the Western Front, at Neuve Chapelle 340 guns, including some super-heavy 9.2-inch and 15-inch howitzers, proved barely adequate to batter down a line of trenches 2,000 yards long.[3] In addition, ammunition for the field artillery at Helles was also short; on 20 May it was rationed to two shells per gun per day. The southern force was also short of men. Reinforcements in the form of a brigade of Indian troops had arrived and the 42 Territorial Division was now in the line. But casualties had been high, especially in the 29 Division which remained the backbone of the Helles contingent but had received only 506 reinforcements by the end of April.[4] The 52 Division, which consisted of 8 battalions instead of 12 and was short of artillery, was due to arrive on 6 June but no one on the British side suggested that an offensive be postponed until it was there. Probably, its weakened condition caused it to be discounted. In addition, the French had suffered so much in the Second Battle of Krithia that the section of line held by them was reduced to just 1,000 yards until reinforcements arrived the night before the battle.

The weakness in the Allied position was compounded by the rapid loss of naval support. Despite the usually ineffective fire from the ships in their attempts to cover land operations, the presence of warships close offshore had a beneficial effect on the morale of the troops. But on 13 May a Turkish destroyer had made good use of a bank of fog in the Dardanelles, eluded the Allied destroyer patrol and torpedoed the battleship *Goliath*. It sank in 2 minutes with the loss of 570 men from a crew of 750.[5] The Admiralty had already received reports that German submarines were approaching the Dardanelles, and these two events caused them to with-draw the *Queen Elizabeth* immediately. Then on 18 May, for similar reasons, Admiral Thursby left on the *Queen*, which was followed by the *Prince of Wales* and *Implacable* and *London*. And with these battleships went their attendant destroyers and light cruisers. None were ever to return to the Dardanelles.[6]

After this, matters got worse. The German submarines did arrive and with devastating effect. On 25 May the *Triumph* was torpedoed and two days later the *Majestic*. The number of ships covering military operations on the Peninsula, already reduced by the sinking of *Goliath* and Thursby's departure, was cut back drastically. There were now no battleships at all stationed off Cape Helles and Anzac. Immediate support for the troops would only be supplied by destroyers, although the heavy units might reappear to assist a major attack.[7] Casting their gaze on the empty seas around them, the troops must have felt that their chance of success was diminishing.

* * *

Despite Braithwaite's perceptive assessment that operations should be confined to limited fronts, at some time towards the end of May the high command decided nevertheless to carry out a general attack on a wide front. Perhaps the news that 3,000 drafts could be expected from England within days for 29 Division, or the fact that quantities of artillery ammunition were on their way, led to more optimistic assessments. In any case the idea of limited operations was quietly shelved. There would be a Third Battle of Krithia and it would take place all along the line on 4 June.

The planning of this battle showed at least some increase in sophistication over earlier efforts. On this occasion Hunter-Weston took pains to make sure that his forces knew where the main Turkish trench lines were and that his own front line was within reasonable assaulting distance from them. Aerial photographs were taken of the Turkish positions, and night advances with digging squads ensured that the British front line actually crept to within 250 yards of its first objective, a vast improvement on the 1,800-yard gap between the lines at the Second Battle of Krithia.

This attack would also use armoured cars. These were almost a private venture: eight Rolls Royce automobiles with armour protection, paid for by the Duke of Westminster, sent out by Churchill and commanded by a Member of Parliament, Josiah Wedgwood. Their use was indeterminate in the operations orders. They were merely to proceed down what few roads the southern Peninsula contained and 'try their luck'.[8]

The bombardment plan was more innovative than previous efforts. The guns would shell the Turkish trenches for two and a half hours and then fall silent. The hope was that the Turks would retaliate with their own artillery thereby disclosing their positions, whereupon they would be subjected to another bombardment by the British and French guns.[9]

The problem with the bombardment lay not with the plan but with the lack of resources with which to carry it out. The shortage of heavy howitzers has already been mentioned. For the battle, the Allies would have just eight between them. Because of the contraction of their front, the French were able to lend to the British some batteries of 75-mm field guns. And at least these guns fired high-explosive shells, which had some chance of damaging the Turkish trenches, unlike the British field guns (18 pounders) which were only supplied with shrapnel.[10]

The objectives demonstrated more realism than hitherto. The first wave of troops was merely required to capture the first line of Turkish trenches, the second wave of troops was to proceed just 400 to 500 yards beyond that to secure the Turks' second main line. Hunter-Weston could not resist including a third objective. In a section ominously called 'Pursuit' he directed the corps reserve to capture Krithia and establish a line running from north-west to south-east beyond it, thus reinstating the complicated 90-degree turn of the First and Second Battles of Krithia. But at least he added that this phase was contingent on the capture and consolidation of the first two objectives.[11] Even Braithwaite had a burst of optimism. On the eve of battle he told Hunter-Weston that if on the attainment of his objectives another advance could be made, 'the enemy must be driven back as far as possible. Every endeavour must be made to press home an advantage and to gain the greatest possible amount of ground.'[12]

The 24,000 men who would launch the Allied attack and the 7,000 in close reserve would face two Turkish divisions (9 and 12) totalling 18,000 men in the front system of trenches. In addition the Turks had two regiments of 7 Division in close reserve and various others, further back, recovering from actions elsewhere.[13] In general, the forces of the two sides were evenly matched in numbers.

The weather on 4 June was fine with a strong wind blowing from the north. When the Allied bombardment opened it was found that this wind blew the smoke and dust kicked up by the shells back over the Allied lines. Within minutes visibility was reduced to a few yards.

On the right it did not take even this long to realize that the French attack had met with disaster. The French were yet again assaulting the Kereves Dere Ravine. Their main problem on this occasion was that the opposing trench lines were so close together (100 yards) that the artillery, in fear of hitting their own men, had landed their shells on the Turkish back positions. This left the defenders in the Turkish front line untouched and able to bring a withering hail of machine-gun and rifle bullets to bear on the assault units of the French 1 and 2 Divisions. Moreover, the area in which the French were operating was so crowded that what remained of their battalions quickly became intermixed. This fatally hampered efforts to organize a subsequent attack but the fact was that the French were incapable of further effort. They had suffered 2,000 casualties in several minutes

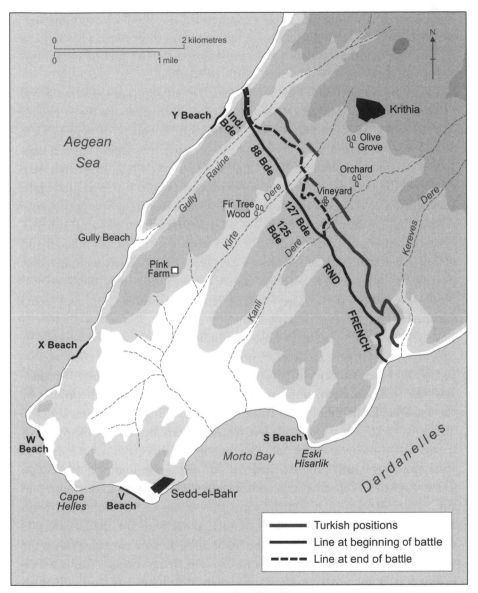

15 The Third Battle of Krithia, 4 June

and were badly shaken. Their commander, General Henri Gouraud, decided that no more attacks should take place until the faith of his soldiers in their supporting artillery had been restored.[14] That spelled the end of French participation in the Third Battle of Krithia.

Attacking on the left of the French were the battalions of the Royal Naval Division. Initially, the French proved helpful to these troops. Their assault distracted the machine-gunners and batteries to the north of Kereves Dere Ravine, and their artillery demolished much of the very shallow trench lines facing the leading battalions. Then it all went wrong. When the French were repulsed, the enemy artillery and machine guns could fire in enfilade into the trenches captured by the Royal Naval Division. This fire was particularly devastating to the Collingwood Battalion which advanced some minutes after the others. In no time at all it had been wiped out, 25 officers and 600 men becoming casualties out of a total force of 850. There were attempts during the afternoon to arrange further operations with the French.[15] Nothing came of them. The right of Hunter-Weston's effort had failed comprehensively.

It also failed on the left where the Indian Brigade led the assault. In this area, the artillery completely missed the front Turkish trench and its protecting wire. Attacking between Gully Ravine and the sea, the Lancashire Fusiliers were cut down in great numbers. Even the expedient adopted by the 1/6 Ghurka Battalion of crawling along the cliff face and attacking the Turks from the seaward direction availed them nothing. Unsupported, because of the check to the Lancashires, the Ghurkas were soon forced to withdraw.[16] The only progress made in this sector was that of the 14 Sikhs. They attacked astride and from within Gully Ravine, which in their area had sides 40 or 50 feet high. On the right they clung to the Worcesters from 88 Brigade who accomplished all of their objectives. On the left, despite the patchy efforts of the artillery, the Sikhs gained some ground. Within the ravine there developed a bitter, hand-to-hand fight with the Turks, which resulted in some early progress and then stalemate. Eventually Turkish machine-gunners in their second line, who had a commanding view of the entire area between the ravine and the sea, decided the matter. The Sikhs, except for a few with 88 Brigade, were driven back to their start line. A total of 29 officers and 514 men had attacked. Just 8 officers and 134 men could be mustered on the following day.[17]

The armoured cars proved useless. Their 'luck' ran out from the first. Some of them ran off the primitive tracks and upended in the complex of trenches behind the British line. Others ran into roadblocks erected by the Turks. Not one car reached any Turkish defensive position before the infantry.

This left the centre formations, the 42 Division (127 and 125 Brigades) and the 88 Brigade, to redeem the battle. Surprisingly, they did so. This was the sector of the front where the heavy howitzers were concentrated, and there is much evidence from the battered state of the Turkish trenches of their destructive force.[18] The 127 Brigade with the 88 Brigade on its left broke right through the Turkish front system and moved on to capture the second line as well. The 88 Brigade were particularly successful. They advanced 1,000 yards, took no fewer than five lines of Turkish trenches and dug in just 500 yards south of Krithia. Their most advanced unit, the 4 Worcesters, described their exploits in a manner that would not have been out of place in *Boy's Own*:

> The whistle was blown by the Officer Commanding the first line as a caution to get ready, and the second [was blown] for them to leap over the parapets and they did it to a man. It was just glorious and magnificent to see our gallant lads get out of the trenches, not a slacker amongst them with the result that the first line was taken with comparatively few losses but resulted in us taking about 200 prisoners, and enabled us to push on to our objective which we gained at 1.45 pm. No fresh orders were received to advance.[19]

Meanwhile, the 125 Brigade was also doing well. By 12.05 p.m. they captured the first line of Turkish trenches and were in occupation of the second objective by 12.30 p.m. Casualties had not been heavy.[20]

So in the centre, the Turks had been pushed back towards Krithia on a front of 1,500 yards. There was in fact only one trench line between the British and the village and there seemed to be no Turks occupying it.

Here then was a chance for Hunter-Weston to initiate the 'pursuit' phase of the battle or at least to implement Braithwaite's exhortation to gain as much ground as possible. And unlike the previous battles for Krithia, the commander was aware of the situation at the front. At 12.40 p.m. he knew that the 42 Division was holding its second objective and that the men were in touch with the Worcesters on their left.[21] Moreover, Hunter-Weston still had the Corps reserve of almost 7,000 men available to him. The decision seemed obvious: reinforce the centre and secure Krithia.

Hunter-Weston did not choose this course of action. Instead, at 12.54 p.m., he dispatched a reserve battalion to the Royal Naval Division to enable them to attack again; at 1.40 p.m. a second battalion was added and finally at 2.55 p.m. the entire 1 Naval Brigade was sent. This left a Ghurka battalion and two battalions from 88 Brigade. They were soon dispatched to the Indian Brigade to attempt another advance on the left. In this manner, Hunter-Weston dispersed his entire reserve to reinforce failure rather than to exploit success.

This approach had little to recommend it. It is true that if the forces in the centre advanced too far, they might be open to flank attack by Turkish reserves to the right and left of them. However, this difficulty could have been foreseen and the reserves given strict instructions to limit their advance to the ridge just beyond Krithia. This position, strongly held, would have placed pressure to withdraw on the outflanked Turkish forces facing the French and the Indian Brigade.

Hunter-Weston's chosen course of action contained a major flaw. It was based on the assumption that an artillery failure on either flank could be redeemed by throwing more infantry against intact trench defences and uncut wire. No amount of infantry could accomplish anything in these conditions, except in adding to the casualty list. In the event, the reserves failed totally on the flanks. As for the battalions in the centre, they were finally forced to withdraw to a distance about 500 yards in advance of their start line because of lack of reinforcements.[22]

* * *

The Third Battle of Krithia was not one of Hunter-Weston's finer moments. By reinforcing failure and throwing his reserves against the strongest sectors of the Turkish line, he almost certainly cast away the chance of capturing Krithia. After the battle, however, there is strong evidence that the British commander took to heart the lessons the battle had to offer. The most important of these concerned the artillery. Success had come where enemy trenches had been subjected to fire from heavy howitzers. On the flanks, where failure had been total, no heavy howitzers had been in operation. There were other lessons to be learned as well, such as the futility of trying to reverse an artillery failure with additional infantry, but there is no doubt that the major lesson concerned the power of the heavy howitzer.

At a series of meetings, Hunter-Weston and Gouraud determined that in future they would avoid large-scale attacks and only assault on a length

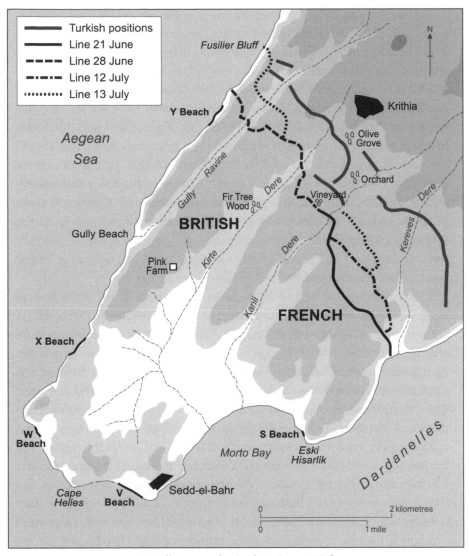

16 Helles: ground gained, 21 June–13 July

of front that could be covered by the combined Anglo-French heavy howitzers. They also determined to limit their advance to distances that could be covered by the majority of their batteries. In short, they would institute a series of 'bite and hold' operations at Helles.

The first experiment took place on the French sector where it was deemed imperative to gain ground towards Kereves Dere Ravine in order to prevent Turkish enfilade fire on the centre of the Allied line. The front of attack was narrowed to 650 yards and the 8 heavy howitzers available to the French were supplemented by 7 from the British. In addition there were 28 × 75-mm field guns, and a new weapon in the form of 16 heavy trench mortars.[23] In all, this gave a concentration of 1 gun for every 11 yards of front attacked, and as the objective consisted largely of the single Turkish front line this actually meant 1 gun for every 11 yards of trench. This was in fact a greater artillery concentration than many bombardments achieved on the Western Front in 1915.

The attack, carried out on 21 June, was a success. The French had an ample supply of shells, so they bombarded the Turkish line for several days before the 21st. Then, on the day of battle, the artillery intensified its efforts for an hour. When the shelling lifted on to the Turkish back lines, men from three assaulting regiments went over the top. On most of the front they found trenches rendered 'useless' and filled with Turkish dead.[24] They occupied their objectives with little loss and set about consolidating the gains. The exception was on the right. There some of the factors that could negate artillery accuracy came into play. The shells missed the trench, the Allied infantry were cut down and it took a re-bombardment and two more infantry assaults to secure the objective.[25] Nevertheless, the lesson was clear: expend sufficient ammunition, and even a trench system upon which much work had been lavished could be captured. This fact is brought home by a comparison of the number of shells fired in the success of 21 June with those used in the failure of 4 June:

Date	Frontage	Shells fired by heavy howitzers	Shells fired by field guns	Shells fired by trench mortar	Total shells	Shells/ yd
4 June	1,500 yd	533	3,500	nil	4,033	2.68
21 June	650 yd	2,700	28,000	700	31,400	48.30

The table shows that on 21 June the French had achieved an artillery concentration almost 20 times that of 4 June.[26] This did not mean that the cost of battle was insignificant. The French lost 2,500 casualties. However, they achieved their objective and inflicted about 5,800 casualties on the Turks.[27] For once the attack had proved cheaper than the defence.

The second operation saw action switched to the left of the line. The idea was that an advance be made astride Gully Ravine to outflank the enemy forces in front of Krithia. The date of the operation was determined by the time it would take to amass the heavy artillery. The French provided nine heavy howitzers and two trench mortars. They would not be in position until the 26 June so the day of battle was fixed for the 28th.[28]

Compared to the French plan, the scheme adopted by Hunter-Weston and General H. de Lisle (commander of 29 Division since 4 June but in overall control of the attack) had serious defects. The length of front to be attacked was about 1,500 yards. Because of the experience of 4 June, the area between the ravine and the sea was deemed to be the most difficult to secure, so it was allocated 20 heavy howitzers, two French mortars and most of the field artillery. But this left just 1 howitzer and 18×18-inch pounders for the attack on the right of the ravine. And because the 18 pounders fired only shrapnel, this meant that a considerable section of the Turkish line would not be bombarded by a single high-explosive shell. Why the length of front was not shortened to take this fact into account is a mystery. Obviously some aspects of artillery concentration remained to be grasped.

There was another factor in play here. The section of Turkish line subjected to the weakest bombardment also had the least-experienced troops. The 52 Division, whose 156 Brigade was given the task of attacking the Turkish line, had not had the happiest of histories. The division had been raised around Glasgow and the Lowlands of Scotland at the outbreak of war. Like all other divisions it had consisted of three brigades. However, just before it sailed for the Dardanelles one brigade had been involved in an horrific train crash near Gretna Green in South-West Scotland. In all, 434 men had been killed or injured and this delayed the dispatch of the unit to the east. When it arrived at Gallipoli (after experiencing yet another accident in the form of a collision with a ship at sea) the division consisted of just two brigades and a reduced quantity of supporting artillery.[29] Here were ample reasons for delaying its baptism of fire while shortening the front of attack, but Hunter-Weston apparently gave no thought to this option.

Following a two-hour bombardment the Allied attack went in at 11 a.m. on 28 June. After much fierce fighting, it succeeded on the left where the howitzers were concentrated and failed on the right where they were not. As a participant from 156 Brigade noted, 'we made very little progress and were effectively held up in a position where an artillery barrage and a supply of bombs [hand grenades] would have been useful but were not available'.[30] In all, 16,000 shells had been expended of which 1,200 were heavy. This was a considerable diminution on the French effort of the 21st, and the 77 guns used represented only about 1 gun for every 200 yards of trench attacked. However, if these figures are broken down into two components—one to the left of Gully Ravine and one to the right—the concentration on the successful left comes out at about 1 gun per 13 yards of trench attacked, a figure similar to the French success on 21 June.[31]

So by the end of June the flanks of the Allied front had been pushed forward and on the left were parallel with Krithia. It was the centre left that was now lagging behind and it was there that Hunter-Weston decided to make his third effort.

The time required to move the French artillery to support the British delayed that attack until 12 July. This allowed the British infantry position to be sorted out. The units of 29 and 42 Divisions were incapable of further effort and were withdrawn from the line. It then transpired that the Royal Naval Division, which was slated to carry out the offensive, was in no better state. Dysentery was rife in the division and exhaustion was also a factor, as some part of the unit had been in the line since the landings. This forced Hunter-Weston to fall back on the recently arrived 52 Division, which would be supported on its right by the French. There were even problems with that unit. Its 156 Brigade had been smashed by the last offensive. This left 155 Brigade and the much battered and delayed 157 Brigade. This was not optimal but if the operation was to go ahead there was no choice. Nor was the artillery position encouraging. Some pieces had to be withdrawn for repair, which left so few howitzers that the command was forced to split the operation in two; the left would attack in the morning and, if it was successful, the right in the afternoon.[32]

The morning attack on 12 July was initially successful. The French artillery alone had fired 500 heavy howitzer shells and 4,000 high-explosive shells from its field guns onto the front Turkish trench system.[33] This effectively destroyed the Turkish position, which was occupied without difficulty. Then the fighting became severe as the British ran into troops who had not been subjected to an intense bombardment. Progress slowed, casualties mounted. There was confusion at headquarters as to the position of the advanced troops. On the right, the French, who had given most of their artillery to the British, could not get further than the first Turkish trench. In these circumstances the decision about whether the afternoon attack should proceed was fraught. In the end it was decided that it should go ahead, if only to relieve the pressure on the 155 Brigade.[34]

The attack by 157 Brigade went in at 4.50 p.m. after a similar bombardment to that of the morning. The results were also similar. The Turkish front trenches were crushed but further back resistance stiffened. The third Turkish trench, which was the final objective of the brigade and which had been identified by aerial photography, was found to consist of a line scratched in the ground. With no protection on offer, the troops were forced to fall back. Confusion reigned for the remainder of the day. At nightfall the British thought they held two lines of Turkish trenches; beyond that there was uncertainty.[35]

The next day did not start well. In the early morning of 13 July elements of 157 Brigade, for reasons that are obscure, panicked and ran back towards their own line. They were halted and 'rallied' by some officers, and sent back before the Turks could take advantage. But the incident drew attention to the poor information the command had about the position of their troops, leading Hunter-Weston to order an attack along the whole line to clarify the situation.[36] This operation was to be carried out by the Royal Naval Division, which despite its reduced condition was the only reserve available. The attack was a shambles, as were many infantry attacks carried out to clarify an obscure situation in this war. On this occasion the troops were not yet in the line when the bombardment took place. They attacked 20 minutes after it had ceased. The only result was that no ground was gained and heavy casualties were inflicted on the already depleted Royal Naval Division.[37]

The Allies had now suffered about 4,000 casualties but had inflicted just over twice that number on the Turks. They had also captured two systems of Turkish trench and advanced their line some 500 yards.[38] Despite some sporadic attempts by small groups to get further forward, the battle was in effect over.

So, as it happened, was Hunter-Weston's career at Gallipoli. Egerton's diary takes up the story: 'The funny thing is that H.W. Whilst going round my lines this morning fell suddenly ill . . . and has taken himself off for two days' rest. He was really bad today.'[39] Hunter-Weston never returned to Gallipoli but his military career was far from over. He would reappear in 1916, once more in charge of VIII Corps, and play a fateful role at the Battle of the Somme.

The three blows struck by Hunter-Weston and Gouraud in June and July have received little favourable comment from historians. They were certainly not masterpieces of military art. On one occasion the front of attack exceeded the ability of the artillery to cover it; on another the fighting went on too long for any good that it did. Nevertheless, there is no doubt that there was a logic underlying the three actions which pointed towards a formula for making small advances at reasonable cost. A determination to withhold battle until the heavy artillery was concentrated and then to limit their objectives to the Turkish front trenches, had the classic characteristics of 'bite and hold' operations later developed on the Western Front. Nor did the Turks seem to have any answer to these tactics. Indeed, it was found later in the war that the only counter to 'bite and hold' was to withdraw troops from the area being bombarded and use them to counterattack later in the battle, and bring up a large amount of artillery in an endeavour to nullify the hostile bombardment. The Turkish army at Helles during this period did not, or could not, embrace either of these options. The idea of giving ground was politically unacceptable and in any case the British were not all that far from the important Kilid Bahr Plateau. Neither did the Turks have the artillery resources to attempt to smother the Allied batteries that were wreaking such havoc upon their trench lines.

This points to another conclusion. Unless the Turks changed tactics, there is no reason to doubt that the Allied armies could have persisted with 'bite and hold'. Whether this would have secured for them Achi Baba or the Kilid Bahr Plateau is mere speculation. But the fact is that there was really no other way of successfully prosecuting the offensive on the Peninsula. No other method even offered the option of forcing the Turks to give ground while inflicting on them heavier casualties than were being suffered. Yet no such operations were ever again conducted at Gallipoli. Having been discovered by the Anglo-French the 'bite and hold' method was immediately abandoned.

There are two possible explanations for this seemingly mysterious phenomenon. The first concerns the fate of the personnel involved. Gouraud did not remain to see even the third 'bite and hold' action.

On 30 June he was seriously wounded by a fragment of shell fired from a battery on the Asiatic shore. He was evacuated to France and did not return. Neither, as we have already seen, did Hunter-Weston. The architects of 'bite and hold' had therefore disappeared from the scene.

The second explanation concerns the reasons that the British in particular embarked upon the Gallipoli campaign in the first place. The impulse behind the naval attack had been, at least in part, an attempt to avoid the killing ground of the Western Front. The decision to commit troops was also made, in part, because Turkey seemed to be an easier enemy that must succumb to Allied firepower and organization. In these circumstances the political and military leadership were hardly going to embrace in Turkey what they had set out to avoid in France. The formula offered by Hunter-Weston and Gouraud was never going to be recognized for what it was.

In any case, the course of the war demonstrates that there was no iron law that compelled commanders to stick to an appropriate strategy even if they happened to find one. The story of the Western Front is replete with commanders abandoning 'bite and hold'. General Sir Henry Rawlinson did so after Neuve Chapelle, General Sir Herbert Plumer after Broodseinde. There is no reason to suppose that Hunter-Weston might have behaved differently. Indeed, Braithwaite, who had first championed 'systematic' attacks on 'certain sections of the front' as now the appropriate means of proceeding, promptly abandoned his own formula when Birdwood submitted a plan to him for a huge manoeuvre battle on the Anzac front. That was the last that was heard of systematic operations. There would be no more attempts at 'bite and hold'. The new operation was designed to win the campaign in one stroke from Anzac.

CHAPTER 11

The Plans of August

In London the progress of the Gallipoli campaign was closely followed by at least one member of the War Council—Winston Churchill. He was particularly well informed about Hamilton's headquarters because his brother Jack Churchill was a member of it. Jack's report of the landings ran over some 3,000 words and was optimistic in tone. 'Things are going very well', he told his brother in late April, 'and I hope ships will be in the Sea of Marmora in a fortnight.'[1] Subsequently the tone changed. It was Jack who alerted Churchill to Hamilton's deep-seated reluctance to ask for reinforcements. In reply, Churchill instructed Jack to ensure that Hamilton asked for the men he required: 'I am sure he would be supported if he asked through regular channels.'[2] The 'regular channels' to which Churchill alluded was of course Kitchener but the response from Hamilton was silence. The First and Second battles of Krithia came and went but there was no request for reinforcements from the commander of the Mediterranean Expeditionary Force.

Eventually, the War Council met on 14 May to consider the 'whole situation of the war'. The meeting was pervaded by gloom. Kitchener set the tone by stating that the Russians were short of shells and ammunition; that it was clearly impossible to break through in the west; and that he was worried about a possible German invasion. He then turned to the Dardanelles, accusing the navy of treachery for withdrawing the *Queen Elizabeth*.

Churchill immediately counterattacked. He argued strongly (if not accurately) that the navy would never have undertaken the initial attack if it had been known that an army of 80,000 to 100,000 men had been available. Kitchener's riposte was to say that he could not see a way forward at Gallipoli and to hint at evacuation. Then, as frequently happened at the War Council, the whole discussion petered out. Nevertheless, Hankey, perhaps on his own initiative, recorded as a decision of the meeting that Hamilton be asked exactly what reinforcement was required to force a decision.[3]

As it happened, this was the last decision that the War Council as a body would make. During the course of the discussion Fisher had struck an ominous note by declaring that 'he had been no party to the Dardanelles operation. When the matter was under discussion he had stated his opinion to the Prime Minister in a private interview.'[4] This statement harked back to the various War Council meetings on 28 January when he had tried to distance himself from the operation but had been persuaded first by Kitchener and then by Churchill to continue to support it. On 15 May even that dubious level of support came to an end. Fisher, wracked with doubt about Gallipoli and worn down by the heavy pressure of his office, suddenly resigned and went into hiding. This was one of a series of events (the shortage of shells for offensives on the Western Front was another) that led Asquith to form a coalition government with the Conservatives. Their *sine qua non* for joining was that Churchill be replaced at the Admiralty. The most forceful advocate of the Gallipoli operation was thus removed from office. Churchill was given the minor and humiliating position of Chancellor of the Duchy of Lancaster (which meant he could appoint members of the judiciary in that area but nothing more). However, he retained his seat on the War Council, now (misleadingly) renamed the Dardanelles Committee.[5]

Hamilton's reply to the now defunct War Council arrived on 17 May. It was riddled with contradictions. On the one hand, he thought lack of space and water would not allow him to absorb any reinforcements at all. On the other hand, two additional divisions and a Balkan ally to distract elements of the Turkish army might allow him to get forward. Failing an ally, he asked for four divisions—provided he could manage to advance a further 1,000 yards at Helles to shelter the new arrivals from shellfire.[6]

This was hardly a decisive response. Hamilton might not be able to take any reinforcements or he might take two divisions or he might be able to use four depending on a (very problematical) advance at Helles. Taken together with the removal of Churchill from high office and Kitchener's gloomy prognosis, it might not have been surprising if one of the first actions of the new Dardanelles Committee had been to end operations at the Dardanelles.

But the Committee did not take this line. Indeed, it decided that Hamilton would have three New Army divisions (ignoring Hamilton's doubts that he might not fit them in) and that he would use them to conduct an offensive in the second week of July.[7] Unfortunately, we cannot follow the trajectory of debate at this meeting; Hankey was absent and no notes were kept. Perhaps Churchill, though now in a subordinate position, was able to persuade members to persevere. For whatever reason, the Committee was obviously not yet of a mind to call off the campaign.

Despite the Committee's new-found optimism, Hamilton did not receive the news of reinforcements with any joy. He replied to Kitchener:

> Every day there are more and more entanglements, trenches and machine guns, and we are in danger of getting ourselves tied up in trench warfare as in France . . . . We have lost . . . a very large proportion of trained officers and soldiers, and the Turks are able to redress the inequality by constant replacement . . . . It is difficult to see what is to alter this situation so long as the Turks are able to draw on the whole of their army, even including the forces in the Caucasus . . . . On the other hand, if I had sufficient troops to enable me to avoid calling on the same units too often I have confidence in the ultimate attainment of Kilid Bahr. As I said yesterday, reinforcements on a considerable scale must expedite decision, but it is quite impossible to forecast time required to gain objectives unless or until I can see some limit to the numbers on which the enemy can draw to oppose me.[8]

The Committee, however, was not to be deflected by the gloomy predictions of the commander-in-chief. At their next meeting Churchill stated that three divisions might be just insufficient to force a decision. He suggested sending out another two divisions to Hamilton. Kitchener, having long banished any thoughts of evacuation, agreed—providing there was sufficient shipping to dispatch them in time for the new offensive. Balfour, now First Lord of the Admiralty, gave a negative response but Churchill pressed the point and persuaded him to investigate the possibility of speeding up the shipping arrangements.[9] In the event Kitchener did not wait for Balfour's reply. Without reference to anyone he decided that the two additional divisions should be sent. When on 5 July the Prime Minister asked what decision had been reached concerning these additional divisions, Kitchener replied that he had already dispatched one, and asked that he be allowed to send the second.[10] There was no discussion. Hamilton was to have five extra divisions.

This news seemed to have a positive effect on the commander-in-chief. Putting aside all his earlier doubts, Hamilton told Kitchener:

> I think I have reasonable prospects of eventual success with three divisions, with four the risks of miscalculation would be minimized, and with five, even if the fifth division had little or no gun ammunition, I think it would be a much simpler matter to clear the Asiatic shore subsequently of big guns etc. Kilid Bahr would be captured at an earlier date and success would be generally assured.[11]

* * *

What was to be done with these considerable reinforcements? There were three options on the table. First was Braithwaite's plan to land a force at Helles behind the Turkish trench lines to speed up the advance on the Kilid Bahr Plateau. This was certainly imaginative and it utilized the power of the navy which, despite the enemy submarines, was still weighted heavily in Britain's favour. But there were problems. Most obvious landing places were defended and the experience at Y Beach on 25 April could have given little confidence in the operation of independent forces behind Turkish lines. The second option was to continue attritional warfare along the lines of Hunter-Weston and Gouraud. There seems little doubt, as noted earlier, that this 'bite and hold' approach was the most realistic option. But it was not cheap, it was not spectacular and it was not the way in which anyone in authority wished to wage war in 1915. It too was dropped.

This left as the third option a plan that had been in the making since May. At Anzac, patrolling by New Zealand forces had revealed that the area to the north of the Anzac perimeter was almost devoid of Turks, and that an opportunity might exist to outflank the enemy defences confronting the Dominion troops. As C.E.W. Bean pointed out, this idea appealed to Hamilton because it held out the prospect of a return to mobile warfare.[12]

Birdwood sent a plan along these lines to Hamilton on 13 May. His aim was to make a sweeping movement from the Anzac perimeter around his left flank to capture the Sari Bair Ridge. Once that was achieved 'it might be advantageous to land a really large force under its cover, and get a position covering Kilia Bay [just north of the Narrows opposite Nagara Point]. If we could get big guns on to such a position, we ought with luck to be able to cut off communications certainly by land and probably by sea.'[13] A few days later he added that the force required to capture the ridge would consist of the Anzac contingent reinforced by the Indian Brigade. An additional division would be required to push across the Peninsula.[14] In that position, supported by heavy guns on the ridge, the Turkish force at Helles would be isolated and the forts at the Narrows captured.

As time passed, however, the objectives of the operation narrowed. On 30 May Birdwood told the commander-in-chief that while he still required the same force, namely, the Anzac Corps plus the Indian Brigade to secure the ridge and the additional division to cross the Peninsula, he was excluding the capture of Hill 971 from his plan because 'it is entirely cut off by precipices from the main ridge' and therefore any assault on it would be isolated from the main attack. He was also becoming concerned about the exploitation phase of the operation. He told Hamilton that the Turkish defences facing him were complex and dealing with them might consume all his reinforcements. Moreover, even if a division managed to push across the Peninsula he doubted whether heavy guns could be placed on Sari Bair to provide it with fire support.[15] This represented a considerable retreat from the ambitions of the first plan.

Further changes followed. By June Birdwood had become convinced that capturing the ridge *would* consume the Anzac Corps, a brigade and the new division. To carry out the advance across the Peninsula at least an additional division would be required, so he now needed to be reinforced by two divisions and a brigade. There was, however, a problem with this because the cramped Anzac position could not accommodate a force of this size. Birdwood's solution was to have the exploitation division available in ships just off the coast and to disembark it immediately the ridge had been captured.[16]

By 1 July this plan had been subjected to major surgery. Indeed, it had segued into two separate operations which would require all three reinforcing divisions. At Anzac, five of their nine brigades would assist in capturing the ridge, which, for reasons not specified, once more included Hill 971. At Suvla Bay, one brigade would land and immediately capture some guns on the Chocolate and W hills to the north of Anzac, which represented a threat to the main force advancing on Sari Bair. (Had

Birdwood undertaken a reconnaissance of this position he would have found that the only guns there were dummies.[17]) The remaining three brigades would also land at Suvla and occupy the ground around the bay to provide a base from which all five divisions operating in the northern area were to be supplied.[18]

This represented a radical change to the plan first proposed. While Sari Bair remained the primary objective, its capture was expected to consume twice the number of men. All other troops would be landed at Suvla Bay to eliminate some guns but mainly to establish a base. Any plan to push troops across the Peninsula to threaten the Narrows had been abandoned. All that was now on offer was the capture of a ridge and the establishment of a base. Although no one commented on it, this ended all hope that the August offensive would produce a decisive result.

Later in early July, Birdwood had a chance to reinstate the advance across the Peninsula when Hamilton informed him that yet two more divisions had been released by Kitchener. Birdwood let it pass, suggesting that they too be landed at Suvla. When the bay had been captured, this force should make it secure by seizing the Anafarta Ridge which overlooked it.[19]

Birdwood's final plan arrived on Hamilton's desk on 30 July. It provided for a covering force to make its way into the foothills to the north of Anzac to drive any Turks from the area. Then three assaulting columns would pass through them and capture the heights. To maximize the element of surprise the force would commence its assault at night and capture the ridge by dawn. In addition to these assaults, the 1 Australian Division would attack Lone Pine on the right of the Anzac line to draw Turkish troops away from the main effort in the north. When Sari Bair was in friendly hands, a converging attack would be delivered by those troops on the ridge in conjunction with the men holding the Anzac perimeter to clear the Turks from the whole position.[20]

By and large, GHQ fell in with Birdwood's wishes. Of the three New Army divisions being sent out for the offensive, Hamilton decided that Birdwood would have five not six additional brigades to assist in capturing the ridge. These would consist of 13 Division (three brigades) and one brigade from 10 Division together with the Indian Brigade already assigned to Anzac.

The remainder (11 Division, two brigades of 10 Division and ultimately the 53 and 54 Divisions) would land at Suvla. Such a large force (designated IX Corps) would need to be placed under a commander of equal rank to Birdwood. This required a general of some authority. Hamilton suggested that either General Rawlinson or General Sir Julian Byng, both then corps commanders on the Western Front, be sent out, but there was no chance of such experienced men being released from France. Moreover, as Kitchener pointed out, both these generals were junior to one of the commanders of a New Army Division, General Sir Bryan Mahon of 10 Division. To respect his seniority, this restricted the choice to Generals Ewart and Stopford. Hamilton chose Stopford on the grounds that Ewart's bulk would not allow him to negotiate trench systems.[21] After the battle, there would be much gnashing of teeth over this sorry farce. However, at the time no one at GHQ entered a protest. Indeed, Hamilton described Stopford as 'undoubtedly the best man available who is at the same time senior to Mahon. In fact if his nerve stands the strain, I could not have a better.'[22] Earlier he had written to the Chief of the Imperial General Staff (CIGS): 'Thanks so much for Freddy Stopford—I mean giving him a favourable impression of me ... I don't like Reed [Stopford's Chief of Staff] ... but then he is calm and tough, exactly the sub-strata most lacking in Stopford's otherwise complete outfit.'[23]

It may be doubted that Hamilton really regarded Stopford as positively as this might suggest. GHQ undertook the task of writing the orders for IX Corps, whereas, as we have observed, Birdwood wrote his own. On 22 July Braithwaite told Stopford what his force was expected to do. He was instructed that the landing would take place at night and that his first objective was to capture three positions (Lala Baba, Nibrunesi Point and Hill 10) which overlooked the landing beaches. He was then to do two things. He was 'to send a small force to secure a footing' on the Anafarta Ridge but it was of the '*first* importance that [the Chocolate and W hills] should be captured by a coup de main before daylight in order to prevent the guns which they contain being used against our troops on Hill [971] and to safeguard our hold on Suvla Bay'. These guns should be attacked from the north as they were protected on the southern and western slopes by trenches and wire. Subsequent to all this it might be possible to move on Hill 971 to aid Birdwood's attack.[24] It is worth noting that this putative aid to Birdwood was a GHQ addition. Birdwood had not asked for anything beyond the establishment of a base and the capture of the guns.

Stopford arrived at Gallipoli in late July. He scrutinized the GHQ plan and declared himself unhappy with it. He noted that to carry out all aspects of it he was expected to land a large and inexperienced force in the dark, advance several miles through difficult country for which there were no maps, attack five defended localities (the three hills overlooking the landing place and Chocolate and W hills), and occupy a ridge 4 miles away and 5 miles long, presumably before dawn. He was then expected to assist another attack several miles to the south, which would have to be approached across some of the most tortuous country on the Peninsula, all with a force of one and two-thirds divisions.

Stopford also observed that all the landing beaches were outside the bay. This meant that if he were to approach the Chocolate and W hills from the north, he would be required to follow a very circuitous route at least 5 miles long. He therefore asked that one landing beach be located inside the bay to shorten this journey. Stopford also had doubts about the timing of this whole enterprise. To capture the positions before daylight he would have to attack dug-in Turkish troops without artillery support (there would be no guns landed on the first day at Suvla). Moreover, he was unsure whether the force advancing on the Anafarta Ridge could reach it by dawn. Finally, he stated that the numerous tasks he was expected to perform would certainly occupy his entire force and he was extremely doubtful whether he would be able to give any help to the Anzac force.[25]

These were thoughtful criticisms. The plethora of objectives, the tight time frame, the long marches and the lack of artillery support revealed grave weaknesses in the plan. Stopford submitted his memorandum to Hamilton and waited for a reply. It was not long in coming. That same day a new set of instructions was sent to the IX Corps commander.

Stopford was now told that 'his primary objective [would] be to secure Suvla Bay as a base' for all northern operations and that this objective would probably occupy his entire force. He should still aim to capture the guns on the Chocolate and W hills because they might make the position of troops on Hill 971 untenable. His route to these positions was made more direct by introducing a landing point inside the bay, but he was only to attack them if this were possible 'without prejudice to the attainment of [your] primary objective'. Moreover, any help he could give to Anzac was only to be undertaken if there were men to spare after his other objectives had been secured.[26]

GHQ had to some extent reverted to the original objective of the Suvla force as outlined by Birdwood: establishing a base for all the troops in the north. They had, however, downgraded the capture of the guns that threatened Anzac to a subsidiary matter, only to be undertaken when the base was secure. In addition, all mention of the Anafarta Ridge and the need to obtain a foothold on it to secure the base, and then to press on and assist Birdwood, had been removed from the plan.

Stopford was not having any of this. In a reply to GHQ he insisted that the elimination of the guns on the Chocolate and W hills was essential for the security of the base and that the Anafarta Ridge was the 'key' to the whole position. It was his firm intention to attack and occupy them seriatim.[27]

The intent of the whole Suvla operation now needs to be summarized. It had begun life as a minor affair to eliminate some guns threatening the left of the Anzac attack. It had eventually changed into the establishment of a base from which the considerable force in the north could be supplied (when 53 and 54 Divisions landed the base would consist of no fewer than the equivalent of seven divisions). But in changing the purpose of the landing something had been lost. Birdwood's original conception had included an exploitation force that was to push across the Peninsula and cut Turkish communications with their Helles contingent. It was this force that was now to be landed at Suvla. In that operation, it needs to be stressed, it would not be involved in exploitation operations of any kind. Indeed, if GHQ had had its way the force might not have even progressed to the Anafarta Ridge. Thanks to Stopford's intervention it would attempt to capture those heights, not as a preliminary to a further advance but to deny them to any Turks who might use their dominating position to threaten the base.

In short, the August operations in the north were now to accomplish just two things: the Anzac operations were to capture the Sari Bair Ridge; the Suvla landings were to establish a base. What was to happen after that was not specified in any documents written at the time. Presumably the successful attainment of the objectives would have led to yet more plans to advance across the Peninsula. But it must be emphasized that the August operations no longer aspired to be decisive events which would bring the campaign to a successful close. They were merely to be the first steps in a long journey.

CHAPTER 12

The Assault on Sari Bair

As finally developed, Birdwood's plan was to attack on the extreme north and south of the Anzac perimeter. The initial attack would occur in the south at Lone Pine. Its intention was to attract Turkish reserves to the area while the main operation proceeded in the north. There, a major outflanking movement would be carried out to secure the Sari Bair Ridge from Hill 971 to Chunuk Bair. Once the ridge had been captured, the troops would attack down its slopes in conjunction with various operations from the existing perimeter (the Nek, Pope's and Quinn's) and so catch the Turks in a pincer movement. At the end the Turks would have been driven back from the Anzac perimeter.

To assist the Anzacs, a diversionary attack was delivered by the troops at Helles on the afternoon of 6 August. It was a complete disaster. The 29 Division faced defences far stronger than anything yet experienced on the Peninsula and their artillery was too feeble to subdue them. The attack gained no ground because of intense Turkish artillery fire and 'cunningly concealed machine guns'.[1] The assaulting brigade suffered 2,000 casualties. The next day, against all reason, the 42 Division renewed the assault. No gains were made and another 1,000 casualties incurred. There is no evidence that a single Turkish unit was prevented from heading north by these operations.

The attack on Lone Pine heralded the opening of the new offensive at Anzac. It was a frontal attack by three battalions on a Turkish position

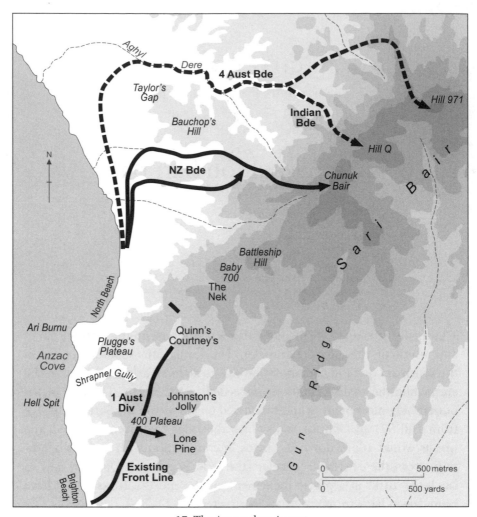

17 The Anzac plan: August

of great strength. As Hunter-Weston and Gouraud had demonstrated, frontal attacks need not be fatal given the correct artillery preparation. Unfortunately for 1 Brigade, which carried out the attack, the supporting barrage was feeble. Just 383 shells were fired at the wire entanglements protecting the Turkish trenches while just eight guns, two of them old and inaccurate, fired at the trenches themselves.[2]

The result was predictable. When the troops dashed across no man's land, some found the wire intact, others found the overhead cover used by the Turks on some of their trenches still in place. As 2 Battalion noted:

> One of the features of the Turkish trenches is the heavy overhead cover on the firing line. In one place heavy sleepers have been put up & earth two feet thick piled on top. The greater part of the firing line is covered, the material being pine or fir tree logs about six to nine inches in diameter and earth on top. In parts great difficulty was experienced by our men in getting in to the trenches owing to this cover but where this was so it was found to be a good plan to cross over the cover & drop into one of the numerous communication trenches in rear.[3]

Turkish machine-gun fire opened on the troops in no man's land and many casualties were incurred before a plan to deal with the covered trenches was worked out. Nevertheless, just after 6.00 p.m. on 6 August Australian troops were fighting inside the Turkish trench system. The Turks launched counter attacks at 7.05 p.m., and 1.20 a.m., and at 1.20 p.m. the following day. The fighting was vicious, often hand to hand, and swayed back and forth among the maze of trenches. Eventually the Australians prevailed. A footing in Lone Pine was secured. The cost was extraordinary: the 1 Division had suffered over 2,200 casualties.[4]

In the end the command would measure the success of the operation not in terms of casualties but in terms of what the operation set out to do. Had it diverted Turkish reserves from the main attack? The answer is ambiguous. The local reserves were immediately drawn in and no fewer than three additional regiments took part in the bloody trench fighting at Lone Pine.[5] And such had been the vigour of the Australian attack that on the evening of 5 August Essad Pasha, commander of the Northern Group, had ordered two regiments of Colonel Kannengiesser's 9 Division from Helles to the vicinity of Lone Pine. Yet, as we will see, these formations took no part in the fighting there but were to play a key role further north.[6]

As the Allied troops were attacking Lone Pine, the small columns of men in the covering force were assembling in the north. Many of them were unwell. At the beginning of August, one in five Australian troops was sick or wounded. Among the sick, fever and dysentery were the main culprits. And it seems certain that many of the men who were to assault Sari Bair were either suffering from these diseases or had only recently recovered from them.[7] It was their task to clear the Turkish troops from the approaches to the ridge. This would allow the three main assaulting columns easier access to their objectives in what was a very tight timetable. The operation was to commence at 6 p.m. on 6 August and the assault on the ridge was to be launched at dawn (4.30 a.m.) on the 7th. That would give the assaulting columns just over ten hours to complete their task.

The plan had four main difficulties. First, it required precise timing with little margin for error if the dawn deadline was to be met. Whether such precision could be maintained by groups of men moving across un-reconnoitred country and with no accurate maps in the dark was problematic.

Second, the assaulting columns themselves constituted a problem, which applied in particular to the one on the left. For the first 2 miles of its 4-mile journey, it would consist of 1,500 men from 4 Brigade, followed immediately by 1,500 men from the Indian Brigade. Given that a marching soldier occupied about 1 yard of space, this column until it divided to attack its respective summits would stretch over a distance of 3,000 yards in tortuous country with ravines and nullahs that were very likely to fragment such an unwieldy formation—especially in the dark.

Third, after the left column split into two, there would be three columns quite widely spaced geographically. Yet the best chance for success required that the dawn assaults be delivered simultaneously. Who was to coordinate this operation? Each brigadier would be with his column while Godley, in overall command, would be out of touch at his headquarters near the beach.

The fourth matter is of some importance as it relates to exactly how the attack on the heights was to be made. A column of marching men has depth but not width. To bring the maximum firepower available against the enemy, the column would have to spread (or deploy) into a line, or more usually, several lines. On a parade ground this was a standard procedure, easily performed by even half-trained troops. But Gallipoli was no parade ground. Those same nullahs, ravines and gullies that could disrupt a march could also play havoc with a deployment, especially one carried out in the dark. The broken nature of the country might well disperse the troops into small packets, thus making a concerted attack with weight of numbers well nigh impossible.

It would be congenial to record that the Anzac command had given these issues their thoughtful consideration. In fact, not one of the four matters discussed was given even a passing mention in the operation orders for the August offensive.

* * *

The covering forces started well. Many small garrisons of Turkish troops simply melted away in the dark. However, as the operation progressed larger Turkish units stood their ground and fought. These fights dislocated the timetable and prevented the Allied troops from clearing the battlefield. Thus, when the assaulting columns crossed the foothills they might blunder into these Turkish forces, which would have the advantage of being concealed by the dark.[8]

From left to right the assaulting columns were commanded by General John Monash (4 Brigade), General Herbert Cox (Indian Brigade) and General Francis Johnston (New Zealand Brigade). All soon lost their way.

Monash at least got off to a prompt start, but the troops had great difficulty in keeping direction in the dark and the column began to straggle.[9] Moreover, those who had started further away from the start line (because of the cramped space on the Peninsula) had to jog to maintain touch with the leading units.[10] For men worn down by combat and dysentery this was an exhausting and debilitating beginning.

It rapidly got worse. To retrieve some lost time, guides suggested that the brigade detour through 'Taylor's Gap' to their first landfall, the Aghyl Dere. This proved to be a nightmarish experience. The Gap was a narrow, rocky, twisting route, covered with prickly gorse. Men soon had to be sent ahead to cut a path for the others. At that moment a few remnant Turks dispersed by the covering force opened fire. The column promptly halted and the entire 13 Battalion was detached from the march to deal with them.[11] Monash's force was revealing itself to be frayed, jumpy and in no physical shape to meet the demands being made on it.

Eventually the Turks scattered and Monash's 4 Brigade crossed the Aghyl Dere. But the brigade then veered off north-west instead of north-east where it ran into more sporadic Turkish fire. This caused a crisis. In one battalion the officers had to 'take exceptional personal risks' to maintain control. In another, there was difficulty getting an attack 'vigorously pushed'.[12] In the end, despite the efforts of the officers, it was the men who decided the issue. They threw themselves to the ground—exhausted, tired, sick and dispirited—and their commanders wisely accepted that they could go no further. They settled down on the Damakjelik Spur, facing away from their objective, Hill 971, and 3 miles from it.

What of Cox's Indian Brigade that was trailing Monash? He had been frustrated by the various delays ahead which had at first reduced his speed to a snail's pace and then halted the brigade altogether.[13] When dawn broke on 7 August his leading unit was just entering Aghyl Dere, and was also 3 miles from its objective, Hill Q. Guides who allegedly knew the country were then called for and they directed Cox's men up various spurs and nullahs which were supposed to bring them out united near their objective. In fact, all the routes chosen dispersed Cox's force over a very wide area. By 9.00 a.m. it had disintegrated. Some troops were with the Australians on Damakjelik Spur, others found themselves with the New Zealanders near Rhododendron Ridge, yet others were north of that point near a feature called the Farm. Only the 1/6 Ghurka battalion, by good luck, were within hailing distance of Hill Q.[14]

Meanwhile, the New Zealand Brigade under Johnston fared slightly better than its northern compatriots. They were late in starting and had to divert men to assist the covering force in ejecting stubborn groups of Turks from some of the lower slopes. But by dawn on 7 August the brigade was in sight of Rhododendron Ridge, the approach route to Chunuk Bair. The leading contingent drove off a small force of Turks on Rhododendron Ridge but they lacked support. The bulk of the brigade became lost in the tangled ravines and eventually made its way back to the start point. A furious Godley directed it back to Chunuk Bair, but this took several hours. In the meantime Johnston and his small group were quite alone and under fire from a group of Turks of unknown size on the crest. Neither was there any sign of support from Hill Q or further north on Hill 971. In these circumstances Johnston decided to wait until the remainder of his force joined him, while instructing his brigade major (Arthur Temperley) to dispatch the news to Godley. Temperley noted later:

> Accordingly I wrote a message to Divisional headquarters saying where we were and how we were disposed but that 'in view of the fact that we were absolutely unsupported on our right or left and could see no sign of any troops we deemed it prudent to remain here and await a further advance on the part of the Indian Brigade'. Colonel Johnston approved

of this message and it was dispatched. The laconic reply received was 'Attack at once'.[15]

No attack could be organized 'at once'. Johnston first had to decide which troops to employ. He eventually chose the Aucklands and two companies of Ghurkas from Cox's force, but to deploy them in attacking order took him over two hours. By then, as the New Zealanders were to discover, it was too late. Ironically, an unintended consequence of the Lone Pine attack was to prove their undoing.

Events unfolded thus. After news of Lone Pine reached Essad Pasha, commander of the northern force, he realized that a major operation was underway but he was uncertain about its objectives. As noted, he had dispatched Colonel Kannengiesser from Helles towards Anzac on the evening of 5 August. This force had bivouacked behind Gun Ridge that night, while Kannengiesser hurried to Essad's headquarters to learn of the situation first hand. He found Essad in a state of some agitation. He was now aware that troop movements had been reported to the north of the Turkish positions facing Anzac, and he also knew that this area was without defenders. He therefore directed Kannengiesser personally to reconnoitre Chunuk Bair and summon his division to the area without delay. Essad also met Mustapha Kemal and ordered him to dispatch two companies of troops to Chunuk Bair and a battalion to Hill 971.[16]

Kannengiesser arrived on the summit of Chunuk Bair soon after 7.00 a.m. and discovered some 20 men and a mountain battery in the area, completely oblivious to the developing situation. It was certainly these men who fired at Johnston's column at around 8.00 a.m. Soon after this incident, Kemal's companies arrived and shortly after that the regiments of Kannengiesser's 9 Division. So by the time Johnston had organized his attack, several thousand Turks were waiting to receive it. In this situation the Aucklands and the Ghurkas never stood a chance. They were swept away by concentrated Turkish fire around 11.0 a.m.

Johnston's decision to await his missing troops and thus forfeit the chance of pressing on to Chunuk Bair has been severely criticized. Two charges are levelled against him. The first is that by not taking Chunuk Bair he dislocated the plan whereby his troops attacking down the ridge would combine with formations on the lower slopes such as the Nek who were attacking up the ridge. This pincer movement was designed to clear all the Turks facing the Anzac perimeter and prepare the way for future operations.

In the event, the non-arrival of Johnston meant the troops attacking at the Nek went in unsupported and were repulsed with much slaughter.

This charge has no substance. Birdwood's staff were aware that no column would make the dawn deadline and had been informed that they were meeting with stiff opposition. This last intelligence was perhaps exaggerated, but on the basis of it Birdwood ordered the attack at the Nek to proceed '*to draw off opposition to a further advance*'.[17] So the bloody rebuff at the Nek took place to ease the path for the New Zealanders, not as part of a failed pincer movement.[18]

The second charge, that Chunuk Bair could have been seized had Johnston acted earlier, has more substance and is more difficult to resolve. Two facts seem clear. Just after dawn on 7 August the hill was bereft of defenders. Had Johnston moved forward he could have occupied it. Thus 1,500 Allied troops armed with some machine guns would have held a key section of the ridge. But there were some negative factors. The men were not in good shape. One account suggests that 30 per cent of the Wellingtons should have been in hospital because of their severe dysentery, rather than conducting offensive operations.[19] The Aucklands were 'worn out by hard work, want of sleep, and weakened by disease'.[20] Whether men in this state could have withstood an attack in divisional strength, which the Turks ultimately mounted, is a doubtful proposition, especially as the New Zealanders would also have been brought under enfilade fire from Battleship Hill.[21] It seems more likely that Johnston's men would have been forced off Chunuk Bair at, say, 9.00 a.m. instead of 11.00 a.m. Like many other 'lost opportunities' of the First World War, perhaps the opportunity was never there to be lost.

All three columns had now failed. But back at headquarters Godley thought he saw redemption. His only reserve was 39 Brigade, newly arrived on the Peninsula and with no knowledge of the terrain. Notwithstanding these drawbacks, Godley instructed it to capture Chunuk Bair and then turn left and assault Hill Q. In issuing this order he was asking an inexperienced unit to accomplish what two battle-hardened brigades had failed to manage earlier in the day. Not surprisingly the attempt failed. Like all other units that ventured into the Aghyl Dere the men became lost. One battalion joined the New Zealanders on Rhododendron Spur while the others described a circuitous route only to finish at dusk near the point where they had commenced in the morning. By then it was too late to launch an offensive and all operations were suspended until 8 August.

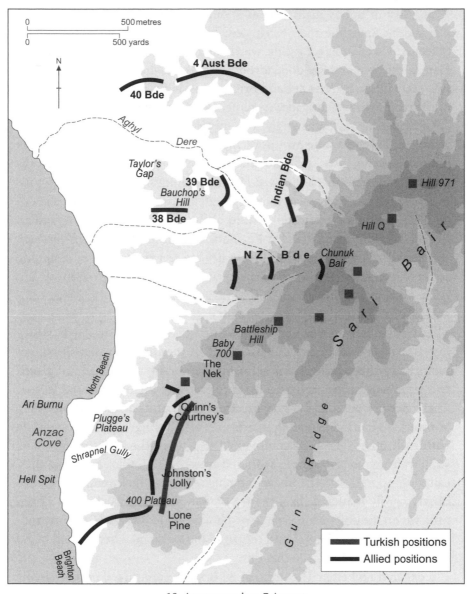

18 Anzac: evening, 7 August

So, to sum up: as night fell on 7 August, Monash's 4 Brigade was on Damakjelik Spur, the men exhausted, demoralized and miles from their objective. Cox's Indian Brigade was scattered between the Australians on Damakjelik Spur and Rhododendron Ridge, although a battalion of Ghurkas was near Hill Q; the New Zealand Brigade was on Rhododendron Ridge with one battalion from 39 Brigade, the remainder of which was in the Aghyl Dere.

Godley took an amazingly optimistic view of this shambles. He reasoned that there were groups of men within striking distance of all the major objectives (he was ill-informed about the position of the Australians in this regard) and that a renewed effort on 8 August would succeed. So his orders for the new day were to a large extent a repeat of those for the 6th and 7th. Monash (4 Brigade) would advance on Hill 971, Cox (Indian Brigade) on Hill Q and the New Zealanders on Chunuk Bair. As 39 Brigade was spread all over the battlefield, Godley made a virtue of it by assigning some of its battalions to each of the assaulting columns. Zero hour would be at dawn on the 8th.[22]

*　*　*

The story of the Australian effort on 8 August is soon told. In the dark they lost their way once again and made off in the direction of Hill 60, yet further away from Hill 971. More misfortune was in store. Essad had placed two regiments in this area, one from reserve and the other from Helles.[23] The concentrated machine-gun fire from these units decimated Monash's leading battalions (14 and 15), which were also having trouble cooperating with each other. The 14th complained that when the Turks opened fire, support from the 15th simply 'withered away'.[24] The 15th claimed that their call for support from the 14th went unanswered.[25] In the circumstances this ill-will hardly mattered. In a matter of minutes 600 casualties had been inflicted on the units. Monash had no choice but to disregard Cox's instruction to advance on Hill 971 and return to the start line. There would be no further action by 4 Brigade that day.

Cox fared no better. The units of 39 Brigade (reinforced in this case by some from the 38th which had arrived on the Peninsula during the night) remained scattered and lost for most of the day. Progress could be glacial:

> Every hundred yards got worse, in some places there were boulders three or four feet high which had to be crossed singly by men heavily armed. Some of these boulders were very smooth and slippery giving no foot hold for men in heavy marching boots. Many of the men fell, and

in order to maintain silence, officers had to be placed at these obstacles. The August night was very hot, the men had had two nights without sleep, and had had a very long and tiring day before commencing the night march. They were all very thirsty [and] I had to halt the leading company more and more frequently as we got higher up the dere.[26]

Eventually, the leading companies of this group made contact with Major Cecil Allanson and his 1/6 Ghurkas. Allanson determined to assault Hill Q with every man he could muster. However, 100 yards from the summit Turkish fire became so intense that he had to dig in and wait for assistance.[27] That was the last action of Cox's column on 8 August.

This left the New Zealand group under Colonel Malone near Chunuk Bair as the only column with a chance of seizing one of the heights that day. Unexpectedly, they succeeded. Augmented by two battalions from 39 Brigade, they charged straight to the top of the ridge without opposition, in the process capturing a machine-gun section.[28]

What had happened to the Turkish defenders who had taken such a toll on the New Zealanders and Ghurkas the previous day? As always, chaos on the battlefield was not confined to one side. Units from no fewer than six Turkish divisions had been thrown piecemeal into the defence of the ridge line between Hill 971 and Chunuk Bair. During the fighting on 7 August two divisional commanders had been seriously wounded and two regimental commanders killed. To add to the confusion, von Sanders had chosen this moment to reorganize the command. He placed this section of the ridge in the inexperienced hands of one of his Suvla generals, thus sidelining Essad Pasha, the man most familiar with the situation. In the absence of firm direction, the regiments on the ridge made their own decisions. Collectively, these amounted to a drift of units, north and south, away from Chunuk Bair. On the summit remained only the single machine-gun detachment captured by the New Zealanders in their assault.[29]

So now an Allied unit was in place on one of the commanding heights. Yet it was far from secure. A murderous enfilade fire was poured into it from the Turks on the right at Battleship Hill and on the left from Hill Q. Indeed, the Allied troops on the summit soon found their position on the crest of Chunuk Bair untenable. The ground was too rocky for them to dig any proper trenches and Turkish bombing parties soon drove them back. Eventually they took up positions offering some protection on the reverse slope of the summit.[30]

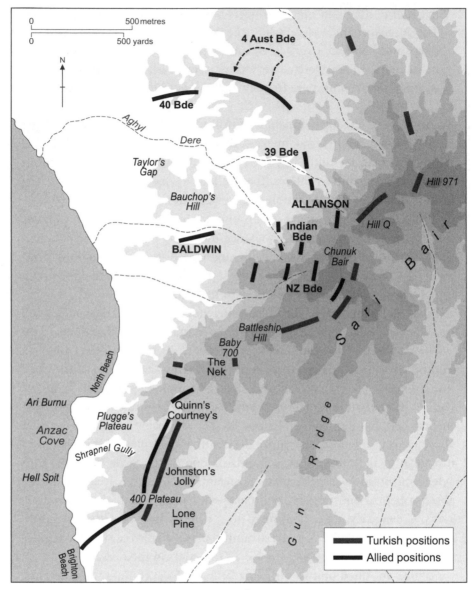

19 Anzac: evening, 8 August

For the remainder of the day the mixed New Zealand and British force endured a series of ferocious counterattacks. These usually took the form of 'bomb attacks followed up by bayonet charges by the Turks creeping up under our crest line'.[31] The first Turkish attack was made by the 64 Regiment from Kannengiesser's 9 Division, but it failed to dislodge Malone's force. A second assault by a regiment of 8 Division (newly arrived from Helles) might well have succeeded against the weary defenders had not some fresh New Zealand troops arrived at the critical time and forced them back.[32] At the end of the day the two sides were within 20 to 30 yards of each other on either side of the summit. The Wellingtons were a shattered force. Of the 750 who commenced the operation only 3 officers and 55 men remained unwounded.[33] But Chunuk Bair was still in Allied hands.

* * *

There could be no doubt regarding Godley's decision for the next day. After three days of thwarted endeavour, he had at last a group of men clinging to one of the key heights of Sari Bair. He determined to widen his hold by capturing Hill Q and the remainder of the ridge between it and Chunuk Bair. There would be the usual three columns. On the right the New Zealand-led force would attempt to strengthen its position on Chunuk Bair. On the left Cox would utilize Allanson with his Ghurkas and a battalion from 39 Brigade to take Hill Q. In the centre, a new formation under the control of General Anthony Baldwin (38 Brigade) would assault between the two summits and occupy the remainder of the ridge. Any attempt to get the Australian 4 Brigade under Monash onto Hill 971 was abandoned.[34]

This plan was far from optimal. The forces on Chunuk Bair were exhausted, those near Hill Q few in number. And the central force, with perhaps the most difficult task of the day, was far away from its objective, quite new to the Peninsula and entirely ignorant of the terrain over which it had to fight. Yet Godley had little choice. The 1 Australian Division had expended itself at Lone Pine; Monash's force was exhausted and the other veteran forces were heavily engaged at points such as Quinn's and Pope's.

It seems likely that the force on Chunuk Bair was never aware that it constituted one column of a major attack on the ridge. The brigade war diary never mentions receiving any orders from Godley. Throughout 9 August the New Zealanders were under such heavy attack from the Turks that they were hardly able to maintain their existing positions, let alone contribute to a general advance. At the end of the day they were where they were at the beginning, clinging to the reverse slope of the Chunuk Bair summit.[35]

Meanwhile, on the left just below Hill Q, Allanson's Ghurkas and three companies of the South Lancashires from 39 Brigade (about 350 to 450 men in all) awaited the arrival of Baldwin's force.[36] When it did not appear, Allanson decided to derive what support he could from the preliminary bombardment by attacking alone. He succeeded in reaching the summit and his men opened fire on the retiring enemy.[37] Then, as Allanson recorded in a message to Cox:

> Unfortunately at 5.25 artillery reopened fire (I think it must have been ours) and a good many casualties occurred among the men; an apparent cross fire also [fell] on us it seemed from Abdul Rahman Bair [to the north] and I regret to say Position was evacuated and the lower position again taken up though many of the troops went farther down the gully. I do not think that the casualties by high explosive should have been sufficient to cause the retirement but all the troops concerned had had an extremely bad night and only just clung on.[38]

This version of events, which is supported by a letter Allanson wrote to his brother in March 1916, should end the controversy that the British lost a foothold on the ridge just because of a few heavy shells.[39] Allanson's force probably was hit by 'friendly fire'[40] but as he stated, his men were also under crossfire from the north and were exhausted. It might be added that they were also very few, certainly far short of the numbers that the New Zealanders had on Chunuk Bair, and that no reinforcements were on offer. In short, Allanson's force was not in sufficient strength to claim anything more than a tenuous toehold on the ridge. It was not therefore 'shelled off the ridge' because it never really occupied it in the first place.[41]

So by the early morning of 9 August Godley's third attempt on the ridge had collapsed on the right and left. This left Baldwin's column in the centre as the last hope.

This meant that there was no hope at all. Baldwin had met Johnston the evening before the attack and was given an approach route to the ridge via Chailak Dere and the Farm. The alternative route was along Rhododendron Ridge to the Apex. Baldwin chose Chailak Dere, almost certainly the wrong decision as his men soon found it impassable because of 'a block of mules, ammunition and wounded'.[42] But the other route was hardly attractive either, as it would have brought the column under enfilade fire from the Turkish defenders around Chunuk Bair. There were no easy options facing

Baldwin that evening and in the event his force, like most others, got lost and did not arrive in time to support Allanson.

Eventually some units of Baldwin's force did attack.[43] But the attacks were made piecemeal and across ground swept by Turkish fire. The result was hardly in doubt—heavy casualties and no ground gained.[44] At the end of the day Godley's men still had one precarious hold on the ridge, that at Chunuk Bair.

They were not to hold it for long. The New Zealand force on Chunuk Bair was exhausted and in desperate need of relief. Two New Army battalions were instructed to take over the positions during the night of 9–10 August. By about 10.00 p.m. the Lancashires were in position but the Wiltshires were nowhere to be seen. In fact, their orders arrived late and at 3.30 a.m. they had just arrived at the lower slopes of Chunuk Bair.[45] Before they reached the summit the Turks attacked.

This operation had been brewing for some time under the direction of Kemal. Although the British were having trouble finding their way to the ridge and then mounting a concerted attack on it, the situation at Chunuk Bair and Hill Q could hardly be looked on with equanimity by the Turkish command. No fewer than three divisions from Helles (4, 8 and 9), one from the central reserve around Maidos and one from the Asiatic shore (near Troy!) had been sent to the Anzac perimeter.[46] In addition, as we will see, other divisions were heavily involved at Suvla. Although the Turkish army had many remaining divisions, these were distant from the battlefield and would take time to arrive. Meanwhile the imperative was to get the British off the ridge. So Kemal designated the 8 Division, which had started the battle just north of Krithia, to push the 'English' forces off Chunuk Bair.[47]

The Turkish forces attacked without a preliminary bombardment at 4.30 a.m. on 10 August. The 700 Lancashires occupying the summit were in no position to withstand a divisional attack:

The Turkish attack on our position at Chunuk Bair was delivered suddenly and with great violence. Of the first three lines, two were dealt with by our fire, but the third swept over our trenches and drove the remainder of the garrisons down the hill. The confused mass of men poured down on to the bivouac of the 5/Wilts . . . so it was too swept away. . . . The Turks at first advanced over the crest of the hill between Chunuk Bair and Battleship Hill in dense masses and suffered severely

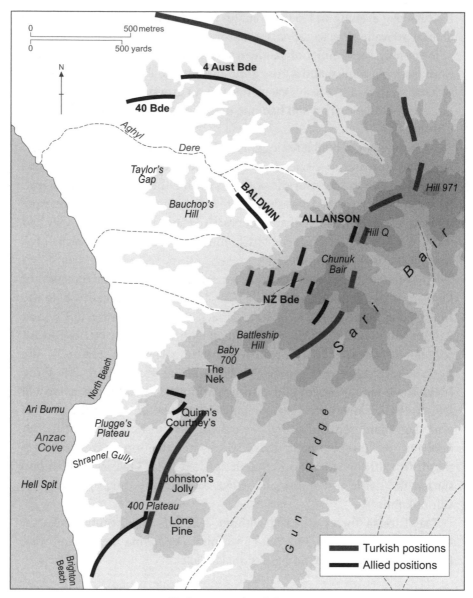

20 Anzac: evening, 9 August

from our Guns and Machine Gun fire. Later they charged across in successive lines, each line as it came on, being engaged by our 18 pr batteries. The Turks behaved with the greatest gallantry but few of them were seen going back over the ridge. . . . A prisoner captured a few days later described the dead on the slopes south of Chunuk Bair as being 'like corn that has been reaped'.[48]

Baldwin's force also bore the brunt of the counterattack, and was driven from its position at the Farm. There was no question that the Turks suffered heavy casualties in this offensive. There was also no doubt that the forces at Anzac had finally lost their tenuous grip on the ridge. The battle for Sari Bair was over.

* * *

Ever since August 1915, historians have argued about the Sari Bair battles. The usual tenor of argument is that on 7, 8 or 9 August the Anzac forces had a grip on the ridge but individual incompetence, be it by Monash, Johnston or Baldwin, caused them to lose it.

However, the only chance of seizing the ridge was by a surprise attack launched simultaneously by all three assaulting columns, and there was never a moment when such an event looked imminent. This was not because of mistakes made by some of the individuals mentioned but because the plan was too ambitious in the first place. It was absurdly optimistic to expect men, either exhausted by months of combat and worn down by disease or completely unfamiliar with the terrain over which they were to fight, to launch a night attack to strict timetable through uncharted country of the most rugged and treacherous kind. In that sense the battle was not lost by Monash in the Aghyl Dere, or by Johnston at the Apex, or by Baldwin in Chailak; it was lost on Birdwood's drawing board before a single soldier had been committed. The troops were asked to do too much and it should be no matter for wonder that they failed.

Many commentators will not accept this scenario. They claim that the operation came within an ace of success. There was nothing unsound about the plan, or if there was, there were still opportunities on offer to seize the ridge.

It is of course true that for intervals troops had attained two of the crucial heights, Chunuk Bair and Hill Q. But several points need to be made about these occupations. The first is that for most of the time the New Zealanders on Chunuk were unsupported. All through 8 August there were no other

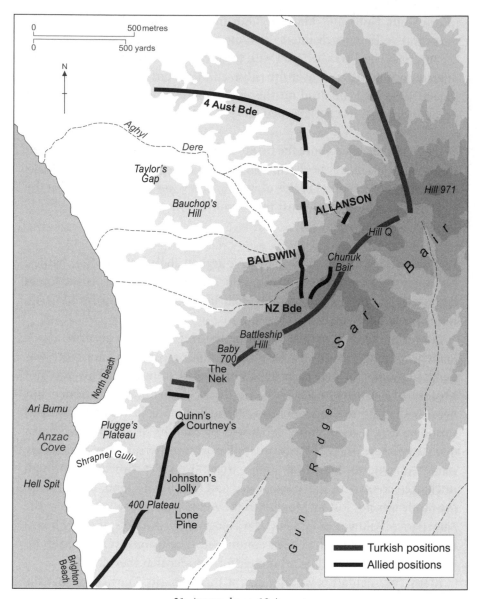

21 Anzac: dawn, 10 August

troops on the heights, and this left Johnston's men open to enfilade fire from north and south. Moreover, when Allanson's Ghurkas appeared on Hill Q on the 9th, they were so few in number and their stay was so brief that they offered no support at all to the force on Chunuk Bair. A group of inopportune artillery shells did not affect this situation. Exhaustion and the small numbers of the men on Hill Q would have soon seen them ejected in any case. The same situation also pertained on Chunuk Bair. The force there was larger than the group on Hill Q but it still succumbed to the first Turkish counterattack in real strength. In this sense the troops on the ridge were never in sufficient numbers or with sufficient support to argue that they 'held' the heights in the first place.

There are other problems concerning the ridge. As the men on Chunuk Bair could have testified, it was futile holding one or two sections of it. Enfilade fire and the constant threat of flanking attacks made such sections extremely difficult to hold and reinforce. To occupy the ridge in safety it was necessary to occupy it entirely or at least the section from Hill Q southwards, but Birdwood's forces never looked like achieving so much.

Even a full-scale occupation of the ridge would have been difficult to maintain. Almost all the troops at Birdwood's disposal would have been required to hold the ridge line. Could such a large force have been supplied with food, water and ammunition across the twisted gullies and ravines that characterized the country between the beach and the crest line? One authority who took part in the offensive answered in the negative, noting that even the few New Zealanders on Chunuk Bair received 'little food, less water, little ammunition and no bombs'.[49]

The mention of ammunition raises the question of fire support for the men on the ridge. Even Birdwood recognized that this was a facet of his plan that presented formidable difficulties. In the first instance he was chronically short of guns, especially heavy howitzers of which he had just eighteen.[50] But in any case it is doubtful whether even these guns could have been moved close enough to the ridge to support the men occupying it. Birdwood had told Hamilton in the planning phase that he doubted whether any heavy howitzers could have made the journey. Many artillery authorities have agreed with him.[51] Without fire support the occupation of the ridge would have been brief.

There is also the issue of what would have followed the capture of the ridge. It is as well to remind ourselves that in Birdwood's conception, the answer was nothing. The troops that Birdwood was to have used as a mobile force to cross the Peninsula near Maidos had all been sent—with Birdwood's approval, indeed at his instigation—to the operation at Suvla. Birdwood had no plan to move on from Sari Bair because he had no force with which to do so. Nothing immediate would have ensued from the capture of Sari Bair. It would only have been the first step in a long journey.

But some historians do not share this view. Indeed, their enthusiasm for what must have followed the fall of Sari Bair knows no bounds. Leading this pack is the Australian official historian C.E.W. Bean. Often seen as a stern realist, Bean has this to say about 9 August:

> The chance which existed during the night of establishing and extending the British foothold on Sari Bair was undoubted. The occupation of the crest might have resulted in the falling back of the already shaken Turks from Anzac, the adherence of wavering Bulgaria, the forcing of the Dardanelles, the fall of Constantinople, the opening of a sea route to Russia, a comparatively early victory, and a complete alteration in the course and consequences of the war.[52]

It is overwhelmingly likely that none of these things would have happened. A full discussion of these matters must wait until the conclusion. Suffice it to say here that there is no evidence to support the contention that the Turks were 'shaken'. They had many more divisions in reserve and would have undoubtedly used them to regain the ridge. As for Bulgaria, it looked to the great events to its north on the Eastern Front as a guide to its policy, and in August the Germans were in the process of driving the Russian armies out of Warsaw.

Bean's other contention equates the capture of Sari Bair with the successful conclusion of the campaign. This is far from being the case. A glance at a map reveals that other ridges stood between the British and the Kilid Bahr Plateau, and although they were not as precipitous, they were still formidable obstacles. As a postwar observer of the Peninsula indicated:

> Between Sari Bair mountain and the Straits is a tumbled mass of hills, little less in height than the mountain itself; this stretch of country is almost indescribably difficult for military operations; it consists of a tangled mass of deep ravines with precipitous sides and choked with scrub. Had we taken Sari Bair we should still have been faced with an advance of some six miles across this type of country *before* we could

have secured positions dominating the Straits. The Sari Bair mountain was in no way a 'key' to the Peninsula.[53]

Given this terrain, it is by no means clear that an advance across this difficult territory would have followed the fall of Sari Bair, even had additional troops been available. While the Anzacs would then have held the highest ridges the Turks might still have held on. After all, had not the Anzacs demonstrated that it was possible to occupy positions that were overlooked and survive? Other issues concern the difficulty of capturing the daunting defences on the Kilid Bahr Plateau, the difficulty of supplying the fleet with the Asiatic shore in enemy hands, the lack of evidence that Constantinople would have surrendered had a hostile fleet appeared, and any discernible difference that could have been made to the German war effort had that city, or indeed the whole Turkish Empire, surrendered. The fact is that there were no large strategic gains on offer on Sari Bair on 9 August or any other day of the campaign.

CHAPTER 13

Suvla Bay
The Scapegoat Battle

The operations at Suvla Bay have gone down in British military history as an example of supine incompetence equivalent to the surrender at Yorktown in 1776 or at Singapore in 1942. The reality is rather more complicated, but before the operation at Suvla is described in detail it may be useful briefly to reiterate the Suvla plan.

The Suvla operation was originally designed to support Birdwood's assault on Sari Bair by capturing some guns on the left flank of that advance and establishing a base for the northern theatre of operations. GHQ suggested that Stopford's force should then seize the Anafarta Ridge and give what other assistance they could to the column advancing on Hill 971. However, when Stopford indicated that he was being asked to do too much with his five brigades of troops, GHQ rethought the entire scheme and suggested that he confine himself to establishing the base. The guns on the flank of the Anzac advance were still to be captured but only after the area around the bay had been secured. GHQ made no mention of capturing the Anafarta Ridge. This was in fact reinstated as an objective by Stopford for the obvious reason that the base could hardly be deemed secure if it remained in enemy hands.

How did Stopford intend to employ his forces? He issued his Operation Order No. 1 on 3 August 1915. The three brigades of 11 Division would carry out the initial landing. They were in the first instance to capture

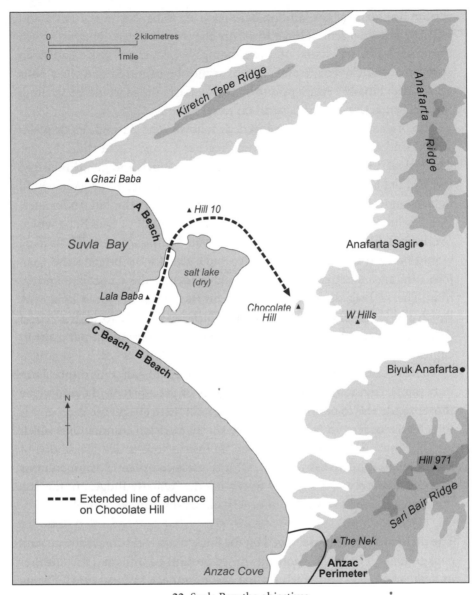

22 Suvla Bay: the objectives

certain heights near the landing beaches (Lala Baba, Nibrunesi Point and Hill 10) and then send a force to secure the ridge Kiretch Tepe Sirt which dominated the left flank of the landing. When these tasks had been completed the Chocolate and W hills would be captured and their guns eliminated. Finally, certain points on the Anafarta Ridge would be secured. Subsequent action would depend on developments.[1]

The brigades would be deployed as follows. The 32 and 33 Brigades would land at night on two adjacent beaches (B and C) outside the bay. The task of 33 Brigade was simple: it would entrench and guard the right flank of the landing and provide a reserve. Meanwhile, 32 Brigade would detach some companies to secure the right arm of the bay (Nibrunesi Point) while the remainder captured the fortified hill of Lala Baba which overlooked C Beach. Once that height had been captured, 32 Brigade would proceed to The Cut where it would wait for 34 Brigade and then join it in an assault on Hill 10, and subsequently the Chocolate and W hills. The 34 Brigade was the key unit in the attack. It would land at A Beach inside the bay, capture Hill 10, which lay directly to its front, and then lead the advance by performing a manoeuvre around the Salt Lake to capture Chocolate and W hills from the north.

There was one curious feature of this plan. Stopford had at his disposal not only the 11 Division but 31 and 32 Brigades of the 10 (Irish) Division (the third brigade was to be employed at Anzac). Yet there was no mention of this force in the orders. In fact, by the time the 10 Division commanders sailed for the Peninsula they had been given no instructions at all.[2] (Did none of these officers think to ask for orders?) It is assumed by some commentators that this division was designated to capture the Anafarta Ridge, but this is a misapprehension; it was without orders and without an objective.[3]

* * *

The men who would be deployed on the Suvla plain had come from varying backgrounds. The 11 Division was raised around Grantham, Lincolnshire, in September 1914 and sailed for the Mediterranean in June 1915.[4] Events conspired against them even before they entered combat. The first troops from the division arrived at the Turkish island of Imbros on 10 July but the others were dispersed around the eastern Mediterranean. Some battalions were not to join their companions on Imbros until 16, 22 and 24 July; others not until 2 August. One entire brigade (33) was put into the trenches at Helles and only arrived at Imbros 48 hours before they were to sail to Suvla.[5] What this meant was that the division could not exercise as a unit and the senior commanders could not familiarize themselves with each other in the war zone until the last moment.

The men were also not fit. They had developed 'at Imbros a particularly weakening form of diarrhea . . . few escaped'.[6] To make matters worse, just before embarkation from Imbros the troops had been inoculated against cholera and many were suffering from the after-effects when they sailed.[7]

The other troops to be used at Suvla were the 10 (Irish) Division. They were raised in Southern Ireland in 1914, transferred to England in 1915 and sailed for the Mediterranean in July.[8] They too were spread all over the eastern Mediterranean. Some were on Mudros, others at Mitylene (Lesbos), southeast of Lemnos. And such was the secrecy surrounding the plan that when the commander, General Mahon, was informed of its details he did not have time to pass on any information to the contingent at Mitylene. The first moment those units discovered that they were being sent to Suvla was when they saw the Salt Lake on the morning of 7 August.[9]

The territory over which these troops would operate requires some description. Suvla Bay itself was semicircular in shape, about 2 miles wide at the entrance and indented $1^1/2$ miles. Directly behind it and connected to it by a narrow channel called The Cut was a large salt lake with a diameter of about 1 mile. The lake was usually dry in summer but military intelligence, which included air surveillance, thought it might still contain water. It was therefore considered an obstacle to be avoided by troops. On the left flank of the landing was a ridge some 150 feet high (Kiretch Tepe Sirt). The other feature was the Anafarta Ridge, 5 miles in length, which overlooked the entire area. Apart from the Chocolate and W hills which lay between the ridge and the sea, the area was flat and known as the Suvla Plain. This territory, although from a distance it looked flat and easily negotiable for troops, was deceptive. Walking over the ground in 1962 Robert Rhodes James had this to say about it:

> The Plain is scored with deep fissures, washaways, unexpected ridges; the ground is coarse, thirsty and difficult. The heat . . . is worse than at Anzac; one finds oneself gasping in the apparently airless atmosphere. Even with a large modern army I would not care to traverse the Plain; it is made for defence, the innocence of the ground luring one into a maze of gullies, and a climb only possible by means of winding goat tracks. It is, of course, far less spectacularly difficult ground to cross than that which confronted Godley's army in its assault on the Sari Bair crests, but

anyone who thinks that it is easy ground should try walking from Lala Baba to Tekke Tepe. This, for me, was one of the major surprises of my visit and made me look far closer at the causes of failure of the Suvla landing with a greater sympathy.[10]

* * *

The 11 Division paraded at Imbros in the late afternoon of 6 August. A battalion commander involved in the initial landing described the scene:

[The battalion] embarked on destroyers and lighters with the object of making a surprise landing at Suvla Bay. Each destroyer towed two lighters which were specially constructed with ramps at either end which could be raised or lowered to allow the speedy disembarkation of troops. [These were the 'beetles' constructed by Fisher and Churchill for their abortive Borkum/Baltic expedition.] All ranks were stowed away below the decks and in silence, with no lights showing we were towed to our allotted landing place. The Battalion with which I was serving, the 9th Battalion, The Sherwood Foresters, were towed to a spot immediately south of the Salt Lake [B Beach] . . ... Our orders were to take up a position from the south west corner of the Salt Lake to the sea, get in touch with the left of the 13th Division, somewhere about Azma Dere, and entrench ourselves forming a covering line to protect the beach. The beach here was ideal for the purpose, a wide open beach shelving steeply to a depth of six feet or more only about 3 or 4 yards out . . ... We affected a landing successfully without any trouble whatever. A few shots were fired at us just before our lighters touched the beach, evidently from a gendarmerie post that were taken by surprise and made off in the dark as quickly as they could. My company was the first to go ashore with orders to cover the disembarkation of the remainder of the Battalion. We doubled off our lighter and in less time than it takes to relate had formed up in attack formation and were moving forward into the dark towards Yilghin Burnu, which loomed up just beyond the Salt Lake.[11]

They then proceeded to entrench and await further instructions.

The two other battalions of the 33 Brigade and the 32 Brigade had an equally uneventful landing. They were unopposed and after forming up on the beach, turned left and made for Nibrunesi Point and Lala Baba. The small Turkish garrison on Nibrunesi Point was easily dealt with. Lala Baba was another matter. It had all-round trench defences and a small but determined

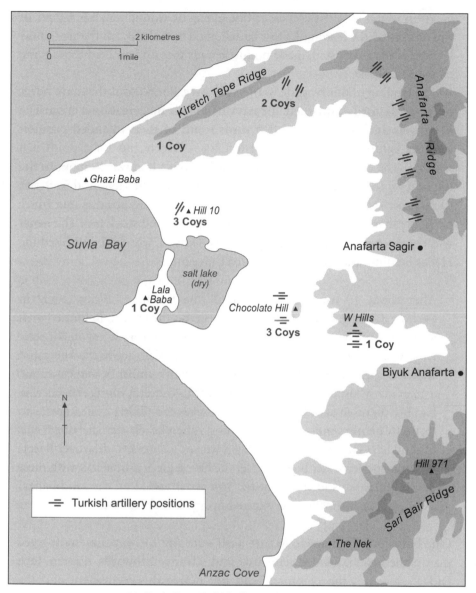

23 Suvla Bay: Turkish dispositions, 6 August

garrison which inflicted 250 casualties, killing or wounding all but three of the officers of the leading British battalions. The hill fell but the men, now leaderless and exhausted, made no further advance and awaited the landing of the 34 Brigade.

The landing of this brigade went badly awry. For reasons that have never been satisfactorily explained, the navy had made a navigational error. The destroyers anchored about 1,000 yards south of their intended position and the lighters therefore headed not for A Beach, but for a point just south of The Cut. Moreover, the leading battalion that was to move to the left and capture Kiretch Tepe Ridge was landed on the right and so it had to clamber over its sister battalion to deploy.[12] In addition, some troop carriers ran into reefs hundreds of yards offshore and stuck fast. The result was chaos on the beaches. Lieutenant I.W. Gibson, who had witnessed the Helles landing, was on hand to record the scene:

> After about 10 minutes I started for the beach. . . . Firing going in onshore & one gun firing from the hills up on the left . . . .. Rather exciting as we grounded some 30 yds from shore as we didn't know in the least what was happening ashore—jumped over the side, above the knees and waded ashore. Couldn't find out much, a certain number of soldiers about, a great many lost ones, mostly rather rattled, & several young officers who had lost themselves or been sent on messages they didn't quite know who to, pretty helpless most of them . . . most rotten beach very shelving & lots of sand bars etc—couldn't have been worse . . . .. Went to destroyer Beagle & commandeered her boats, she let me have a gig & a whaler & with these & our cutter we somehow got the troops [stranded on the sand banks] ashore but very slowly & very mixed up, most unfortunate.[13]

One battalion did manage to sort itself out. The 11 Manchesters formed up on the beach, headed leftwards and advanced towards Kiretch Tepe Ridge. However, the command did not notice this movement and the battalion lost touch with their comrades for at least 24 hours.[14]

Meanwhile, some companies of the other assault battalion (9 Lancashire Fusiliers) thought they had located Hill 10:

> We started [towards the hill] in extended orders in three lines, the men going forward splendidly, led by their platoon commanders in the most superb manner imaginable, with shells and bullets coming thicker and

thicker, every man tearing forward, eager to get to the objective. . . .
There was a check just before we got to the foot of the Hill. Then in one
'mad' rush we carried the hill at the point of the bayonet.[15]

The Lancashires had not captured Hill 10 but a sand dune just inland from
the beach, manned by a Turkish patrol. Fire from the real Hill 10 now
poured in on them. They were pinned down, and without reinforcement
could do nothing more.

The British advance inland (apart from the unobserved 11 Manchesters)
had therefore stalled. But reinforcements were on the way. Stopford had
finally decided what to do with the two brigades (30 and 31) of 10 Division.
They were directed to land inside the bay at A Beach. Their objective was the
Kiretch Tepe Ridge but they could then assist in the capture of Hill 10 and
later advance on Chocolate and W hills.[16] However, their landing was also
about to go awry. Stopford's naval commander, Admiral A. Christian,
offshore in the yacht *Jonquil*, had been alerted to the disruption to
34 Brigade's landing. Assuming the reefs in question were adjacent to A
Beach, he redirected 31 Brigade and two battalions of 30 Brigade to land
outside the bay at C Beach, thus depriving the left of much needed reinforcement. But this was not quite the end of the story. In the meantime
the true situation regarding A Beach had been discovered, therefore General
Mahon and the remaining two battalions of the division were landed there.
Due to these misunderstandings, 10 Division was scattered across the Suvla
Plain and the bulk of it separated from Mahon.[17]

Meanwhile General Frederick Hammersley, the commander of
11 Division, had landed at B Beach just after midnight and established his
headquarters south of Lala Baba. In the early hours of 7 August he had been
unable to get in touch with any of his brigadiers and was uncertain of the
situation apart from the fact that Lala Baba had fallen. Then at 4.45 a.m. a
message was received from General H. Haggard (commanding 32 Brigade)
that the 34 Brigade seemed to be held up. Hammersley replied that Haggard
should gather what forces he could from 32 Brigade and assist 34 Brigade in
capturing Hill 10. This he did. Battalions from both brigades charged the hill
and dispersed the hundred or so Turks that had so ably defended it.[18] Just
after 6.00 a.m. the last of the strong points near the beaches had been cleared.

The situation facing the British at daybreak was certainly ambiguous
but not without hope. Operations were well behind schedule. The
Chocolate and W hills were to have fallen before dawn but no British

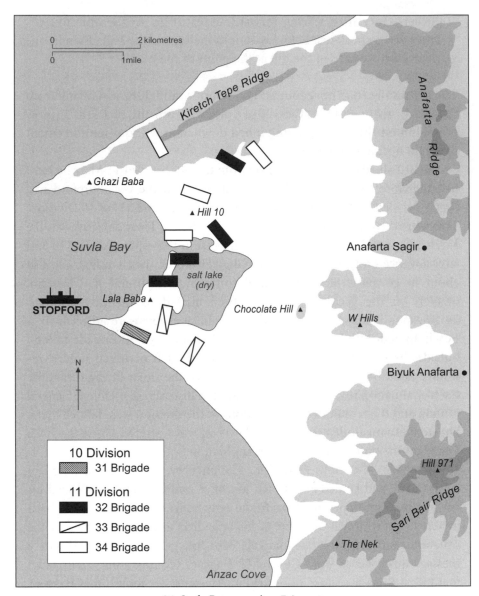

24 Suvla Bay: morning, 7 August

troops were yet within miles of them. The dispersal of 10 Division added an element of chaos. However, the beaches were secure and there were no large enemy groups in sight. Moreover, the battalions in the vicinity of Hill 10, though intermixed, amounted to some 3,000 men, which was more than enough to secure Chocolate and W Hills. In other words, the landing mishaps could be redeemed if prompt action were to follow.

In the event, there were many orders but not much action. Between 8.00 a.m. and 2.40 p.m., Hammersley issued three sets of written instructions and various verbal instructions concerning the attack on Chocolate and W hills to one of his brigadiers and a senior staff officer.[19] All these missives, to some extent, contradicted each other. The result was paralysis, especially as the senior brigadier, the appropriately named Sitwell of the 34 Brigade, was in any case reluctant to move from his position on Hill 10. Sitwell, it seems, had been badly shaken by the disruption of the landing, by the confusion in taking the hill and the intermixture of his units with those of 32 Brigade. Nevertheless, his reluctance to advance was to some extent soundly based. An attack by his forces on Chocolate and W hills would expose his left flank to attack from Kiretch Tepe and perhaps Anafarta Ridge. What friendly or hostile forces were lurking in those heights was unknown to him. Also unknown were the enemy forces he might encounter on the way to Chocolate and W hills. There was much sniping and a sporadic rain of shrapnel shells coming in on his positions. Moreover, many of his troops were sick and the heat of the day was taking its toll. Finally, he had received a series of orders so confusing as to leave him uncertain of his role.

The situation was of course much more favourable to the British than Sitwell knew. The 11 Manchesters were advancing on Kiretch Tepe, where they were to be joined about midday by the two battalions of 10 Division that had been landed at A Beach. There were also only small detachments of Turks between Hill 10 and Sitwell's objectives, and very few on the Anafarta Ridge. But this is hindsight. On 7 August Sitwell knew nothing of these matters.

Nevertheless, it seems fair to say that Sitwell was not at the dynamic end of the spectrum of command. General Hill of the 31 Brigade and General Maxwell of the 33 Brigade were more willing to venture into the unknown. At 2.30 p.m. units from these brigades moved on Chocolate Hill. (In the confusion of orders, all thought of seizing the W Hills had vanished.) They were immediately held up by snipers and subjected to harassing shrapnel fire, thus seeming to confirm all Sitwell's fears. But the enemy were few in number and the British gradually worked forward. At 5.15 p.m. some guns, which had been hauled up Lala Baba, opened fire on the Turks on Chocolate Hill.[20] Under this thin but helpful barrage the Lincolns and Borders of 33 Brigade, followed by elements from 31 Brigade, stormed the hill. The small Turkish force was overwhelmed, the survivors of the attack retreating to the W Hills to the north.[21] The British also made a startling discovery. There were no defences to the south of Chocolate Hill. The whole elaborate plan to march around the salt lake (which in any case proved to be dry) and take the hill from the north had been unnecessary. It could easily have been taken by direct assault from B and C beaches. Nevertheless, as darkness fell, Chocolate Hill, one of the major objectives for the first day, was secure.

Summing up the first day at Suvla, the British were reasonably placed. They had secured the hills around the beaches and could land stores and supplies without interference from enemy infantry. Some shrapnel was still hitting them from the heights but it was not intense. A start had been made to capture ground inland; some of Kiretch Tepe had been taken as had the first of the hills between the beaches and the ridge. Certainly everything was running behind schedule, but no additional Turks had yet arrived on the battlefield and night would provide some time for rest and reorganization. All depended on the events of 8 August.

* * *

The Turkish command took steps on the night of 7 August to make the 8th as uncomfortable as possible for the British. Twenty miles away Turkish reserves at Bulair gathered to attack them. As soon as he had heard of the Suvla landing, von Sanders dispatched a regiment from 7 Division towards the bay. When the full extent of the operation became known to him, this force was increased to two divisions (7 and 12). However, not everything favoured the Turks. Most of those marching towards the British were recovering from the battering they had received at Helles in June and July. Their commander, Feizi Bey, was sick and the road to Suvla rough and winding.[22] These troops had no chance of arriving on the 7th. Whether they would arrive in time to forestall the British on the 8th was also an open question. The 'race' for Suvla was about to be conducted by two tortoises, or at best two sick hares.

For the British local command at Suvla, the overwhelming difficulty was the chaotic state of their brigades. A glance at the map will show that at

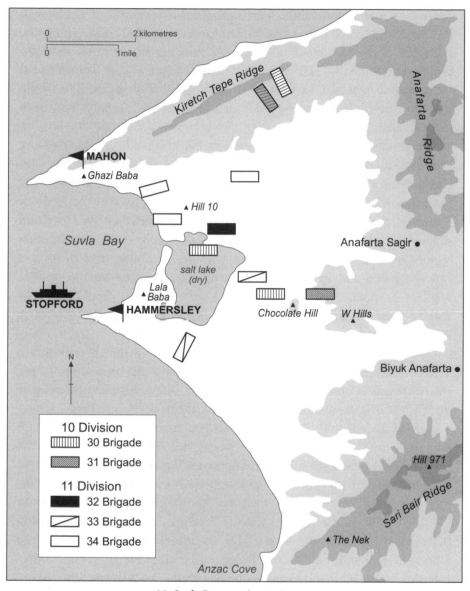

25 Suvla Bay: evening, 7 August

dawn on 8 August four of the five brigades at Suvla were scattered all over the battlefield; some battalions from the same brigade were separated by the width of the battlefield, others were on the beaches or in the foothills. Only one brigade (32) was concentrated. In as much as they had trained at all, brigades expected to fight as distinct units. The inclination would therefore be to take no concerted action until the brigades had been consolidated.

A commander of ruthless disposition might have been able to force groups of men forward even though their units were mixed. Hammersley was not that man. He visited the brigadiers in the early morning with the intention of organizing an early advance. But the response he received was entirely negative. The men were not only disorganized, they were tired and sick as well. He was also told that supplies, especially water, were in short supply and the columns of mules that would distribute these stores had not yet landed. Finally, there were just three batteries of guns to provide artillery support. The brigadiers urged that 8 August should be spent sorting out the brigades and resupplying and resting the troops. A concerted attack could then be made early on the 9th.[23]

Confronted with these arguments Hammersley immediately capitulated. There would be no offensive action of any kind at Suvla on 8 August. Only the intervention of a IX Corps staff officer modified this plan. He pointed out that 32 Brigade was concentrated to the north of the Salt Lake and that a short advance would close the gap between the troops on Chocolate Hill and those on Kiretch Tepe. Hammersley agreed but he stipulated that the brigade was 'not to fight but to take up a position and entrench'.[24]

So, at 9.30 a.m. units of 32 Brigade tentatively moved forward and established a connection (although not a continuous one) across the plain from Chocolate Hill on the right to Kiretch Tepe on the left. One enterprising battalion even captured Scimitar Hill, an intermediate position between Chocolate Hill and the Anafarta Ridge. And that, as far as forward movement went, was all that happened that day on the front line at Suvla Bay.

Back at GHQ Hamilton was becoming increasingly worried about Suvla, not because he was *au fait* with the situation but because he was not. On 7 August just one message had arrived from Stopford, to the effect that as yet he had not advanced much beyond the beach.[25] After that there was silence. Amazingly it took Hamilton nine hours to reply. He said that he hoped Stopford was taking every opportunity to advance before he was forestalled by Turkish reserves which must soon arrive. A further 16 hours passed. Then a second message from Stopford arrived. The IX Corps was ashore and consolidating on the Suvla Plain.[26]

Hamilton finally acted. Before Stopford's second message had arrived, he had ordered his staff officer (Colonel Cecil Aspinall, later Official British Historian of the campaign) to Suvla. Due to the non-arrival of a destroyer, Aspinall did not land at Suvla until noon. Here he found that Hamilton had telegraphed to Stopford an aerial reconnaissance report to the effect that no Turks could be seen on Anafarta Ridge and that 'you will be able to gain early footing'. In case Stopford had missed the point, Hamilton added, 'very important'.[27] Aspinall then went ashore to see Hammersley who rehearsed all the familiar reasons for inaction. An alarmed Aspinall, who had observed groups of men bathing and lying around the beach, at once telegraphed Hamilton that he must come to Suvla as 'golden opportunities' were being lost.[28] Hamilton set out at once, but not before signalling Stopford that an assault on the ridge must be undertaken immediately.[29]

As a result of Hamilton's signal, Stopford and Hammersley decided to mount a two-brigade attack on Anafarta Ridge, not immediately, but at 5.00 a.m. the following day, 9 August.[30] Soon after these orders were issued, Hamilton arrived. He summarily rejected the plan. The advance must commence at once. Hammersley claimed that it could not be done; by the time the two brigades were concentrated it would be dark. The territory was unknown. Confusion was bound to result. Hamilton reluctantly agreed but he insisted that 32 Brigade be concentrated and then send its leading battalion without delay to secure key positions on the ridge.[31]

As it happened, Hamilton's intervention only made matters worse. The battalion designated to lead the advance was out of touch with the remainder of the brigade because it was occupying Scimitar Hill, one of the key heights north of Chocolate Hill. When the battalion finally received orders (they took six and a half hours to arrive) to concentrate with the bulk of the brigade, the battalion withdrew from Scimitar Hill, which incidentally was never again held by the British.[32] In the event, the advance only began at 4.00 a.m., just one hour before the much-derided attack ordered by Hammersley. It was too late. The troops ran into a hail of gunfire from Scimitar Hill and the ridge. They were soon forced back to their start line.

The main attack fared no better. As 33 Brigade moved forward, most battalions were stopped in their tracks by heavy fire. The exception was the 6 Borders. They advanced into a gap in the Turkish line and almost made it to the top of Anafarta Ridge. But they were unsupported and Turkish counterattacks drove them back.[33]

Stopford and Hammersley have been much criticized for the lack of action on 8 August at Suvla Bay. However, there were factors at work that day hampering the ability of any commander to accomplish much more than what was achieved by IX Corps. First we must consider supply and logistics. To fight, an army needs three items above all: water, food and ammunition. Of these, because of the soaring temperatures at Suvla, water has good cause to be considered first. Provision had been made regarding this matter. Four lighters carrying a large amount of water left Imbros on 7 August.[34] However, one of these grounded on a reef in the bay, a second was hit by shrapnel and also grounded, a third arrived late on the 8th and the fourth never even left because it grounded at Imbros.[35] In time, platforms were built out to the lighters and water got onshore. But that was by no means the end of the problem. The mule teams that were to distribute the water to the men inland were late in disembarking.[36] And, as the only water the men were carrying was in small water bottles, supplies would soon be exhausted. This was no trivial matter. Had they reached the Anafarta Ridge, some 4 to 6 miles from the beaches, it might have been impossible to supply them at all.

The same argument can be made for food and ammunition. In the absence of pack transport, it also might have been impossible to distribute these items at great distances from the beaches. Nor must the poor condition of the troops be overlooked. Could a force suffering from dysentery, diarrhoea and the heat have been capable of a substantial advance?

Meanwhile, on the other side of Anafarta Ridge, the Turks were grappling with problems that were not all that dissimilar from those facing the British.

The conventional view of what happened on the Anafarta heights is that the dynamic Mustapha Kemal, who had just taken command at Suvla, thwarted the British by the ruthless use of his divisions, and that similar action on the part of Stopford or Hammersley would have resulted in a quite different outcome.

The real story hardly involves Kemal. Feizi Bey had set his two divisions (7 and 12) in motion early on 7 August. But, as noted, his formations were not in optimal condition. They were weak in numbers, the distances they were required to march were long (between 25 and 36 miles), the day was hot and they were tired. As a result, they made very slow progress. While

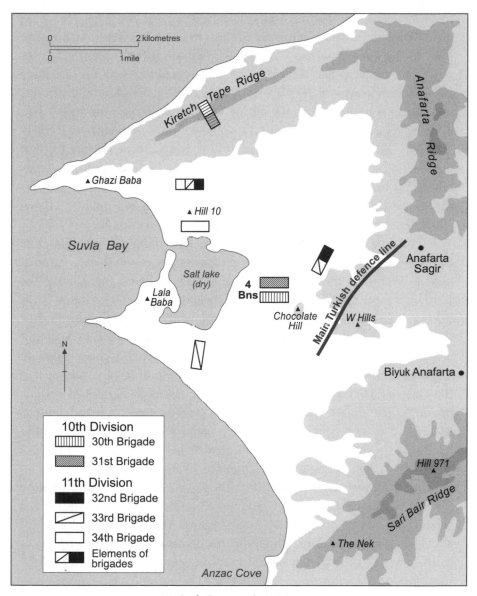

26 Suvla Bay: evening, 8 August

they were plodding towards Anafarta, Feizi developed his plans. He would use 12 Division to attack across a wide area from Kiretch Tepe to Chocolate Hill. At the same time the 7 Division would advance towards Hill 60 to relieve any threat to Sari Bair from Anzac. He then met with his divisional commanders to explain the plan. At this meeting he was told that the troops were in no condition to attack on the 8th. So, much as Hammersley had done, he recast his orders. The attack would commence at dawn on the 9th. This plan did not meet with the approval of von Sanders. He insisted that the assault be delivered on the night of the 8th. Feizi disagreed and was relieved of his command. Enter Kemal. He arrived at Suvla at 1.00 a.m. on the 9th, whereupon he confirmed all Feizi's plans. There would be a dawn attack because the troops were incapable of anything else.

That attack, again contrary to legend, was something of a shambles. The three brigades of 12 Division started at different times and there was much loss of direction in the dark. (It was one of these instances that allowed the Borders almost to reach the Anafarta heights.) Nevertheless, the Turks outnumbered the British and were in command of the high ground. Not surprisingly they drove the British back. More surprisingly they were not able to force them back far. The Turks soon suffered a check from an improvised British firing line well supported by machine guns. On the left, the Turkish 7 Division was actually driven back by a battalion of 33 Brigade operating near the Anzacs.[37] At 6.00 p.m. Kemal ordered a halt and directed that his forces entrench. For the first time continuous trench lines began to be dug on the Suvla Plain. Yet again stalemate had been reached. [38]

However, this fact was not recognized by the British command. So fighting continued around Scimitar Hill and Kiretch Tepe, conducted by the recently arrived and barely trained 53 and 54 Divisions.[39] Finally, a broader attack was made on 21 August against the W Hills, Scimitar Hill and Hill 60 by these units which on this occasion were joined by forces from Anzac and the 29 Division, brought north from Helles for its final martyrdom.[40] Most of these actions gained no ground. On the one occasion when some Turkish trenches were captured (by the Anzac forces on Hill 60), it was found that the Anzacs still did not command its summit.

A common feature of these operations was their poverty of purpose. All of them were designed only to improve the local tactical situation on various parts of the line. None were attempts to seize the Anafarta Ridge and so could have made no substantial difference to the overall position of the IX Corps. What they did do was add to the casualty bill. Exact figures are hard to come by, but the total casualties caused by these futile actions cannot have been fewer than 10,000 and the attack on the 21 August alone cost 6,500 men. One additional horror was added to the sufferings of the troops in these actions. In many places the scrub caught fire because of the shelling and trapped those unable to drag themselves away.[41]

These last fiascos were not presided over by General Stopford. He had counselled against them and been replaced by General H. de Lisle who, as 21 August testified, only proved that Stopford's protestations had been well founded.

* * *

Is the Suvla Bay operation to be equated with other disasters in British military history such as Yorktown in 1776 and Singapore in 1942? Surely not. The Suvla operation was undertaken to establish a supply base for all forces on the Anzac Peninsula north of Helles and in this it was successful. Certainly, there was a codicil to this instruction which said that if the base was established, additional help might be given to the Anzac operation, but in relation to the plan this was a secondary matter. Despite the failure to seize the Anafarta heights, which overlooked the area, the base was established and Suvla remained the main source of supply for the northern forces from late August until the evacuation. The Turkish troops on those heights conspicuously failed to deny the lower ground to the British by artillery fire or by mounting a major attack to drive them into the sea. The reasons for this are not hard to find. Turkish artillery resources had to be spread over a wide number of fronts and were manifestly insufficient at Suvla to blast the British from their beachhead. As for undertaking a full-scale attack in the open, the experience of 19 May at Anzac demonstrated to the Turks the futility of such a manoeuvre. If they could not drive the invader from their shores, at least by occupying the heights they could intern them.

To observers such as Aspinall and Hamilton at the time, and to a raft of historians since, Suvla was not about establishing a base. Though they should have known better, in their minds Suvla became part of a great attempt to drive the Turks back across the Peninsula, open the way for the fleet and bring the campaign to a successful conclusion. We have already seen how the appearance of a few men on Chunuk Bair had been identified as a potential turning point of the campaign, lost through a supine command. The same phenomenon can be observed at Suvla. The failure of Stopford and Hammersley on 8 August—to seize the moment and seize the heights—became established as yet another step along the way to the ruination of the Gallipoli operation. Yet a moment's thought should give us pause. If the heights had been seized, what would have followed? Certainly, the base would have obtained absolute security and the Turks been denied some high ground. But the fact remains that no objectives of note lay beyond the Anafarta Ridge. Indeed, the angle of the ridge in relation to the Peninsula meant that the further the troops advanced from the ridge, the further they were from Sari Bair. In the words of one commentator, 'the terrain at Suvla forced eccentric advances which could not have supported, in any direct sense, the main attack on Sari Bair'.[42] Moreover, a glance at a map shows that any force advancing from Anafarta was also increasing its distance from the real objectives of the campaign—Maidos, the Kilid Bahr Plateau and the Narrows.

Why then have writers on the campaign been so eager to condemn the actions of the Suvla force? In the case of Aspinall and Hamilton the explanation is obvious. They made the overall plan for Suvla. How convenient it was to have a scapegoat of the nature of Stopford on whom to blame the whole fiasco. When Aspinall (transmogrified into Aspinall-Oglander) came to write his official history of the campaign, there was little doubt as to what line he would take. Stopford had ruined everything by failing to advance on 8 August, the day when 'golden opportunities' were cast away. In this way the attention shifted from the shortcomings of Aspinall's own plan onto the hapless IX Corps commander.

Birdwood and the Australians were very willing to fall in with this line of argument. This served to divert attention away from the considerable defects of Birdwood's own plan, and partly reflected Anzac attitudes to the soldiers of the Kitchener armies who landed at Suvla Bay, whom they regarded as the rankest of amateurs. Indeed, in describing these men the Australian official historian, C.E.W. Bean, speaks of race degeneracy, the evil effects of big-city living—ideas then popular in the eugenics movement in which he had a great interest. While this merely demonstrates that Bean was a man of his time, there is no need now to seek such explanations for failure when there is a surfeit of military factors available.

However, Aspinall, Birdwood and Bean had other accomplices quite ready to place the blame for the Suvla 'failure' on Stopford. There was Winston Churchill, still eager to show that the whole campaign turned on the inaction of commanders like Stopford; Roger Keyes, who considered that the failure at Suvla denied him an opportunity to demonstrate that a revived naval attack could have succeeded; and a whole raft of historians since. As a scapegoat, Stopford was perfect. There was the ridiculous circumstance of his appointment, the Ruritanian flavour of his previous appointment as Lieutenant of the Tower of London and the obvious fact that he was not a commander of the first or even of the second order. However, Stopford and his men succeeded in their main task of establishing the base. And even a commander of genius might have accomplished little more. Great deeds, the vanquishing of important foes, the conclusion of important campaigns were not on offer in the sideline to a sideshow that was the operation at Suvla Bay.

CHAPTER 14

'War as we must'
The Political Debate

The failure of the August offensive caused much anguish for the Dardanelles Committee. The reinforcements had produced no result. Hamilton was now asking for a further three divisions to achieve success.[1] But winter was approaching and, as rumour had it, so were German heavy guns and troops. The Committee agonized but in the end factors extraneous to Britain would render much of their discussions irrelevant.

The French, the Committee was soon to be reminded, wished to rid their soil of the German invader. Two colossal efforts in the spring had proved fruitless, at a cost of 250,000 casualties. Now the French were determined on an autumn offensive to redeem the earlier failures.

On 16 August, as British troops struggled towards Scimitar Hill, General Joffre put his new plan to Kitchener. The French would launch a massive attack south of Lens. The British were required to guard the left flank of the French armies near Loos. Joffre claimed that the offensive was a necessity to restore French morale. (He was exaggerating here, for many Frenchmen in high authority actually opposed the offensive.) But Joffre also pointed out that the Russians were under great pressure in the east (Warsaw had fallen on 6 August) and the new operation in the west would give them a breathing space.

Kitchener was loath to agree; Joffre's plan looked no improvement on those in the spring. Yet he felt that Britain was bound to come to the aid of its ally. So he committed the government to the offensive and broke the news to the Dardanelles Committee on 20 August. He explained that as a result there could be no large reinforcement for Hamilton, who must make do with the drafts already promised for his existing divisions. This decision was energetically opposed by Churchill, who pointed out that the Allies did not have the necessary preponderance in numbers to mount a successful attack on the Western Front and that the whole venture might cost them 200,000 or 300,000 men—about accurate as it happened. Kitchener admitted that 'there was a great deal of truth in what Mr. Churchill had said, but unfortunately we had to make war as we must, and not as we would like to'.[2] On the one hand this was an extraordinary statement, that huge losses might be incurred without the expectation of a decisive result. On the other hand it was merely recognition of reality. The French were the senior Alliance partner and if they had decided on a major effort on the Western Front, their ally must, despite misgivings, support them.

The next blow to the Gallipoli campaign also came from the French. The event that occasioned it was a change in German policy in the Balkans. Until the latter half of 1915 Germany had been quite willing for the Austro-Hungarians to take the lead in dealing with Serbia. The armies of Franz-Joseph were eager for the task but incompetently led, all their attempts at invasion having been beaten back by their much smaller adversary. Yet Germany wanted Serbia overrun as a matter of urgency. The stalemate on the Western Front made the need to attract allies to the Central Powers imperative. With Serbia to parcel out, Bulgaria and Rumania, countries that coveted Serbian territory, might come in on the German side. So in September it was decided that a German army would 'assist' its ally in overrunning its small Balkan protagonist.

The massing of German and Bulgarian forces on the Serbian frontier in late September did not go unnoticed by French intelligence. The question was: what aid could the French send to the land-locked Serbs? The easiest route was through the northern Greek port of Salonika, and as the Greeks were bound by treaty to go to the aid of Serbia in the event of an attack, this seemed a convenient landing point. After much discussion and after an invitation to land at Salonika had been extracted from the (still neutral) Greek government, the French decided to dispatch 75,000 troops there. They also pressured the British to contribute a like number of men. The reluctant British therefore found themselves involved in a Balkan imbroglio.

It is no part of this book to delve into the sorry story of the Salonika expedition. For our purposes all that need be recorded is that the first two divisions to be sent (10 Irish and a French division) came from Gallipoli. They sailed for Salonika at the end of September. Hamilton's force was thus diminished by 25,000 men. And these troops would constitute just the first Allied contribution to Salonika. By November the British would have four divisions in the line, the French nine. In this situation Hamilton's chances of attracting reinforcements for a new offensive at Gallipoli were practically nil.

Yet Hamilton continued to call for new divisions. The Dardanelles Committee (with the exception of Churchill) proved reluctant to participate in what Bonar Law described as another 'useless sacrifice of life'. In the end their debates were irrelevent. With a pending offensive on the Western Front and an additional theatre of operations opening at Salonika, there were just no more troops to send to Gallipoli.

Hamilton's repeated requests for troops raised the whole question of the command at Gallipoli. While he remained at the helm another offensive would always be in the offing. But after failure in August, Hamilton was rapidly losing the confidence of the decision makers in London. In addition, two rather strange events may have hastened the decline in Hamilton's fortunes.

The first came in the form of a letter written to Asquith by an Australian journalist, Keith Murdoch. The origins of this letter are bizarre. Murdoch was visiting the Peninsula on behalf of the Australian government to inquire into the postal service. While there, he was handed a letter, addressed to the Prime Minister and highly critical of Hamilton, by the self-styled strategist and war correspondent Ellis Ashmead–Bartlett.[3] The military got wind of this exchange and when Murdoch landed in Marseilles they arrested him and confiscated the letter. Murdoch was then released and on arrival in London wrote his own letter to Asquith, even more critical of the Dardanelles command than Ashmead-Bartlett. Asquith had the letter printed as a state paper and placed on the agenda of the Dardanelles Committee. It made the most sensational claims. Murdoch asserted that there was a general lack of confidence in the command on the part of the troops; that the British soldiers at Suvla had shown an 'atrophy of mind' that was appalling; that at Anzac morale was better but the men had 'nothing but contempt for Hamilton and the staff' who live in luxurious surroundings; and that 'sedition is talked round every tin of bully beef on the peninsula'. Not surprisingly, his conclusion was that Hamilton and Braithwaite should be recalled immediately.[4]

As Hamilton's supercession followed shortly after this letter was circulated, it has often been suggested (not least by Murdoch) that the letter was the instrument of Hamilton's removal. This is certainly an overstatement. When the Dardanelles Committee finally got around to discussing the letter on 6 October, it was in the general context of the failure of the new armies at Suvla. Kitchener admitted that there had been a great deal of criticism of Hamilton, but Asquith immediately interrupted him to remark that as far as Murdoch was concerned the letter was a 'bitter document with many misstatements of fact', which rather begged the question of why he had circulated it to the Cabinet in the first place. Hankey added that he had met Murdoch and that he had been unable to substantiate many of his statements. Discussion then turned to the French and their attitude to a Balkan campaign, and that was the last time that the letter was formally discussed in high places.[5]

But there were mutterings about Hamilton from closer to home. A member of his staff, Captain Orlo Williams, chief cipher officer at GHQ, had this to say in his diary about Hamilton's modus operandi:

> I have talked to Deedes & Dawnay about . . . the G.C. [Hamilton]. I find that my ideas are quite correct, that he really does nothing at all, never has a scheme, has a shallow, at times obstinate mind, no grasp of detail. His first despatch, so perceived in London, was almost wholly written by his staff. The plan of the 2nd big push, not only was not thought out by the General, but was Dawnay's idea which, supported by Dawnay's arguments, induced him to give up his own idea of still plugging at Achi Baba . . . . He doesn't for a moment realize how serious and extraordinary the situation is here. If this next attack fails, it means, in all probability, thorough and complete failure. This campaign is practically run by Dawnay and Aspinall, 1 adjutant captain & the other a Capt in the Munster Fusiliers. I wonder how many people realize that. It is also run by Hunter-Weston & F.S. Skeen, Birdwood's GSO 1.[6]

This is a curious document in that the staff seem eager to take responsibility for devising a series of plans that had utterly failed. But there is no doubting their opinion of Hamilton. Yet so out of touch was Hamilton with the thinking of his staff that at the end of August he decided to send Major Guy Dawnay to London to explain the Gallipoli situation to Kitchener. This Dawnay did but not in the manner expected by Hamilton.

Dawnay saw Kitchener and practically all the members of the Dardanelles Committee. His opinion, though always couched in diplomatic terms, was that evacuation was inevitable unless 150,000 new troops could be provided and supported by sufficient heavy howitzers to blast the Turks from the main ridge.[7] In the end he could have left no doubt that whatever policy the government adopted, Hamilton was not the man to carry it out.

It is probable, however, that the Dardanelles Committee did not require Murdoch or Dawnay to alert them to Hamilton's shortcomings. After all, the Committee had before them the evidence of a series of defeats followed by promises of victory which stretched back to late April. Finally, at a meeting on 11 October, Sir Edward Grey came to the point. Alternate strategies were being discussed. Should the British increase their commitment to Salonika or look once more to Gallipoli? Hamilton was not the man to adjudge these matters. A new commander was needed in the east to advise the Committee. Balfour, Lloyd George and Asquith were quick to agree, the latter even suggesting that Haig (at that time a senior army commander in France) should be sent out or that Kitchener should go himself.[8]

At the next meeting, on 14 October, the Committee decided that Hamilton and Braithwaite would be recalled but that neither Haig (now described by Asquith as 'indispensable') nor Kitchener (not described as indispensable but too canny to absent himself from the seat of power) would go. Instead, the Commander of the Third Army in France, General Sir Charles Monro, would be sent. Churchill queried Monro's ability but Kitchener defended him. Monro, he said, was a man of much ability whose judgement could be trusted.[9]

So Hamilton departed. His successor was a man of a very different stamp. Monro had fought on the Western Front since the beginning of the war and had risen to the rank of army commander in early 1915. He was a thorough, determined man, who perhaps lacked imagination but that may have been considered a virtue rather than a drawback in any successor to Sir Ian Hamilton.

Kitchener's instructions to Monro on 20 October were quite explicit. He was to report 'fully and frankly' to the government on:

> the best means of removing the deadlock on the Gallipoli Peninsula and the means required to carry it out

whether it was the better policy to evacuate the Peninsula and the losses that might be incurred in such an operation.[10]

* * *

The decision to attack in the west, the French reaction to the plight of the Serbs and the removal of Hamilton all pointed towards the termination of the Gallipoli campaign. But events and opinion did not follow such a smooth trajectory. At various times during the period under discussion, the Gallipoli campaign underwent various, but usually short-lived, revivals in its fortunes.

Astonishingly, given French policy elsewhere, the first Gallipoli revival also had its source in French policy. In late August, after the western offensive had been approved, the French suddenly announced that they were to send an expeditionary force to Gallipoli of no fewer than six divisions to operate on the Asiatic shore of the Straits.[11] This prospect produced great excitement in London. Having just ruled out any reinforcement, Kitchener immediately earmarked two new army divisions to bolster Hamilton. There was much talk about a renewed naval attack to support the French effort. Churchill urged that the offensive in the west be postponed until the new campaign at Gallipoli had concluded.[12] Then it all evaporated. It was soon revealed that the French government's main motivation for sending a new army to the east was to give a recalcitrant senior military figure (General Maurice Sarrail) something to command as far away from France as possible. When Joffre heard of this move he vetoed it, not so much because of Sarrail, whom he too regarded as a nuisance and a rival, but because he wanted the six divisions for his new western offensive. That was the end of French adventurism at Gallipoli.

The second Gallipoli revival was led by the British navy. Since the failure of the August offensive (and in some cases even earlier) several naval officers had been calling for a resumption of the naval attack. Among the leading advocates of this plan was Roger Keyes, in charge of the destroyers at the Dardanelles, and Captain Godfrey, de Robeck's Chief of Staff. These naval officers considered that many of the guns defending the minefield had been removed to supplement the firepower of the Turkish army on the Peninsula.[13] In addition, they thought that the minefield defences had been neglected by the Turks since the military landing and would not therefore represent such an obstacle as they had in February and March.

These premises had little substance. The Turks had removed 82 guns from the Straits defences for use by the army.[14] Yet in the same period 43 guns had been added to sea defences, mainly on the Asiatic shore.[15] This meant that instead of the 119 guns faced by the fleet early in 1915, from July to November it would have faced 80, certainly a lesser number but still a formidable obstacle to a flotilla of slow-moving vessels. As for the mine defences, they remained intact through the entire operation, and the addition of extra searchlights would have made the task of the sweeping force more difficult.[16]

So the fleet would have faced defences almost as formidable as those that defeated it in March. Did Keyes and Godfrey have a new method with which to deal with them? Essentially they did not. They realized that the minefields, their protecting batteries and the big guns in the forts formed part of an interlocking defensive system. They therefore called for all three elements to be attacked simultaneously, but this had been done on 18 March with disastrous results. There were some minor innovations. A group of monitors would bombard the Narrows forts from across the Straits, a more modern force of aeroplanes would spot for the ships and only a narrow channel on the European side of the Straits would be swept. Through this would steam four of the most modern British pre-dreadnoughts, which would dominate the Marmara, sever the lines of communication between the Turkish army on the Peninsula and its base, and bring about the downfall of the Turkish Empire.[17]

There is little that was new here. The monitors had few heavy guns and were hardly a substitute for the *Queen Elizabeth,* which had been the only ship to hit an enemy gun from across the Straits. As for the spotting force, it was doubtful whether it could have been assembled. In late September one of the ships reported that only once had an aircraft been provided to aid its fire.[18] As for the sweepers, they would have faced the same formidable minefields that had been in place in March. No doubt the force would have been more robust, being manned this time by naval personnel, but there was no indication that new sweeping methods had been thought out or that the guns protecting the minefields could have been dealt with.

One matter however had changed. Between April and September the ships of the fleet had constantly been in action in supporting land operations. The inevitable result had been severe wear on the ships' guns and a resultant drop in accuracy. For example, it was discovered that the rifling on one of the guns of the *Vengeance* had worn completely away and that its accuracy within a distance of 1,000 yards was questionable.[19] How such guns were to fire with the pinpoint accuracy needed to destroy guns in forts was never revealed by Keyes.

Finally, the main problem with a renewed naval assault again came down to what those four pre-dreadnoughts might do if they broke into the Marmara. De Robeck, who had allowed Keyes to travel to London to put his plan to the Admiralty, commented thus:

> In regard to his [Keyes's] proposals, they would not lead to any result if we got through with a few ships. . . . The Turks would not lay down their arms if we bombarded Constantinople, nor would they abandon the peninsula because four or five [of] our ships got into the Marmora (a most unlikely thing). They have several months supply on the peninsula & unless we can pass our colliers & supply ships through the Straits we cannot carry out an effective campaign in the Marmora. To do so we must take and destroy all the Turkish forts in the Straits & it must be a combined operation with the army.[20]

That was not quite the end of the attempt to revive the naval plan. In November de Robeck was replaced by Admiral Wemyss who asked Keyes to draft yet another plan for an assault on the Narrows. But by then the moment had passed.[21] The Dardanelles Committee was too busy with the military consequences of General Monro's report to concern themselves with naval adventures.

*   *   *

Monro arrived at Gallipoli on 28 October. After consulting the staff, he telegraphed Kitchener for some experienced company commanders and for building materials to provide winter shelter. He also noted that he had seen the corps commanders who reported that the morale and health of the troops were improving.[22]

This rather mild, even optimistic assessment, elicited the most extraordinary reply from Kitchener: 'Please send me as soon as possible your report on the main issue at the Dardanelles, namely leaving or staying.' Undoubtedly, this peremptory note was the result of the pressure that Kitchener was under in the Dardanelles Committee. In a series of meetings the War Minister had come down firmly against evacuation, even stating that such an operation 'would be the most disastrous event in the history of the Empire', only to be met by a wall of scepticism from Bonar Law, Crewe and Lloyd George.[23] Unwittingly, however, his telegram forced Monro's hand. The newly appointed commander left for the Peninsula immediately he received it, surveyed the scene from the three landing places and reached a rapid conclusion. He told Kitchener that the troops, with the exception of the Anzacs, were incapable of sustained effort. The Turks held all the high ground, which meant that only frontal attacks were possible and these had no prospect of success. There were reports of ammunition and heavy guns arriving from Germany, and he recommended a speedy evacuation so that the force could be redeployed in the defence of Egypt.[24]

Before the Committee could digest this advice, General Monro elaborated. He had now consulted the corps commanders regarding evacuation. General 'Joey' Davies and Sir Julian Byng were favourable. Birdwood was afraid that British prestige in the east would suffer and that the operation might be impossible because of the inclement weather. Monro considered these options and concluded that evacuation should be immediate and that those troops not needed for the defence of Egypt be sent to the Western Front. Almost as an afterthought, he announced that the Committee could expect the evacuation to cost 30 to 40 per cent of the Gallipoli force.[25]

Having rushed Monro into making a speedy response, Kitchener found it not to his liking. The Dardanelles Committee, now renamed the War Committee, which had dispatched Monro to the east, agreed with the War Minister. Recently they had contemplated evacuation with equanimity. Now the prospect of 40 per cent losses refocused their minds. Monro was to be ignored. Kitchener was to be sent to Gallipoli to provide more palatable advice.[26]

Kitchener left for the east full of contradictions. On 4 November he instructed Birdwood to work out in the strictest secrecy a plan for evacuation.[27] However, the very next day he informed Asquith that such an operation would be 'a disaster'.[28] He finally arrived at Gallipoli on 9 November. His first thoughts were that the Peninsula need not be abandoned but that if such a decision was reached, a new landing at Alexandretta on the Turkish coast should be made in order to cut the railway line to Egypt and, although this was not said explicitly, to cover the humiliation of defeat.[29]

After touring the battlefields on the Peninsula, Kitchener's thoughts were more sombre. He told Asquith that the country was much more difficult than he had imagined and that the positions could not be held if German troops arrived to assist Turkey. He believed that an evacuation would not necessarily entail losses of the proportion suggested by Monro, but still favoured the Alexandretta landing for 'prestige' purposes.[30]

In London, the War Committee (without the presence of Winston Churchill who was excluded from the new Committee, and had as a consequence left for the trenches of the Western Front) was quick to seize on the fact that despite having spent a week at the Dardanelles, Kitchener had made no definite recommendation. They were, however, firm in the opinion that there must be no more Middle-Eastern adventures such as Kitchener was proposing at Alexandretta.[31] Meanwhile they had received from General Robertson (Chief of Staff to Sir John French) and General Archibald Murray (Chief of the Imperial General Staff, or CIGS) papers recommending immediate evacuation.[32] Eventually their resolve hardened to the extent that they were prepared to order the evacuation of the Peninsula. But at this point Asquith intervened. He insisted that such a grave decision be taken by the Cabinet. This was no doubt constitutionally correct but would also ensure that the responsibility for terminating the campaign (and for the expected losses) would be spread as widely as possible.[33]

Asquith miscalculated. No doubt he considered Cabinet approval a foregone conclusion. But Lord Curzon, former Viceroy of India, self-styled expert on the East, and an implacable foe of Kitchener, led a revolt. He asked to see the General Staff papers on Gallipoli and be allowed time to write a rebuttal. He had enough support from Lord Lansdowne, the Earl of Selborne, Crewe and others in the Cabinet to win his point.[34]

Curzon's paper, which was produced on 27 November, made many cogent points. In summary his arguments in favour of staying amounted to prestige factors, the vacillation of the military leadership (he meant Kitchener) on the question of evacuation, the dubious assumptions that either the Turks or Germans could bring up sufficient heavy guns to render British positions untenable and the scale of the losses that were predicted to occur in the operation.[35]

He was immediately supported by a paper from Hankey, who made many of the same points but also emphasized the danger to Egypt if Turkish forces were freed from their commitments on Gallipoli. Russia, he thought, might also take a dim view of evacuation to the extent that they might be induced by the Germans to sign a separate peace.[36]

All this made the War Committee wobble. Their nervousness was exacerbated by the return of de Robeck, who under examination by the Committee seemed to admit the possibility that the Narrows forts might after all be captured. The ensuing discussion showed how tenuous the Committee's decision to evacuate had been. Reginald McKenna (Chancellor of the Exchequer) leapt at de Robeck's statement to ask whether an advance from Suvla was possible.[37] Kitchener surprisingly agreed that it was. He thought four fresh divisions might carry the day. At the next meeting it was decided to send a telegram to Monro asking whether he could carry out a further offensive with such a force.[38]

Monro supplied the necessary douche of cold water to the overexcited Committee. Four new divisions would result in impossible congestion on the Peninsula, the weather remained treacherous and the preparations would take a long time to complete. He strongly advised against it.[39]

That really was the end. On 8 December the Cabinet finally decided to evacuate Suvla and Anzac.[40] Helles was to be retained for a period, ostensibly to prevent the Germans and Turks from establishing a destroyer and submarine base there, but actually to save whatever face remained to be saved. As far as the politicians were concerned the Gallipoli adventure was over. All that remained was for the military to carry their wishes into effect.

CHAPTER 15

A Campaign Not Won

While the War Committee deliberated on the future of the operation, at Gallipoli the command grappled with the aftermath of the August failure.

At Suvla, scapegoats in the persons of Stopford and Hammersley had been identified and dismissed. The new officer in charge was General de Lisle, the commander of at least part of the 29 Division for some of the time at Suvla.

At Anzac, Birdwood maintained his post, the prevailing view (almost certainly incorrect) being that his scheme had come within an ace of success, only the want of initiative and of every other military quality by the New Armies to his north having thwarted his design.

At Helles, General Davies had taken command in early August. No major operations had taken place in this sector since July, just so-called diversionary attacks in support of various offensives at Anzac and Suvla.

We happen to have detailed knowledge of one of these operations because a Committee of Inquiry was set up to examine why it failed. Although the operation had no military importance, the evidence taken at the inquiry is worth studying because of what it tells us about the state of the army and the style of its leadership.

On the night of 15–16 August, about 100 men from the 1/6 Highland Light Infantry were ordered to capture 120 yards of trench at a location known as the Vineyard. The attack was to take place in three waves, each consisting of an officer or non-commissioned officer (NCO) and 30 men. The operation had some unusual features. There were no written orders: they were given verbally to the officers and NCOs just before the attack, and it was 'optional' how much of the so-called 'orders' they took down. In the event, such was the level of sickness in the Highland Light Infantry that no more than 60 men moved to the attack, most of them without the slightest idea of what they were to do.

In addition, it is clear from the testimony of some of the officers that the men were exhausted from an extended period of trench digging just prior to the attack. Most of the men had also been involved in a night attack on 12 July where no ground had been gained at the expense of heavy casualties. Finally, neither the officer who ordered the attack nor his second-in-command was anywhere near the front when the attack went in and thus could exert no control.

What happened when the attack went in can be established in some detail. First, only some groups possessed a watch so each section advanced at a slightly different time, allowing the Turks to concentrate all their fire first on one group and then on another. Second, the men had no fire support, the artillery having missed the Turkish trench by a considerable margin. Third, the small numbers involved meant that the men had to be spread thinly to cover the front of attack. In the dark they were too distant from their flanking colleagues to be sure whether they were supporting them or not. Essentially, each man advanced alone.

In these circumstances the attack just melted away. Most officers testified that when they reached the Turkish front line they found themselves utterly alone and that if the men had got out of their trenches at all, they had certainly not advanced more than a dozen or so yards. Any attempt to get the men forward failed as they drifted back in the dark. The feebleness of the effort, its want of leadership and organization and the utter exhaustion of the participants had brought the men to the sensible decision that this was not an attack worth the candle. If the 1/6 Highland Light Infantry was anything to go by, the Mediterranean Expeditionary Force was in no state to continue operations.

In one sense the command accepted this view. They stated that the men were 'not very lively', or were 'lacking in keenness and energy', or they showed 'a great want of energy, initiative and interest' in the operation. There was of course no explanation of why the men were reduced to this condition. In any case, a riposte to the command might be that it was because the men wished to remain 'lively' that they had used a great deal of initiative to survive this sad affair.

General Davies, however, was made of sterner stuff. In summing up the reasons for failure he commented:

> The operation failed for one reason only, namely the misconduct of the men whose duty it was to carry out the attack.
>
> I have not the slightest doubt that if these men had possessed any proper military spirit, the Turkish trench would now be in our possession.
>
> The cowardly behaviour of the men 1/6th Highland Light Infantry has brought great discredit on the regiment to which they belong and on the land of their birth [Scotland].[1]

There seems little doubt about why the command reacted by setting up a full-scale Court of Inquiry—not, let it be noted, into the shortcomings of the plan but into the men's response to it—nor why Davies condemned the men in such savage language. In the First World War men were repeatedly asked to undertake hare-brained operations and repeatedly did so without question. Here was a small example when they had chosen to act otherwise. The command could neither comprehend such behaviour nor condone it. However, the normal response—court-martial and punish—was not available to the command because in the dark it could never be ascertained with certainty who advanced and who did not. It is this frustration that explains Davies' actions in setting up the Inquiry and the language he used in his summary statement. As for the men, it may be assumed that they did not long dwell on their 'cowardly behaviour' or the supposed disgrace they had brought on their country. They had lived to fight another day.

* * *

The significance of this small affair of the 1/6 Highland Light Infantry is that it illustrates how the Mediterranean Expeditionary Force was fading away as an effective army. At Helles by October the divisions needed 30,000 men to bring them up to full strength. At Anzac the numbers were 32,000 and at Suvla 33,000. So while the nominal strength of the force was around 200,000 men, its actual strength was just over 110,000. Nor were these deficiencies in men made up by a sufficiency of firepower. At Suvla there were just 20 heavy guns, at Anzac 35 and at Helles 22. The entire force therefore had 77 heavy guns, far fewer than a single assault division would have had on the Western Front. Moreover, in August, shortage of ammunition reduced the daily ration to two rounds per gun, hardy enough shells for the Turks to notice.[2]

And then there was the truly alarming rate of sickness. In October the force was losing at least 5,000 men per week to dysentery and related diseases. The dribble of drafts sent from England and Australia (the 2 Australian Division arrived in late August to early September) could not compensate for even these numbers, let alone casualties caused by the sporadic fighting.

What was life like for the men in this debilitated force, which was so obviously incapable of sustained action? It was the usual mixture of terror, boredom and misery. The terror is typified by the activities of a tunneller at Anzac. In September Sergeant Cyril Lawrence was still constructing tunnels at Lone Pine as he had been in May:

Near one of our tunnels, old Johnno [the Turks] had been working against us for some days and it was decided to blow him. The mine was laid and fired in due time, poor Johnno working away right up to the last moment. What happened to him we never found out, but as the trenches were so close we could not place a large charge for fear of damaging our own lines. Consequently all we did was to blow a hole into their tunnel. Immediately both sides erected barricades . . . and for some days firing went on from both sides, no one being hit.

During this time we started further back in our tunnel and burrowed in and down eight feet-odd . . .. We eventually blew the whole concern up—Turk and all.

This little incident will give an idea of what our work is like at times. No wonder we have casualty lists and yet we never appear in the showy nerve tinglers in the dailies.[3]

By way of contrast, at Helles in November an engineer set down for his family what he saw as the tedium of his daily life. It consisted of inspecting trench works dug overnight, collecting the post, parade and inspections, visiting the workshops where trench signs were made (and crosses for graves), eating 'tea' (jam, tea and biscuits) and then dinner (soup, meat, jam roll pudding 'Oh so Heavy') and then a game of auction bridge before lights out around nine o'clock.[4] He continued:

Besides these [things] . . . I have to answer official letters, see the rations are all right, inspect the Water-cart, see Clothing, Boots, Shirts are issued properly—see daily sick report—grumble at dirtiness of Dug-outs if necessary—draw and issue money—censor the letters (& cross out many things I put in my own!!)—be at the beck & call of the C.R.E. and Adjutant and any Staff Officer who wants information—attend to any urgent jobs such as are necessary when Johnny Turk blows up a mine or blows down our trenches with shells or bombs. . . . I wonder if you will read this I hope you have plenty of 'leisure' if you are to wade thro' you will want it.[5]

The misery was encapsulated by the weather. There was a taste of what was to come in early October when a heavy gale damaged piers at Suvla and Anzac, beached ships and buckled some of the light railway supplying the troops. Later in the month similar storms stopped all boats putting in to Anzac Cove, damaged the recently repaired piers and drove lighters and tugs ashore.[6]

The really ferocious weather, however, did not arrive on the Peninsula until late November. Then, a 'fierce south-westerly gale, which started on the afternoon of the 26th, veered next day to the north. It continued with considerable violence for three days, and throughout that period it was impossible for any boat to approach the Gallipoli beaches.'[7]

The storm struck with peculiar ferocity at Suvla, where the low-lying ground and the exposed positions on Kiretch Tepe Ridge offered little protection. In that area were located the 1 Lancashire Fusiliers, who had been in the thick of the fighting since landing at W Beach on 25 April. Their War Diary indicates what happened in graphic detail:

November 26th.

1900. Very severe thunderstorm, with very strong gale, and torrents of rain.

2000. All telephone communication was cut off, and all dug-outs flooded out.

2100. Reported to Bde Hqrs that all trenches were flooded, water had come in as though it had been a tidal wave, that many men must have been drowned, and few had been able to save their rifles and equipment. The men were standing up to their knees in water, behind the parados of the trenches . . ..

By midnight the men who were capable of work had thrown up for themselves in most places sufficient cover to protect them from shrapnel fire. The water had subsided in the trenches to an average depth of 4 feet. A few overcoats, rifles and a certain amount of ammunition were recovered. Great difficulty was experienced in bringing up rations for the men, but eventually Bully Beef, a few biscuits and a little rum issued. The conditions during the day were trying, men were huddled together in shallow trenches, dug behind the parados during the night with any implements they could lay their hands on . . . .

A cold N E wind blew all day with a little rain and sleet at intervals and it is feared that a great number died from exposure. Towards evening the weather got worse, down to ambulances in large quantities.

0200. The blizzard continued all through the night and the condition of the men so deplorable that orders were received from the brigadier that any man not fit to fire a rifle had to be sent to the ambulances.

0400 Orders received . . . to move to reserve . . . . It was very fortunate that during this period the blizzard became heavier, therefore hiding the movement of the troops from the enemy, consequently there was no shelling.[8]

Similar conditions were experienced at Anzac, where drowned Turkish soldiers were often swept into Australian trenches, and at Helles, where so many small craft were destroyed as to throw thoughts of evacuation into doubt. In all it is possible that about 8,000 men suffered from frostbite and that more than 500 were drowned. Only the similar experiences of the Turkish troops prevented them from taking any military advantage of the situation.

* * *

Meanwhile, the higher command had been preparing plans (not yet sanctioned by the government) to evacuate the entire Peninsula. This was an extraordinary decision. While the government dithered, many generals decided as early as November that the game was up. Consequently, they had taken the opportunity gradually to reduce the garrisons, stores and guns on the Peninsula. This 'preliminary' stage was not part of a concerted plan but there is little doubt that the prudence of the generals considerably aided the actual plan when it was put into place. Thus at Anzac and Suvla when the order to evacuate was received from the government, the garrisons had been reduced from 92,000 to 83,000 and a number of guns had also been sent away. In this instance the great storm aided the process by providing an excellent cover for men to leave the Peninsula and not return.

On 8 December when the order was finally received from London, the number of men on Gallipoli totalled about 80,000 men. There was also an immense quantity of stores, ammunition, animals and building and trenching materials of all kinds.

The plan was to evacuate Suvla and Anzac at the same time but retain Helles for naval purposes for an indefinite period. This was merely a sop to the anti-evacuationists; there was no question that the Helles garrison would be retained indefinitely, although the lack of small craft to lift 80,000 men simultaneously was a more tangible reason for retaining it for a few more weeks.

The basic plan for the evacuation was worked out by the Chief of Staff of the Anzac Corps (the newly promoted Brigadier-General Brudenell White) and the Chief of Staff of IX Corps, General H.L. Reed. A committee of staff officers from both corps was set up to ensure that the exit of the adjacent forces from the Peninsula would be properly coordinated. The most difficult question was whether a fighting retreat from trench line to trench line to the beaches would be conducted or whether the front line would be held to the end by reduced garrisons of men. White had strong views about this. He pointed out that the opposing trench lines at Anzac were so close together that the slightest withdrawal might alert the enemy. And in that instance, because there was so little distance between the front line and the beach, his men might be caught in the open and slaughtered or driven into the sea.[9]

That settled matters. In the 'intermediate period' of 10 days the trench lines would be thinned until no more than 20,000 men remained at Suvla and at Anzac. Then the majority of these men would be evacuated, leaving just a rearguard in place. Finally, if possible, these men would be removed. All evacuations would take place at night.

At first only the corps commanders and their staff officers were told about this plan. The troops were merely informed that the garrisons were being reduced to facilitate supply during the stormy winter months, and that some of the guns were being removed to Salonika where they were urgently needed. On 12 December the divisional and brigade commanders were let into the secret. However, by then rumours had begun to circulate. An Anzac gunner, sent to Mudros on Lemnos to obtain stores, was told not to bother because the whole force would soon leave the Peninsula. Moreover, troops at the front soon began to draw their own conclusions about what was happening. It rapidly became impossible to conceal the

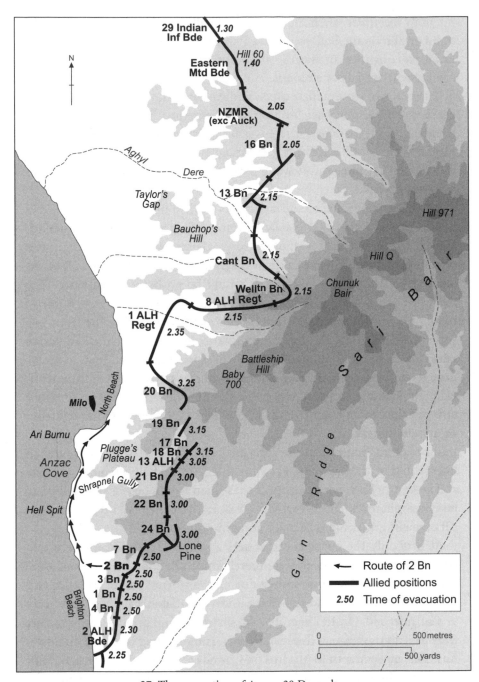

27 The evacuation of Anzac, 20 December

intent of the withdrawals and the whole force was informed of the evacuation on the evening of the 13th.[10]

There is no doubt that the planning of the northern operation was a masterpiece of precision and cunning. This demonstrates two things: first that these were staff officers of the highest calibre; and second that evacuations, despite their complexities, are usually easier to plan than battles.

The first matter to settle in the intermediate period was the exact order in which the reductions of troops, stores, guns, pack animals and equipment was to take place; the second was how to keep the Turks in the dark about the whole process.

We happen to know, in great detail, how the first of these matters was carried out at Suvla and Anzac. The plans of each corps were different only in minor ways and worked towards the same end—to leave 20,000 men and as small a quantity of stores as possible by 18 December.

In IX Corps at Suvla, it was decided to commence the evacuation on the night of 10–11 December by removing much of the artillery, together with some machine guns, vehicles and ammunition. This was followed on the next night by lifting more vehicles, 400 horses and mules and 32,000 pounds of fodder. The field ambulances and their personnel (1,700 men) were sent away on the following evening. Then, in successive nights, ammunition and a combination of troops and equipment were removed. By the evening of the 18th, just 19,500 troops, 28 artillery pieces, a small number of pack animals and millions of rounds of small-arms ammunition remained to be evacuated in the final period.[11]

The IX Corps also practised a series of deception methods. To maintain the illusion that the front-line troops were continuing to be supplied, empty carts, making as much noise as possible, were sent to the front at night and then, with wheels padded, silently withdrawn fully laden. In addition, although the field ambulances and casualty clearing stations were emptied early in the period, none of their tents were struck, this semblance of normality being maintained until after the evacuation was completed.[12]

The navy also played its part. Some stores were sent by lighter to the transport ships in broad daylight, their loads concealed under dark tarpaulins. This equipment was then offloaded onto the side of the ship furthest from the enemy. The lighters then returned empty, hiding the fact by leaving the tarpaulins in place. This ruse had the added advantage of freeing up the night for the more bulky cargoes of troops, guns and animals.[13]

At Anzac the pattern of withdrawal was similar to that at Suvla and a number of deception operations were used to convince the enemy that all was business as usual. For example, 'silent periods' were instituted when no guns of any kind were fired. This was designed to accustom the Turks to periods of quiescence, during which many guns and quantities of ammunition were withdrawn.[14] At other periods, rifle and machine-gun fire was maintained at the usual rate, towards the end by a small number of men moving from loophole to loophole along the trenches. Then there were the famous, if rather overrated, 'automatic' rifles, which fired when water was dripped into a tin until it was heavy enough to exert pressure on a string attached to the trigger.[15]

The navy also assisted at Anzac. Between 6 and 10 December two heavy bombardments were fired by the ships on the concentration of Turkish batteries near the Olive Grove, south of Gaba Tepe. These batteries were well placed to enfilade the beaches at Anzac. The aim of the naval attack was to deter the batteries from coming into action during the embarkation period. In the event, the shelling reduced the fire of these batteries in the final period to an acceptable level.[16]

The intricate detail regarding the embarkation of the last troops can be examined by looking at the arrangements employed by an Australian battalion during their last week on the Peninsula. The 2 Australian Battalion was holding a section of the front just south of Lone Pine. Their plan was that most men and stores would be embarked on 18 and 19 December. For the last night this would leave just over 60 men per company to hold the line. These troops would consist of 45 hand-picked men, 2 machine-gun detachments (12 men), 1 cook, 2 of the 'best' subalterns, a medical officer, a stretcher party and the company commander. After these men had been selected, they would be divided into three sections, A, B and C. A section would consist of the 'least active' men and be the first group to go. B would be made up of the 'next best' and C would be the cream, picked for their discipline, steadiness and shooting ability. As C section would be the last to go, their packs would be taken by A section and their blankets by B to ensure that they had maximum freedom of movement.

Routes from their position south of Lone Pine via Victoria Gully to Milo Pier, just north of Anzac Cove, were carefully traced out. Boots would be muffled by sandbag coverings and the march rehearsed to ascertain the exact time taken from the trenches to the pier (28 minutes as it happened).

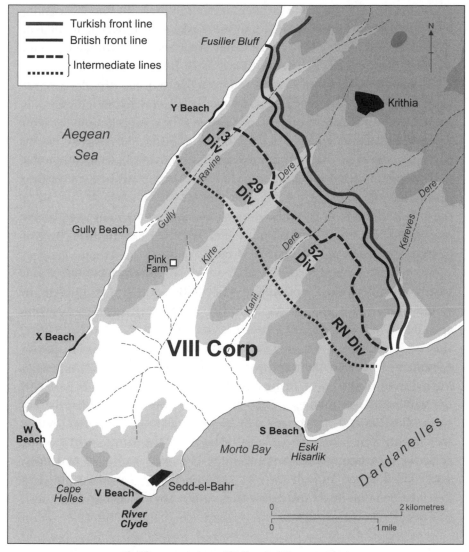

28 The evacuation of Helles, 8–9 January 1916

Arrangements were made for silent periods in the front line, followed by heavy bouts of sniping to 'educate' the Turks to a different if reduced volume of fire. During the last days rolls of barbed wire would be pushed out from the trenches to deter any curious Turkish patrols.

Random movements of men to and from the trenches were made in full view of Turkish observers at Gaba Tepe, or (it was hoped) they would be sighted by Turkish reconnaissance planes. These actions brought some Turkish shells down on these areas, but it was considered essential that the enemy be convinced that normal movements near the front were continuing.

It was emphasized in battalion orders that there must be no straggling during the march to the piers. Each column of troops was to close up to the extent that a man could hold on to the coat of the man in front. No one was to be permitted to fall out even if the line of march was checked. Complete silence was to be imposed and all lights banned.[17]

In the end, with the considerable aid of a sustained period of fine weather, it all worked smoothly.[18] The sandbagged boots muffled the sound of marching and on the night of 19–20 December first A section and then B moved off to their beach in small parties at ten-minute intervals. By 2.30 a.m. only ten men and a small number of officers constituting C remained to hold their company's section of the line. These groups moved from post to post, firing a round each, 'giving the impression that the whole line was manned'. Then at 2.40 a.m. this last group embarked from Milo Pier and was conveyed by beetle barge to the SS *Heroic*. Similar movements were taking place along the length of the Anzac perimeter and at Suvla. In a final act, mines under the Nek were exploded and many Turks killed. When Turkish patrols crept forward they found the positions deserted. So far as Suvla and Anzac were concerned the Gallipoli operation was over.[19]

*   *   *

Helles was now all that remained. The War Committee soon abandoned the facade that a beachhead was to be retained for naval purposes. General Davies, the corps commander, was told that evacuation would take place early in January. This represented a considerable challenge to the Helles commanders. On the one hand they had the experience and plans developed by the staff officers at Suvla and Anzac. On the other hand the Turks would be expecting the British to leave. Furthermore, Davies soon realized that there were some differences between conditions at Suvla and Anzac and those he faced at Helles. He identified three main issues distinct to his situation. First, the distance between the front-line trenches and the beaches was over 6,000 yards. This was much further than at either Suvla or Anzac. The troops would take considerably longer to traverse this area than in the north, and Davies was concerned that groups making the march might be open to attack in force if the Turks managed to break his front. He therefore determined to hold the line in strength until the last moment. This would mean lifting no fewer than 17,000 men on the final night and sacrificing much materiel to allow the maximum amount of shipping to be devoted to troops.

Second, the exposed position of the beaches at the southern end of the Peninsula meant that the entire operation would have to be as rapid as possible to take advantage of what might prove to be a small window of good weather. The great storm in late November had destroyed all the piers at Helles. Such an event in the middle of a lengthy evacuation could hardly be contemplated, so the operation was reduced to just six nights.

Third, the French still had a brigade of colonial troops at Helles and Davies determined that his task would be greatly simplified if they were evacuated first, leaving the final operation as an all-British affair. The French showed no disposition to dispute this rather offhanded assessment and left without any discernible regret on New Year's night 1916.[20]

While all this was being decided, there was much shuffling of troops at Helles. The 42 Division was deemed quite exhausted and left the Peninsula in December. Late in the month they were replaced by two brigades of the hapless 13 Division (already evacuated from Suvla and resting at Mudros) and a brigade of the even more unfortunate 29 Division, who also thought their labours on the Peninsula had come to an end. Then the departing French were replaced by the Royal Naval Division. The only unit to hold its position in the south was 52 Division, which had carried out a diversionary attack to mask the northern evacuations.[21] Whatever the military justification for all these last-minute troop movements, they might well have had the effect of confusing the Turkish command about what British intentions were in the southern zone.

Despite the fact that he planned to hold the front line in strength up to the last moment, Davies was still concerned that he might face a concerted Turkish attack towards the end of the operation when the garrison was at its weakest. In an attempt to forestall such an event, several lines of resistance were therefore constructed between the front line and the tip of the Peninsula. A telegraphist describes how it was done:

Trip mines were placed in front of [these lines] in every conceivable place. Tons of barbed wire and entanglements [were placed] across the road & Communication trenches with only space for our troops to finally pass thro' but to be closed after the passage of the last man. Special routes were marked off for the final retreat. Special roads were made & sandbags placed along the edges & sprinkled with flour so as they could be seen in the dark. Along the routes control stations were placed & reported the passage of each body of troops as it returned. My job as telegraphist was at one of these & I had to remain with the controlling officer till I could report the last man as having passed through & then retire ourselves.[22]

In other ways, the evacuation proceeded in rather similar manner to the Suvla and Anzac operations; the same kinds of deception regarding rates of fire, 'silent periods' and the removal of the sick and wounded took place.

By the morning of 7 January the garrison had gradually been reduced to the required 17,000. At this point, however, events seemed about to take a dangerous turn for the British. A ferocious two-hour bombardment was opened by the Turks on the left of the British line opposite 13 Division. Our telegraphist found himself in the centre of the maelstrom:

The Turks were enfilading [Gully] Ravine with as much shrapnel & high explosive as possible. I thought this was strange as during all my sojourns in Y Ravine previously they had never shelled it. I was soon stopped musing by a shell too close to be pleasant. I retired round the corner of the ravine & sat down under a huge rock. From there I had a fine view of the ships bombarding. Again I was interrupted. This time by a high explosive on the cliff above. The splinters flew down the cliff side & struck the ground with an unhealthy thud. They came down like rain & no mistake & have beautiful jagged edges. My word! I had a hot time there! 4 more of these beauties very near falling about a yard away together with shrapnel.[23]

According to Liman von Sanders, this bombardment was meant to be the preliminary to a major attack designed to catch the British in mid-retreat. Some time after 4.00 p.m. when two large mines had been exploded, the trenches opposite 13 Division began to bristle with Turkish bayonets. But nothing followed. A few half-hearted attacks by small groups of Turkish infantry were easily beaten off with the help of a huge volume of shells from the supporting naval contingent. What the Turkish intent actually was is still uncertain. Perhaps the Turks were staging a mock attack in an attempt to get the British to reveal their positions and the strength with which they still held the Peninsula. Perhaps most Turks could not be induced to attack an entrenched enemy across open ground. In any case, nothing came of it. The evacuation continued.[24]

The only possible factor that could have hampered the operation now was the weather. On the evening of the last night, 8 January, the breeze freshened and by 9.00 p.m. it was blowing at 35 mph. The newly reconstructed piers took a pounding, lighters found it hard to get alongside and by 3.30 a.m. on the 9th the sea was running so high that it seemed the removal of the last contingents might have to be delayed. But just at this moment the rearguards appeared on the beaches and at the cost of much sea-sickness, steamed off to Mudros.

Unlike the northern operation, much equipment and many animals were destroyed. Over 500 mules were shot, 15,000 vehicles of all kinds disabled and hundreds of tons of stores torched or set alight by naval gunfire. In all, considering that original projections were that 30 to 40 per cent of the entire force would be lost during the evacuation, these losses were deemed a small price to pay. The sombre fact was, however, that the Gallipoli operation was over and it was the Turks who wandered victorious through the abandoned British positions on the next day.

*   *   *

The great question regarding the evacuation is: how much were the Turks aware of British intentions? On all three beachheads the Turks occupied the high ground, yet every account we have from them and their German advisers insists that they had been gulled by the British deception plans. Perhaps they had been. Perhaps, on the other hand, the Turks were unwilling to admit that their army remained quiescent in the presence of the evacuation. The usual explanation given for this passivity is the 'low morale and will to win of the Turks'.[25] This explanation makes no sense. An army observing its adversary leaving its shores has surely already won and in that case the matter of willpower or its lack is hardly a factor. The Turks might instead have reflected on the occasions where they had launched attacks across open ground. At Helles on 28 April, at Anzac on 19 May and at Suvla on 9 August these manoeuvres had resulted in much slaughter to their troops, inflicted by groups of defenders often in the most rudimentary defensive positions. The ferocious naval bombardments of early December and 7 January might have been timely reminders of what might happen to a new series of attacks. In other words, it was probably not low morale that kept the Turks in their trenches on those last days, but prudence in the face of a defeated enemy.

Moreover, C.E.W. Bean makes the cogent point that to optimize their chances of success, the Turks would have required detailed knowledge of the Allied evacuation timetables. To attack too early might risk slaughter; too late and it could not be hailed as a major victory.

But the Turks were not alone in perpetuating the myth of the 'perfect evacuation'. Whether Allied commanders had supported the operation (such as Birdwood and Churchill) or opposed it (Monro and Davies) or planned it (Aspinall and Dawnay), it suited them to emphasize the cunning of the deception plan. This would not only draw attention to the role of staff and commanders in the final planning but help portray the end of the affair as some kind of victory. In the end, they could claim that British and Anzac planning had confounded the stolid and unimaginative Turk. This is of course the merest sophistry. However cunning the final plan, it was after all a plan for an evacuation—an operation that set the seal on a failed endeavour. As a statesman not unconnected with the Dardanelles operation might have said, 'campaigns are not won by evacuations'.

Reflections on Gallipoli

The Gallipoli campaign was conceived initially as a limited naval operation that offered potentially large gains for relatively small losses. By the
time it ended in disaster, it had evolved into a full-scale military operation.
How had this situation come about? If there is a popular view it probably
is something like this: Winston Churchill had wanted to attack Turkey ever
since it sided with the Central Powers. As head of the Royal Navy he was
anxious to use that instrument to assist the land war and in the process
boost his standing in the country. He therefore devised the naval attack,
bulldozed it past his naval advisers despite their objections, and then used
the same methods to convince his Cabinet colleagues that the plan had
naval approval and that it should be attempted. These circumstances led to
the naval attack and its failure led inexorably to the military campaign.
Churchill is therefore to blame for the whole sorry fiasco.

This is in my view at best a caricature of what happened and at worst just
plain wrong. Churchill was certainly to the fore in devising plans to use the
navy to materially assist the land campaign in the west. Initially, he focused
on plans that might lure the German fleet into battle, and there is little
doubt that he was frustrated by the failure of the Germans to oblige in
launching an attack on the Grand Fleet which they were bound to lose. He
felt that, in Asquith's phrase, the navy was not 'breaking any crockery' and
that such a mighty force must be able to make a greater contribution to the

war. In thinking thus Churchill certainly had in mind his own reputation, but he had other motives as well. He wanted a shorter and cheaper war and, unlike many of his colleagues, he was aware of what a prolonged war on the Western Front would mean in terms of casualties. He therefore put forward various operations designed to make the German navy fight in circumstances (so he thought) much to their disadvantage. All these schemes—the attack on Borkum, the entry of the British fleet into the Baltic, the Belgian coast operation, the plans to use naval pressure to induce Holland to enter the war—failed for one of two reasons. First, many of the schemes risked the Grand Fleet in waters dominated by mines, submarines and coastal batteries. Second, the plans failed to win the support of Britain's major ally, France or, in the case of Holland, defied attempts even to produce a workable scheme.

Churchill only turned towards Turkey as a poor alternative to his northern plans when it became clear that his admirals would not cooperate in carrying them out. Indeed, his attention was refocused on Turkey by others. Hankey had mentioned operations against the Ottoman Empire, Fisher took up the idea with alacrity and Lloyd George saw an attack on Turkey as part of a larger series of operations in the Balkans. Even Kitchener was not averse, providing no troops were to be used.

Churchill's contribution was to take those parts of the various plans for action against Turkey, weed out the impractical aspects such as the use of huge British armies or those of obviously reluctant Balkan states and produce the plan to attack the Dardanelles 'by ships alone'. However, this plan was not foisted on his advisers by the First Lord. Churchill had the plan discussed by the Admiralty War Group at some length. It was approved without a dissenting voice. The old battleships that were to be used were clearly surplus to requirements in the North Sea. The core of the Grand Fleet would not be put at risk. The admirals were all for it. However, it *is* possible that Fisher's support was illusory and that he was using the 'Turkey Plan' to deflect Churchill from his dangerous northern schemes, but there was no way that Churchill or anyone else could have known that at the time.

Having won naval support, Churchill then took the plan to the War Council which on 13 January approved it unanimously, the members having no doubt that the Royal Navy could dispose of an enemy such as Turkey with ease. As Prime Minister, Asquith must bear a large share of the blame for this. Yet so far from giving a lead to the War Council, he appeared merely a spectator to the discussions led by Churchill and Kitchener. In wartime this is not sufficient. The decision to launch the naval attack therefore must be shared between Asquith, Churchill, the War Council and the Admiralty.

The period from 13 January to the opening of the naval attack on 19 February must rank as one of the strangest in Britain's military history. The confidence in the naval-only attack disappeared almost the day after the War Council decided to carry it out. At the Admiralty, Richmond, Jackson and most importantly Fisher called for troops to support the naval endeavour. What caused this sudden switch is difficult to establish. Probably, the Admiralty experts thought it prudent to have troops on hand to destroy any guns that could not be dealt with by the fleet. This left Churchill in a considerable dilemma. It is obvious that after the War Council decision he was determined that the naval attack would proceed. But he had been shaken by Admiralty opinion that troops might be needed. Consequently, he took up the seemingly contradictory stance of calling for a division of the Regular Army to be sent to the east (which implied that he expected heavy fighting) and insisting that the naval attack would still succeed (which implied that there would be no fighting by the army). Partly, however, he was able to take such a position because of the lamentable quality of naval advice he was receiving. Jackson and Richmond in particular were reluctant to take a firm stand. While still claiming that some ships would get through to Constantinople, they expressed concern as to what those ships might achieve without military support. They were thus able to call for troops without voicing doubts about the naval-only attack. As for Fisher, he finally showed his hand in his memorandum of 25 January. In that paper he came out against *any* extraneous operations involving the fleet, a respectable strategic position but confused by his nonsensical notions about the war as a whole.

Nevertheless, by early February it was clear that Admiralty opinion had turned against the naval-only attack. It is also clear that members of the War Council were well aware of this shift. Hankey had informed anyone who would listen, and then there was Fisher's public dissent at the meeting of 28 January. What is equally clear is that having taken Fisher's view into account, the War Council discounted it. Why they took this position is quite clear. Many thought that Fisher was hardly capable of rational thought, and were more influenced by other experts who had after all stated that a portion of the fleet would get through. This was enough for a group of politicians. The appearance of a British fleet had wrought many diplomatic changes in the past. There was no reason to think that this would not continue, especially against a second-rate power such as Turkey. Troops would indeed be a bonus but the navy should continue with its plan.

The next two weeks, however, saw a decisive change in naval and military opinion regarding the use of troops. De Robeck bluntly told the Admiralty that troops would be needed to assist in the destruction of the Turkish guns. This might be expected to have marked the end of any plans for a purely naval attack. Churchill perhaps concealed this opinion from his colleagues, but with Birdwood telling Kitchener the same thing, political opinion in London must have been aware of the change. Curiously though, there was no call from any party to delay the naval operation until an army had been assembled. If there was a consensus emerging that troops would be needed, this was surely the prudent step to take. Churchill is particularly culpable in not suggesting this course of action. As head of the navy he had the authority to postpone naval operations. Moreover, in calling for Regular soldiers he clearly had a view that all might not go well with the naval attack. So a peculiar situation developed where confidence in an operation was receding at the same time as preparations for its implementation were steaming ahead.

Once the naval attack had commenced, there was no chance that the War Council would take a firm line on the use of troops. In this period they showed often euphoric confidence in the ultimate success of the naval attack. Indeed, it was only necessary for Carden to announce the demolition of a Turkish gun for the War Council to begin parcelling up the Ottoman Empire. And it was not just Churchill who exhibited this confidence. Some of the strongest proponents of sending troops to the Dardanelles—Hankey, Richmond, Asquith, Lloyd George and even Fisher—all expressed satisfaction with what they took to be the progress of the fleet. This mood demonstrates, as nothing else, that the naval attack had its adherents even after the call for an army to be assembled had become deafening.

As for the naval attack itself, the men who could have stopped it in its tracks were Jackson and Oliver. If they had paid any attention to what rate of hitting could have been expected from the old guns of the pre-dreadnoughts on targets at long range, and placed these facts before the Admiralty War Group, the Dardanelles plan would have gone the same way as Borkum. Instead they neglected this issue, as they did those of aerial spotting and minesweeping. This is not to say that efficient spotting and sweeping forces would have converted failure into success, but it would be pleasant to record that the Admiralty had given Carden's squadron a decent chance.

* * *

As for the efforts of the bombarding squadron to carry out the naval plan, the episode was without question the nadir of all British military actions against Turkey, with the possible exception of Charles Townshend's surrender at Kut-al-Amara in April 1915. Over a period of four weeks Carden conducted a lackadaisical, half-hearted series of attacks against the Strait's defences. In that time he fired such a derisory amount of shells at the forts, that he stood little chance of disabling them, given the inaccuracy of the guns of the pre-dreadnoughts. Exactly why operations were so desultory is hard to explain. If he was running short of ammunition, Carden should have placed this fact squarely before the Admiralty. Perhaps he had lost confidence in his own plan and while loath to admit the fact, found it impossible to prosecute it with any enthusiasm. It should be conceded however that with the force available, no admiral could have conquered the Straits defences unless the Turks threw in the towel. This was probably the hope of the British all along, but unfortunately for them the Turks showed no signs of obliging.

* * *

The bizarre way in which the naval operation segued into the landings on 25 April has not often been appreciated by commentators. The War Council had in fact agreed to a landing well before the navy had failed. Indeed, the attack on the forts had only been underway for two days when Kitchener issued his 'no going back' statement. The War Council meekly accepted this dictum, although there is no doubt that much of the initial appeal of the project lay precisely in the ability to 'go back' at any time. Thus, the War Council should share in the responsibility for the Gallipoli operation as well as the naval attack. Certainly Kitchener and Churchill gave the lead but no member of the Council dissented, including the Prime Minister. Indeed, Asquith ignored the advice of Hankey, one of his principal confidants, who warned him that 80,000 troops might not prove able to defeat the Turkish Empire.

To sum up, it seems that when the deadlock on the Western Front became manifest in late 1914, members of Britain's politico-military elite were determined to find a fresh field in which to prosecute the war. Churchill, Lloyd George, Hankey, Balfour, Asquith and at times the Admiralty War Group, all sought an alternative theatre of operations. It was

Churchill who eventually came up with a plan that could at least be put into effect. But so wedded were his colleagues to the concept that when the high authorities at the Admiralty started hedging their bets they were ignored. And when the naval attack failed, so determined were the decision makers to persist against Turkey that they did not consider it necessary to reconvene to give formal approval or even to scrutinize the military plan. United they stood for the Dardanelles, united they were to stand, in the medium term at least, for Gallipoli.

*   *   *

The military attack lasted from 25 April until 9 January, a period of 260 days. During that time contingents from Britain, Australia, New Zealand, France and India fought contingents of soldiers taken from various provinces of the Turkish Empire. Despite the obvious fact that the Allies were defeated, can we apply a 'blood test' to establish the price each army paid for the campaign to see whether this produces a different perspective on Gallipoli? Battle casualties for the various Allied contingents are given in the table below.

Contingent	Killed	Wounded	Total
British	26,054	44,721	70,775
French	8,000	15,000	23,000
Australian	7,825	17,900	25,725
New Zealand	2,445	4,752	7,197
Indian	1,682	3,796	5,478
Total	46,006	86,169	132,175

In addition to these figures there are the non-battle casualties. These are available in the case of the British where they amount to double their battle casualties. Assuming the non-battle casualty rate for the other contingents is proportional, this gives a figure of about 260,000 in total. So the total casualties suffered by the Allies at Gallipoli amount to about 390,000.[1]

Of more interest, however, is the number of these men who never fought again. By adding to the dead those proportions for the wounded, sick and injured who were invalided out of the army, we arrive at an Allied figure of about 90,000 men who were permanently lost to the war. The Gallipoli campaign, over a period of about eight months, consumed just over five divisions of troops. So about 30 per cent of the infantry who fought at Gallipoli (just over 16 divisions were engaged at one time or another on the Allied side) never fought again. This does not match the lethality of battles such as the Somme when one soldier in two did not fight again. But it demonstrates that the Gallipoli campaign was more lethal than is generally recognized. And, of course, the campaign had been carried out in the first place to avoid the killing ground of the Western Front, not to duplicate it.

The Turkish casualties are much harder to establish. It might be thought that they were fewer than the Allied casualties because for the most part the Turks were on the defensive. Certainly, it is highly likely that for the three landings—Helles, Anzac and Suvla—the Turks inflicted more casualties on the attackers than they suffered themselves. The same seems to have been the case in the three battles of Krithia, directed with such ineptitude by Hunter-Weston. To set against these propositions, however, are the Turkish counterattacks at Helles, their disastrous foray at Anzac on 19 May and the major counterattack at Suvla on 9 August. In all of these actions it is certain that the Turks lost more heavily than their adversaries. Moreover, the actions undertaken by Hunter-Weston and Gouraud at Helles in late June and July certainly cost the Turks dear. Taking all these factors into consideration, it seems reasonable to assume that the battle casualties for each side were about even.[2] As for the non-battle casualties it is also a reasonable proposition that the Turks, because of their more primitive medical arrangements, could not return as high a proportion of their wounded, sick and injured to the battle as could the Allies. The Turks therefore might come out on the negative side of the casualty equation, but not by much. In short, there is little comfort to be had for the Allies in looking at comparative casualty statistics.

* * *

What of the fighting qualities of the armies? It may be useful to compare them, beginning with the infantry and moving up the chain of command.

All armies have their moments of panic or doubt. This was true at Gallipoli. The 29 Division at Y Beach was certainly less than steady. The French Colonial Division broke under the weight of the Turkish counterattacks in early May. Part of the 52 Division streamed back to its start line in July. The Highland Light Infantry adopted survival tactics in August. At Anzac there was the drift back to the beaches on the evening of 25 April. Monash's 4 Brigade decided on 8 August that they had had enough. At Suvla there were various incidents in which the troops showed a reluctance to move.

Nevertheless, these are isolated incidents which usually indicate that the units involved were poorly led or were pushed too far. In the overwhelming number of cases the men were quite willing to place their lives at risk for what, even at the time, must have seemed the slimmest chances of success. Most men most of the time fought well, with a tenacity that often stopped attacks that were delivered in great force.

Much the same points can be made for the Turkish army. On 25 April its troops proved resolute in defence and later in the campaign they launched various attacks (the night offensives at Helles, 19 May at Anzac, 9 August at Suvla) which must have cost them dear. It is true that on the three major battlefronts they held the most advantageous ground, but they were subjected to fire from the battleships which, if not very accurate, was certainly frightening. Yet only a few units of this force broke under fire and in those cases the troops soon steadied or were stiffened by fresher units from reserve. Turkey might have been classed as a second-rate power but its troops on Gallipoli proved able to stop those units from first-rate powers that were sent against them.

The junior officers (battalion commander and below) were a mixed bag. Matthews on Y Beach and the leaders of the units on X Beach seemed devoid of initiative. In the 29 Division, Major Frankland was quite the exception at this level and Captain Geddes showed initiative and common sense in the extreme conditions at V Beach. The officers who led the abortive attack of the Highland Light Infantry in August were not generally of the first rank. Surfacing during the August attack there also seem to have been problems among the junior officers within and between the 13 and 15 Australian Battalions. Generally, however, we know very little about this class of men. What we do know is that on virtually every occasion the troops followed these officers into battle, and that when an attack went wrong it was usually because the plan was bad, fire support non-existent or because the enemy was too strong. The fact is that as soon as the lines were entrenched, no junior officer had much scope to demonstrate initiative. It was firepower that became the determinant of victory and neither side had enough to allow officers of skill the opportunity to practise it.

The brigade and divisional commanders were in a similar position. They were often required to carry through a plan that had been made by those above, whether they thought it reasonable or not. It is doubtful, for example, whether Monash, who has been much criticized by some authorities for his efforts in August, thought very highly of Birdwood's plan. The fact that

Monash's brigade could not carry it through is a comment on the plan, not on him. No doubt there are other examples. It would be interesting to know what Sinclair Maclagan thought of Birdwood's change of plan for the landing. On 25 April Maclagan probably should have disobeyed orders and attempted to seize the dominating high ground. But this ran counter to ingrained habits in 1915 and Maclagan had little time in which to make a decision. It is hardly surprising that he took the obvious route of obeying orders.

In some cases brigadiers showed as little initiative as those below them. Sitwell, especially, at Suvla was cautious to the point of paralysis. But as so often at Gallipoli, had there been more adventurous brigadiers, the character of the battle would have been little changed. Problems such as lack of water or ammunition or artillery support were often more crucial to an advance than the personalities of the men in command. In short, the leadership might have exhibited few desirable qualities but that did not necessarily mean that different leaders would have accomplished more.

The divisional commanders had slightly more scope but not much. Bridges (1 Australian Division) was killed before he could demonstrate competence in a military situation. Walker, who succeeded him, showed admirable steadiness when evacuation of the Anzac force was raised. In the static situation that followed he had little opportunity to shine. His counterpart, Godley in the NZ & A Division, often thought he was controlling the battle when he was not, so his orders during the August offensive often bore little relation to what was happening on the ground. Hammersley (11 Division) stands out but only for his lack of grip. His inability to organize an advance at Suvla on 8 August shows him in a poor light. Mahon (10 Division) had little in his favour except seniority. Of the others, General F.C. Shaw (13 Division) saw his troops used by Godley and Birdwood for their own purposes. Egerton (52 Division), General J.E. Lindley (53 Division) and General Francis Inglefield (54 Division) are little more than names at Gallipoli. De Lisle, who succeeded to the command of 29 Division and then IX Corps, is often thought of as a new breed at Gallipoli, but there is no evidence that he performed with greater skill than his predecessors.

We know much more about the corps commanders. Hunter-Weston has been portrayed as a byword for brutal incompetence. His handling of the landing and the three battles of Krithia merit the description. There was, however, a little more to him. He showed prescience in warning against the landings as sound military operations. And in June and July he worked out with Gouraud an (admittedly imperfect) method of gaining ground at moderate cost. This aspect of Hunter-Weston is little remembered, though perhaps there is some justice in that.

Birdwood has perhaps received the best press of all the commanders at Gallipoli. It is less certain whether he deserves it. His plan for the landing was appallingly vague and it is notable that he made no attempt to clarify the exact landing place for the Anzacs. There is no question that he favoured evacuation on the evening of 25 April, or that if it had been carried out much of the force would have perished. His August plan was fatally flawed and took no account of the decrepitude of the soldiers who were required to carry it out. Only the evacuation was a triumph and that was planned by Brudnell White, his staff officer.

Stopford was not quite the buffoon of legend. His criticisms of Hamilton's plan were acute and to the point. In battle, however, he showed no grip and allowed operations to drift without much attempt to contact his men or the higher command. But at least he realized when the game was up at Suvla, which is more than can be said for his superiors.

What of Hamilton? A general who was willing to speak his mind no doubt would have informed Kitchener that Turkey could not be defeated by 80,000 men and some old battleships. Probably, given the military authority of the Secretary of State for War, no such general existed in the British army. Nevertheless, a large question mark still hangs over Hamilton's reputation. He was reluctant to ask for reinforcements, put an unwarranted gloss on events in his reports to Kitchener and generally adopted an air of optimism (or was it insouciance?). Certainly, pessimism in a commander is hardly a desirable attribute. But realism certainly is, and it was not until July that Hamilton assessed the situation with a clear eye. The irony is that the Dardanelles Committee persuaded him to accept reinforcements and try again. This saw the end of Hamilton's realism. He soon returned to his naturally optimistic stance, a position he maintained until he was removed.

Hamilton's overall plans for the campaign demonstrated varying degrees of competence. The plan for the landing had its merits. It confused the defence and forced the Turks to disperse their reserves. However, Hamilton could have been clearer about the objectives at Anzac and at Helles. In the last instance it remains a puzzle that he decided to attack the Turks where they were strongest and leave his flanking units with no instructions. He never grasped what Hunter-Weston was up to in June–July, but probably would have disapproved if he had. It was the Anzac outflanking movement that attracted his attention, though he presided over the muddled development of the plan which saw the decisive movement across the Peninsula removed in favour of Suvla Bay. No doubt any dash for the Straits would have come undone, but Hamilton was striving for a decisive battle. For him not to notice that the plan did not provide for such an encounter was, in this sense, an egregious error.

We know much less about the imperatives that acted upon the Turkish command. There is some memoir literature but the detailed operation orders and war diaries are still not available. However, it is still possible to arrive at some conclusions regarding the Turkish and German commanders. Of the junior officers we know almost nothing. The actions of Sergeant Yahya at Helles are revealing but quite exceptional. Higher-ranking officers, such as Sami Bey, had a mixed campaign. He was saddled with Liman von Sanders's troop dispositions which spread his force too thinly to prevent the lodgement at Helles. On the other hand, the counterattacks he ordered in late April and early May were desperate affairs, always likely to meet with disaster. On the positive side, his timely dispatch of troops to Anzac on 25 April was probably more decisive than Mustafa Kemal's in dislocating the Anzac plan. Essad Pasha seems to have done well. Certainly, his actions on 7 and 8 August (together with Kannengiesser) were of great importance in halting the Allied advance on Sari Bair. His removal at a critical time of the battle almost cost the Turks some of the most important heights.

Over all these commanders looms the imposing figure of Kemal. He was obviously an officer of the first rank, but legend and perhaps political imperatives in Turkey often portray him as having thwarted the attacks in the north single-handedly. There is no need to take all of this on board. Kemal's appearance on 25 April denied the Anzacs heights such as Battleship Hill but, as argued here, Sami Bey's actions were probably just as important. We must also remember that Kemal presided over (but did not originate) the disastrous counterattack of 19 May, hardly his finest hour. Kemal was also important in thwarting the advance on 7 August, but so were Essad and Kannengiesser. On 9 August Kemal merely took over the plans of Feizi Bey for the great counterattack against the British. To what extent responsibility for the botched operation that followed can be placed at Kemal's door will remain a mystery until the Turkish war diaries are released. In sum, Kemal made mistakes at Gallipoli but it would not do to overstate them. As the key commander of the northern force he ultimately prevailed against the Anzacs and had the satisfaction of watching them leave Turkish shores.

In one sense Liman does not emerge well from Gallipoli. He dispersed his troops too thinly to have any chance of preventing the Allied landings. His fixation on Bulair almost deprived his army of the necessary reinforcements to halt the Anzacs. He also tended to micro-manage operations to ill effect, as his removal of Essad at a crucial time in August demonstrates. Yet Liman was hobbled by the limited resources available to him in the form of heavy artillery, and after all he too emerged on the winning side. In that sense, as Army Commander, he could claim that he presided over the Turkish victory on the Peninsula.

The civilian direction of the campaign has received little attention in the literature. We have already noted the role of the War Council in its origins. Once fighting was under way, the Council played a curious role. While perpetually dissatisfied with Hamilton's progress, the council members were so eager for results that in July they doubled his force without perhaps noting that the commander-in-chief was having severe doubts about his ability to win. From then until the end of the campaign they fluctuated between optimism and despair but proved mighty reluctant to call off the operation. Kitchener must bear a great deal of responsibility in all this. He sidelined the General Staff, who were opposed to the whole venture, to the extent that he became almost the government's sole adviser on the campaign. It took the civilians some time to conclude that Kitchener was not the all-knowing authority on the east that he continually claimed. They were then caught in a trap of having a figure who was immensely popular with the public but with feet of clay. It was fortunate that in the end it was Kitchener who authorized the evacuation. Had he not reached that conclusion it is doubtful whether the civilian leadership would have overruled him.

Once more we know little about the impact of the Turkish civilian leadership on operations. Enver Pasha certainly ordered on more than one occasion that the Allies be pushed back to the sea, when such actions had little chance of success. However, he often had the agreement of his local commanders for such operations. There was also the imperative, as the French could have testified, to remove an invader from the homeland. It would have been politically unacceptable to remain on the defensive throughout the campaign, even though this might have been the most prudent course of action.

* * *

It is time to turn to the 'terrible ifs' (the phrase is Churchill's) that have
plagued the historiography of the campaign for so long. In brief the main
'ifs' are these: What would have happened *if* the fleet had persevered after
18 March? What would have happened *if* the Sari Bair Ridge had been
captured in August? What would have occurred *if* the fleet had broken
through to Constantinople? And finally, what would have followed *if*
Turkey had been knocked out of the war?

The first two of these have already been dealt with and it is only necessary here to summarize the conclusions. If the fleet had persisted after
18 March nothing would have resulted. The Turkish guns still had sufficient
ammunition but the main point is that the British had no method of
dealing with the real obstacle in the Straits: the minefield. As for the capture
of Sari Bair in August, nothing would have followed from that either.
Hamilton and Birdwood had no reserves to send across the Peninsula, even
had that proved possible. All British reserves had been landed at Suvla Bay.
There were no further prospects on offer even if the ridge had fallen.

The next matter cannot be dismissed with the same dispatch. What
would have followed if, against the odds, the fleet or a portion of it had
broken through to Constantinople? The answer must remain speculative
but it is by no means certain that de Robeck's ships would have been left
unopposed to threaten the capital. The Turks had certainly made plans to
attack the fleet as it passed Nagara Point. They hoped that the British ships
would approach in a single line, which would have enabled the *Goeben* or
other craft to attack them one at a time.[3] Moreover, if no dreadnought had
been present it is possible that the *Goeben* might have wrought considerable havoc on the pre-dreadnoughts before weight of numbers told. Nor
would the Turkish fleet have been the last of de Robeck's problems, for the
Turks had placed batteries of guns on the Princess Islands past which the
fleet would have to sail.[4] Furthermore, Constantinople was defended by
five batteries of guns capable of inflicting damage on the fleet.[5]

Of course the optimists among the British thought that such impedi-
ments to the progress of the fleet were unlikely to occur because the
approach of the armada would spark some kind of coup or revolution in
the Turkish capital. It is difficult to find hard evidence to support this view.
The American ambassador in his memoirs mentions the exodus of women
and children from the city, as well as most of the diplomatic corps, the gold
reserves, the archives and many civil servants.[6] The Director of Naval

Intelligence, Admiral 'Blinker' Hall, drew the same conclusions as Morganthau in his evidence to the Dardanelles Commission.[7] But none of these moves signified an impending revolution. These were merely wise precautions to place persons and property out of harm's way. Similar precautions were in fact taken by the French in 1914, and no one has suggested that these moves were the preliminary to seeking an armistice or to surrender.

There is, however, evidence that the Turks intended to defend their capital. Trenches were dug in the city and additional artillery was brought forward to protect it.[8] Moreover, Constantinople was in military hands and there is no evidence to suggest that the army leadership was about to desert Enver and the Young Turk government.

We must now take the next step and ask what might have happened if Constantinople had surrendered. There is no doubt that the political leadership in Britain and France expected that a Balkan bloc would be immediately formed. Churchill sums up the argument most succinctly:

> The whole of the forces of the Balkan confederation [which he estimates at just over 1 million men] could then have been directed against the underside of Austria in the following year [and that this] must have involved the downfall of Austria and Turkey and the speedy victorious termination of the war.[9]

To reiterate, there is no evidence that Turkey would have been out of the war even had Constantinople fallen. In all likelihood the Turks would have continued to fight from Anatolia. However, the interesting question is the prospect of a Balkan coalition and the state of their armies in late 1915 or early 1916.

The first problem is that in adding up the Serbian, Greek, Bulgarian and Rumanian armies, observers such as Churchill take no account of how armies with no common language and equipment could have been combined in an efficient way. Moreover, the internecine hatreds of the Balkan states for each other would not have made the traverse of, say, Bulgarian armies across Serbia an easy matter to arrange. There were formidable difficulties over communications as well. There were only two railway lines linking the Balkans with Austria in 1915 and it is certain that these narrow-gauge links would have proved insufficient to supply armies of the size suggested.

Then there is the state of these armies to consider. The Rumanian army may be taken as an example. In 1914 this army had little modern artillery and was particularly deficient in heavy pieces. What they had was pulled by oxen because of the shortages of tractors and horses. Machine guns were in very short supply, eight divisions of the Rumanian army having none at all. The Rumanians had ammunition for only two months of heavy fighting, and one shell factory which delivered two shells per day. They had no gas, virtually no aircraft and no equipment such as trench mortars.[10]

There is no reason to believe that the other Balkan armies were in any better condition. The Greek army was in the process of changing much of its equipment and in 1914 was not in a fit state to take the field. The Greeks had no armaments industry and were looking to the major powers to re-equip them. That prospect vanished at the outbreak of war when the major powers found that they had insufficient equipment for their own forces.[11]

These then were the armies that Churchill and others expected to take on and defeat the armies of Austria–Hungary and Germany. It seems certain that the Austrians alone would have had the capacity to deal with this motley array. If by mischance they had been forced back, the Germans would have rushed to their aid. The issue would then have been beyond doubt.

Any Balkan alliance then was probably chimerical, but even if one had been formed and their armies placed in the field their prospects were dismal. More likely is that no such alliance would ever have been formed even if Constantinople had fallen.

Indeed, this investigation lays bare the fallacy behind the entire Gallipoli adventure. Turkey and the Balkan states were but minor players in the war. Rather than prove an accretion of strength to either side, they would certainly have become a burden or rapidly exited the war as Rumania did when it was attacked by Germany in 1916. The great engine of the war from the point of view of the Central Powers was the German army, and it happened to be on the Western and Eastern Fronts. As far as Britain and France were concerned, they had to defeat the Germans in the west or lose the war. In this sense there was no way around. The defeat of Turkey in 1915 would have saved temporarily the lives that were lost in the Palestinian and Mesopotamian campaigns from 1916 to 1918. But had Turkey fallen in 1915, those troops would have been transferred to the killing fields of the Western Front. How many would have survived this ordeal is speculative, but it seems certain that the overall death toll might well have been higher than it was.

All this leads to an unwelcome conclusion about Gallipoli and the Dardanelles. Despite the bravery of the Allied troops who fought there, the campaign was fought in vain. It did not shorten the war by a single day, nor in reality did it ever offer that prospect. As Churchill said (and then promptly forgot), 'Germany is the foe & it is bad war to seek cheaper victories'. Gallipoli was certainly bad war. As it happened, it did not even offer a cheaper victory or in the end any kind of victory. But even if it had, the downfall of Turkey was of no relevance to the deadly contest being played out on the Western Front.

Notes

Introduction

1. For examples of this type of history one only need turn to the work of C.E.W. Bean, Winston Churchill, Alan Moorehead, John North and (perhaps surprisingly) Robert Rhodes James. Details of these books can be found in the bibliography.
2. To cite just a few examples: there is the estimable book by Jenny Macleod, *Reconsidering Gallipoli* (Manchester: Manchester University Press, 2004); Frank Glen, *Bowler of Gallipoli* (Canberra: Army History Unit, 2004); *Gallipoli: Our Last Man Standing: The Extraordinary Life of Alec Campbell* (London: John Wiley, 2003); and, from the Turkish side, Mehmed Fasih, *Gallipoli 1915: Bloody Ridge (Lone Pine) Diary of Lt. Mehmed Fasih 5th Ottoman Imperial Army Gallipoli 1915* (Istanbul: Denizler Kitabevi, 1997).

Chapter 1: The Origins of the Naval Offensive

1. A clear exposition of the first part of Churchill's plan can be found in a memorandum written on 2/12/14 in Admiralty Papers, ADM 137/452, National Archives, Kew. There are numerous other examples. The Baltic section of the plan can be found in a memorandum by Churchill on 19/8/14. See *Winston S. Churchill, vol. 3, Companion, Part I, Documents, July 1914—April 1915*, ed. Martin Gilbert (London: Heinemann, 1972), pp. 45–6. (Hereafter *CV3*.)
2. Lord Fisher, 'On the possibility of using our Command of the Sea to influence more drastically the Military Situation on the Continent', ADM 116/3454.
3. Fisher to Churchill 21/12/14, *CV3*, pp. 322–3.
4. Lady Richmond Diary 5/1/15, Richmond Papers, RIC 1/17, National Maritime Museum, Greenwich
5. Churchill to French 9/12/14, *CV3*, p. 300.
6. War Council Minutes 7/1/15, Cabinet Papers, CAB 42/1/11, National Archives, Kew.
7. Fisher to Churchill 9/1/15, *CV3*, p. 399.

8. Ibid.
9. Fisher wanted one of the admirals responsible for the escape of the German ships, Sir Berkeley Milne, shot. Henceforth he addressed him as Sir Berkeley Goeben, the name of the German battlecruiser.
10. Churchill to Sir Charles Douglas (CIGS) 1/9/14, *CV3*, p. 75.
11. Callwell memorandum 3/9/14, in ibid., pp. 81–2.
12. See T.M. Cunninghame [British Military Attaché in Athens in 1914], 'The Greek Army and the Dardanelles', *National Review*, vol. 92, September 1928, p. 124.
13. War Council minutes 25/11/14, CAB 42/1/4.
14. Ibid.
15. Asquith to Venetia Stanley 5/12/14, *CV3*, p. 297.
16. See footnote 24.
17. Valentine Fleming to Churchill, November 1914, *CV3*, pp. 272–3.
18. Churchill to Clementine Churchill 23/11/14, in ibid., p. 274.
19. Lt-Col Hankey memorandum 28/12/14, in ibid., pp. 337–43.
20. Ibid.
21. Churchill to Asquith 29/12/14, in ibid., pp. 343–5.
22. Ibid.
23. Lloyd George memorandum 31/12/14, in ibid., pp. 350–6.
24. Lloyd George memorandum 31/12/14.
25. Fisher to Hankey 2/1/15, Hankey Papers, CAB 63/4, National Archives, Kew.
26. Fisher to Churchill 3/1/15, *CV3*, pp. 367–8. This last exhortation was strange. Fisher disliked Sturdee, whom he blamed for allowing a German cruiser to escape at the recent Battle of the Falklands in November 1914.
27. Fisher to Churchill 21/12/14, in ibid., pp. 322–3.
28. Sir George Buchanan to Sir Edward Grey 1/1/15, in ibid., pp. 359–60.
29. Kitchener sent two letters to Churchill on 2/1/15 to this effect, in ibid., p. 360 and pp. 360–1.
30. Note by Greene, August 1916, Greene Papers, GEE/11, National Maritime Museum, Greenwich.
31. Ibid.
32. Churchill to Admiral Carden 3/1/15, *CV3*, p. 367.
33. Churchill to Jellicoe 4/1/15, in ibid., pp. 368–9.
34. Churchill to Fisher 4/1/15, in ibid., pp. 370–1.
35. Fisher to Churchill 4/1/15, in ibid., pp. 373–4.
36. Richmond Diary 19/1/15, RIC 1/9.
37. Jackson memorandum 5/1/15, *CV3*, pp. 376–7.
38. Carden to Churchill 5/1/15 in ibid., p. 380.
39. Churchill to Carden 6/1/15, in ibid., p. 381.
40. War Council Minutes 7/1/15, CAB 42/1/11.
41. All quotations above come from the War Council Minutes 8/1/15, CAB 42/1/12.
42. Jellicoe to Churchill 8/1/15, *CV3*, pp. 397–8, and Fisher to Churchill 9/1/15, in ibid., pp. 399–400.
43. Carden to Churchill 11/1/15, in ibid., pp. 405–6.
44. All quotations above are taken from the War Council Minutes 13/1/15, CAB 42/1/16. Asquith's admission of where his attention lay is to be found in a letter to Venetia Stanley of 13 January in *CV3*, p. 412.

Chapter 2: From Ships to Troops

1. Churchill to Fisher and Oliver 13/1/15, *CV3*, pp.412–13.
2. Ibid. Emphasis added.

3. Lady Richmond Diary 14/1/15, Richmond Papers, RIC 1/17, National Maritime Museum, Greenwich.
4. Ibid., 20/1/15.
5. Oliver, Draft Autobiography, p. 147, Oliver Papers, OLV/12, National Maritime Museum, Greenwich.
6. Jackson memorandum 5/1/15, *CV3*, pp. 376–7.
7. 'REMARKS ON VICE-ADMIRAL CARDEN'S PROPOSALS AS TO OPERATIONS IN DARDANELLES,' *CV3*, pp. 419–21.
8. At the Dardanelles Inquiry, Jackson was no clearer. When asked whether he endorsed the 'ships alone' plan he replied: 'Oh, dear no'. But when the Commissioner probed further and asked, 'Admiral Carden said it would be impossible to rush the Dardanelles, but I understand he thought you might get through by attacking the forts one by one. Was not that your view?', Jackson replied 'Yes; possibly'. See Dardanelles Commission Evidence Q2049 to Q2057, Cabinet Papers, CAB 19/33, National Archives, Kew.
9. Fisher to Oliver 12/1/15, *CV3*, pp. 406–7.
10. Fisher to Tyrell 12/1/15, quoted in ibid., p. 407, note 1.
11. Churchill to Carden 15/1/15, *CV3*, pp. 415–16.
12. Churchill to the Comte de Sainte-Seine (the French Naval Minister) 16/1/15, in ibid., pp. 421–2.
13. Churchill to Grand Duke Nicholas 19/1/15, in ibid., pp. 430–1; Buchanan to Grey 25/1/15, in ibid., pp. 455–6.
14. Oliver memorandum 25/1/15, and memorandum 2/2/15, in ibid, pp 450–1 and 478–80 respectively.
15. Richmond to Leveson 3/2/15, RIC 1/12.
16. Fisher to Churchill 18/1/15, *CV3*, p. 428.
17. Fisher to Churchill 20/1/15, Churchill Papers 13/65, Churchill College, Cambridge.
18. See their exchange or correspondence on 20/1/15 in *CV3*, pp. 433–5.
19. Fisher to Jellicoe 19/1/15, *CV3*, pp. 429–30.
20. Fisher's evidence to the Dardanelles Commission, Q3124–3148, CAB 19/33. The statement (unlike much of Fisher's evidence) has a ring of truth.
21. Asquith to Venetia Stanley 20/1/15, *CV3*, pp. 431–2.
22. Fisher's memorandum can be found in ibid., pp. 452–4.
23. Ibid.
24. This might have reflected an 'orientalist' view of the Turks held by Churchill and his colleagues. On the other hand it could merely have been a misjudgement about the grip on the army and therefore on the capital which the Young Turk government possessed. For 'orientalism' see Edward Said, *Orientalism* (London: Penguin, 1977).
25. Churchill to Fisher 26/1/15, *CV3*, p. 458.
26. Fisher to Churchill 28/1/15, in ibid., p. 460.
27. Fisher to Asquith 28/1/15, in ibid., p. 461.
28. War Council Minutes 28/1/15, in ibid., pp. 463–70.
29. War Council Minutes 28/1//15, CAB 42/1/26.
30. Fisher to Churchill 29/1/15, *CV3*, p. 471.
31. Oliver memorandum 2/2/15, in ibid., pp. 478–80.
32. Sir Henry Jackson, 'ATTACK ON CONSTANTINOPLE', 13/2/15, *CV3*, pp. 506–12.
33. See this document in the Richmond Papers, RIC 1/9.
34. Hankey to Balfour 13/2/15, *CV3*, p. 500.
35. Asquith to Venetia Stanley 13/2/15, in ibid., pp. 512–13.
36. Richmond had written this paper on 14 February and shown it to Fisher who thought it 'EXCELLENT'. See *CV3*, p. 513 and note 3.
37. War Council Conclusions 16/2/15, *CV3*, p. 516. Hankey was not present at this meeting. Asquith communicated the conclusions to him later and Hankey thought them of sufficient importance to record them.

38. 'Report of the Committee Appointed to Investigate the Attacks Delivered on and the Enemy Defences of the Dardanelles Straits', London, Naval Staff Gunnery Division, 1921, in AWM 124, Chapter 2, pp. 3–20, Australian War Memorial, Canberra. (Hereafter Mitchell Committee Report.)
39. War Council Minutes 19/2/15, CAB 42/1/36.
40. Ibid.
41. Ibid.
42. 'The Dardanelles Operations', undated note by the Director of Military Operations (DMO) in War Office Papers, WO 106/1538, National Archives, Kew.
43. Ibid. After the war the official historian, Cecil Aspinall-Oglander, saw this memorandum and littered its margins with comments such as 'Ye Gods!' or '!!'. He did not, however, feel the need to cite it in his history.

Chapter 3: The Worst-Laid Plans

1. Mitchell Committee Report, Chapter 2, pp. 3–4.
2. Details from the Mitchell Committee Report, pp. 3–19.
3. Carden to the Admiralty 11/1/15, *CV3*, pp. 405–6.
4. Jackson's paper of 15/1/15 is to be found in *CV3*, pp. 419–21; Oliver's memorandum of 25/1/15 is on pp. 450–1; Oliver's memorandum of 2/2/15 is on pp. 478–80 and his operations orders to Carden on pp. 485–90; Jackson's second paper is on pp. 506–12.
5. Mitchell Committee Report, p. 78.
6. Mitchell Committee Report, p. 51.
7. Oliver memorandum 2/2/15, *CV3*, pp. 478–9.

Chapter 4: The Rise and Fall of the Naval Attack

1. De Robeck to Admiral Arthur Limpus 3/6/15, Admiral Limpus Papers, LIM 66, National Maritime Museum, Greenwich.
2. Wemyss to Limpus 4/6/15, in ibid.
3. Sir Julian Corbett, *Naval Operations, vol. 2* (London: Green, 1921), p. 145. (Hereafter *Naval Operations V2*.)
4. Mitchell Committee Report, pp. 34–5.
5. Mitchell Committee Report, p. 34.
6. Admiral Carden, 'Narrative of Events 19th February to 16th March', Admiralty Papers, ADM 137/38, National Archives, Kew.
7. Carden to the Admiralty 3/2/15, ADM 137/96.
8. I. W. Gibson Diary 20/2/15, uncatalogued, Imperial War Museum (IWM), London.
9. Ibid., 24/2/15.
10. Mitchell Committee Report, pp. 35–6.
11. Quoted in Corbett, *Naval Operations V2*, p. 160. Something seems to have got lost in the translation of this passage.
12. Mitchell Committee Report, pp. 38–41.
13. Ibid.
14. Ibid., p. 42.
15. Gibson Diary 26/2/15. He wrote '45 knots' in his diary but it is obvious that he meant degrees.
16. Ibid.
17. The figures come from the Mitchell Committee Report, pp. 44–55.
18. Mitchell Committee Report, pp. 503–10.
19. Carden, 'Orders for the forcing of the Dardanelles by the Allied Squadron', ADM 137/38.

20. A. T. Stewart and C. J. E. Peshall, *The Immortal Gamble* (London: A & C Black, 1917), p.17, and Note by Admiral de Robeck on *Prince George*'s Report 3/3/15, ADM 137/38.
21. Churchill to Carden 11/3/15, *CV3*, pp. 677–8.
22. See Mitchell Committee Report, pp. 51–9.
23. See J. H. Godfrey Papers, 69/33/1, Churchill College, Cambridge, and Notes by Captain P. Dent in War Office Papers, WO 95/4263, National Archives, Kew.
24. Ibid.
25. Mitchell Committee Report, p. 60.
26. Martin Gilbert, *Winston S. Churchill vol. 3 1914–1916* (London: Heinemann, 1971), p. 348.
27. Account of Lt D. H. Hepburn, P232, Imperial War Museum, London.
28. De Robeck's Report 24/3/15, Admiral de Robeck Papers 4/4, Churchill College, Cambridge.
29. De Robeck to General Ian Hamilton 19/3/15, Hamilton Papers 5/4, Liddell Hart Centre, King's College, London.
30. For a full discussion of this question which details all the estimates of Turkish ammunition supply, see Robin Prior, *Churchill's 'World Crisis' as History* (London: Croom Helm, 1983), pp. 97–9.

Chapter 5: No Going Back

1. Fisher to Hankey 19/2/15, Cabinet Papers, Hankey Papers, CAB 63/4, National Archives, Kew.
2. Lloyd George, 'Some Further Considerations on the Conduct of the War', 22/2/15, CAB 42/1/39.
3. Cabinet memorandum by Churchill 23/2/15, CAB 37/124/43.
4. War Council Minutes 24/2/15, CAB 42/1/42. All subsequent quotations from this meeting are from this source.
5. War Council Minutes 26/2/15, CAB 42/1/47.
6. The diplomatic traffic reveals that Bulgaria, Greece and Italy had been most impressed by Carden's activities. No doubt these countries were fairly uninformed on the actual details of the naval attack.
7. Sir Frances Elliot (British Minister in Athens) to Grey 1/3/15, *CV3*, p. 603.
8. Lady Richmond Diary 1/3/15, Richmond Papers, RIC 1/7, National Maritime Museum, Greenwich.
9. Ibid., 4/3/15.
10. Hamilton to his son 1/3/15, Hamilton Papers HTN/120, National Maritime Museum, Greenwich.
11. Fisher to Beatty 20/2/15, Beatty Papers, National Maritime Museum, Greenwich. Was Beatty aware that it had been Fisher who had added the *Queen Elizabeth* to the bombardment fleet?
12. Fisher to Jellicoe 28/2/15 in A. Marder (ed.), *Fear God and Dreadnought: The Correspondence of Admiral of the Fleet Lord Fisher of Kilverstone*, vol. 3 (London: Jonathan Cape, 1959), pp. 161–2.
13. For Hankey's Paper, see CAB 42/2/1.
14. War Council Minutes 3/3/15, CAB 42/2/3. All subsequent quotations from this meeting are from this source.
15. One can imagine a headline, 'Turkish Army Besieges Vienna', and the appeal that would have had to the former Turkish colonies in the Balkans.
16. Churchill to Kitchener 4/3/15, Kitchener Papers, NA 30/57/61, National Archives, Kew.
17. For Bulgaria see Bax-Ironside to Grey 4/3/15 and 10/3/15 in Admiralty Papers, ADM

137/109 and ADM 116/1336, National Archives, Kew. For Rumania there is a good account in Lt-Col H.D. Napier, *The Experiences of a Military Attaché in the Balkans* (London: Dranes, 1924), p. 126. For anti-Entente moves by the Balkan states, see Elliot to Grey 4/3/15 in Foreign Office Papers, FO 371/2243, National Archives, Kew.

18. Birdwood to Kitchener 5/3/15, Birdwood Papers, DRL 419/10/17, Australian War Memorial (AWM), Canberra.
19. Maxwell to Fitzgerald (Kitchener's Military Secretary) 8/3/15, Kitchener Papers, NA 30/57/61.
20. De Robeck, 'Appreciation of present position in Dardanelles and proposals for future operations', 9/3/15, Godfrey Papers, 69/33/1, Churchill College, Cambridge.
21. Carden to the Admiralty 10/3/15, ADM 137/1089.
22. War Council Minutes 10/3/15, CAB 42/2/5.
23. Ibid.
24. Dardanelles Commission, Hamilton's Evidence, CAB 19/33.
25. 'Instructions For The General Officer Commanding-in-Chief The Mediterranean Expeditionary Force 13/3/15', *CV3*, pp. 684–6.
26. C.F. Aspinall-Oglander, *Military Operations: Gallipoli*, vol. 1 (London: Heinemann, 1929), pp. 101–02. (Hereafter, Aspinall-Oglander, *Gallipoli V1*.)
27. Hamilton to Kitchener 19/3/15, *CV3*, p. 710.
28. Orlo Williams Diary 18/3/15, Williams Papers, 69/78/1, Imperial War Museum, London.
29. Kitchener to Hamilton 19/3/15, Hamilton Papers, 15/17, Liddell Hart Centre, King's College, London.
30. Lord Wester-Wemyss, Admiral of the Fleet, *The Navy in the Dardanelles Campaign* (London: Hodder & Stoughton, 1924), p. 43. For the captains, see 'Meeting of Captains 19/3/15', de Robeck Papers, 4/5, Churchill College, Cambridge.
31. Admiral of the Fleet Baron Keyes, *The Naval Memoirs of Admiral of the Fleet Sir Roger Keyes: The Narrow Seas to the Dardanelles 1910–1915*, vol. 2 (London: Thornton Butterworth, 1934), p. 186.
32. War Council Minutes 19/3/15, CAB 42/2/14.
33. Churchill to de Robeck 23/3/15 [not sent], *CV3*, pp. 724–6.
34. For this see the documents in *CV3*, p. 788.
35. De Robeck to Churchill 27/3/15, ADM 116/1348.
36. Churchill to de Robeck 27/3/15, *CV3*, p. 753–4.
37. Actually, the Cabinet was the body that should have made the final decision on these matters. However, the Cabinet had long given up strategic decision making. As will be shown, they were to make a late intervention in the Gallipoli campaign.

Chapter 6: The Military Plan

1. This at any rate was the experience of the author in more recent times.
2. The description of the topography of the Gallipoli Peninsula is taken from the Mitchell Committee Report and from 'The Defences of Constantinople', a document prepared by the General Staff of the War Office in 1909. It can be found in War Office Papers, WO 32/2333, National Archives, Kew.
3. Edward E. Erickson, *Ordered to Die: A History of the Ottoman Army in the First World War* (Westport, Conn.: Greenwood, 2001), p. 7. Much of the information on the Turkish army that follows comes from this invaluable source.
4. Ibid., pp. 76–7.
5. Mitchell Committee Report, pp. 153–4.
6. Captain F.A. Rayfield, 'Notes on the Turkish Army in 1914', p. 4, Rayfield Papers 69/61/5, Imperial War Museum, London. It is difficult to describe these papers, but in essence they consist of an enormous manuscript history (unfinished) of the Gallipoli campaign in addition to some very useful source material which Rayfield gathered for his history.

7. Ibid., pp. 5 and 6.
8. Rayfield claims this, as does von Sanders in his memoirs.
9. Erickson, *Ordered to Die*, pp. 82–3.
10. Ibid., p. 83.
11. Otto Liman von Sanders, *Five Years in Turkey* (London: Baillière, Tindall & Cox), 1928), p. 55.
12. Peter Chasseaud and Peter Doyle, *Grasping Gallipoli: Terrain, Maps and the Failure at the Dardanelles, 1915* (Staplehurst: Spellmont, 2005), p. 157. This important book is an essential reference for any future work on Gallipoli and I am grateful to the authors for their assiduous scholarship, even if I cannot agree (as will be seen later) with some of their conclusions.
13. Hamilton to Kitchener in GHQ War Diary 18/4/15, WO 95/4264.
14. GHQ Intelligence Summary 29/3/15, WO 157/647.
15. This was expressed in a letter to Birdwood on 3/4/15. See Birdwood Papers, Australian War Memorial, DRL 419/10/7, Box 209, Canberra, but similar sentiments were expressed in a letter to Hamilton just before the landing. See Maxwell to Hamilton 25/4/15, Hamilton Papers, 5/12, Liddell Hart Centre, King's College, London.
16. Appreciation by General Paris 19/3/15, Hamilton Papers, 17/7/31.
17. Ibid.
18. Aspinall's Appreciation 23/3/15, in ibid., 17/15/2.
19. Ibid.
20. Braithwaite's Appreciation 23/3/15, in ibid., 17/15/2.
21. Birdwood to Kitchener 4/3/15, *CV3*, p. 638.
22. Birdwood to Hamilton 1/4/15, Birdwood Papers, DRL 419/10/7, Box 209.
23. Hunter-Weston to Hamilton 30/3/15, Hamilton Papers 17/7/30.
24. Braithwaite to Fitzgerald 10/4/15, Kitchener Papers 30/57/61, National Archives, Kew.
25. Lord Kitchener's Instructions to Sir Ian Hamilton 13/3/15, quoted in *Military Operations: V1, Gallipoli 1, Maps and Appendices*, Appendix 1, p. 1 (hereafter, *Gallipoli Maps and Appendices V1*.)
26. Dardanelles Commission, Hamilton's Evidence 13/10/16, Q4385–6, Cabinet Papers, CAB 19/33, National Archives, Kew.
27. Hamilton to Kitchener 30/3/15, Hamilton Papers, 5/1.
28. Hamilton to Kitchener 4/3/15, Kitchener Papers, NA 30/57/61.
29. Hamilton, Force Order No. 1, *Gallipoli Maps and Appendices V1*, Appendix 3, pp. 7–11.
30. All these instructions are to be found in 'Instructions for Helles Covering Force', 19/4/15, in ibid., Appendix 4, pp. 12–15, and 'Instructions to GOC A&NZ Army Corps', 13/4/15, in ibid., Appendix 5, pp. 16–18.
31. Hamilton to Kitchener 15/4/15, Kitchener Papers, NA 30/57/61.
32. See this note by Hamilton in *Gallipoli Maps and Appendices V1*, Appendix 13, pp. 34–6.

Chapter 7: Bodies Everywhere: The Helles Landings

1. See Diagram of Helles Landing in Aspinall-Oglander, *Gallipoli V1*, sketch opposite p. 217.
2. 29 Division, Operation Order No. 1, in *Gallipoli Maps and Appendices V1*, Appendix 17, pp. 49–52.
3. See 29 Division, Operation Order No. 1 and 'Instructions for the Helles Covering Force' in ibid., Appendix 18.
4. See Lt-Col G.E. Matthews' evidence to the Dardanelles Commission 16/2/17, Q18,674, Cabinet Papers, CAB 19/33, National Archives, Kew.
5. All these details are taken from Aspinall-Oglander, *Gallipoli V1*.
6. Orders Issued by the Naval Commander-in-Chief 12/4/15, in *Gallipoli Maps and Appendices V1*, Appendix 7, pp. 21–3.

7. Ibid. Emphasis added.
8. See Dardanelles Commission Evidence—Statement by Captain H.P. Douglas, R.N. Hydrographic Department, CAB 19/32.
9. 'The Landing from the "River Clyde" at V. Beach April 25th 1915 By A Company Commander In The 1st Royal Munster Fusiliers' (Captain G.W. Geddes), 86 Brigade War Diary April 1915, War Office Papers, WO 95/4310, National Archives, Kew.
10. Mitchell Committee Report, p. 169.
11. Ibid., p. 162.
12. Turkish General Staff, *A Brief History of the Canakkale Campaign in the First World War (June 1914–January 1916)* (Ankara: Turkish General Staff Printing House, 2004), p. 105. (Hereafter *Turkish Staff History*.)
13. 2 South Wales Borderers War Diary 25/4/15, WO 95/4311.
14. *Turkish Staff History*, p. 105.
15. 2 South Wales Borderers War Diary 25/4/15, WO 95/4311.
16. Ibid.
17. Ibid.
18. 1 King's Own Scottish Borderers War Diary 25/4/15, WO 95/4311.
19. Aspinall-Oglander, *Gallipoli V1*, p. 205. Tim Travers states that an entire company of the KOSB actually entered Krithia. See his *Gallipoli 1915* (Stroud, Gloucestershire: Tempus, 2001), p. 59.
20. Report by Lt-Col G.E. Matthews, Commander Plymouth Battalion 27/4/15, GHQ War Diary, WO 95/4264.
21. Ibid. Colonel Koe of the KOSB, who had been too ill to attend briefing sessions before the battle, imagined that he was in charge of the Y Beach force. He certainly acted as if this was the case. He claimed to have ordered the withdrawal to the cliff face and sent a message to X Beach to this effect. The message was not acknowledged by anyone at X. Koe was mortally wounded during the night and died the next day. See Aspinall-Oglander, *Gallipoli V1*, pp. 202, 206 and 208.
22. *Turkish Staff History*, pp. 104–5.
23. Ibid., p. 107.
24. This account is based on the *Turkish Staff History*, p. 109, and Aspinall-Oglander, *Gallipoli V1*, pp. 207–8.
25. This account is based on Matthews' Report and his evidence to the Dardanelles Commission 16/2/17, CAB 19/33. In particular, see his evidence between Q 18,674 and 18,685, and Aspinall-Oglander, *Gallipoli V1*, pp. 208–10.
26. Aspinall-Oglander makes these claims in *Gallipoli V1*, pp. 214–15.
27. '29th Division Order for Landing' and '29 Division Instructions for the Helles Covering Force', *Gallipoli Appendices V1*, Appendices 17 and 18.
28. Much is made of this in a letter from a 29 Division gunner, Brigadier Alan Thomson, to the historian John North, in the Lockyer Papers, Imperial War Museum, London, 75/56/1. H.C. Lockyer was the captain of the *Implacable* and had done a fine job in giving such close support to the troops. He was not to know that the enemy consisted only of some piquets.
29. The *Turkish Staff History* says 9 (p. 103), Aspinall-Oglander says 12, *Gallipoli V1*, p. 225.
30. This account is pieced together from the *Turkish Staff History*, pp. 103 and 107, which unfortunately is incorrect in the timings given for most attacks; 'Report on Landing of 29th Division in the Neighbourhood of Cape Helles', 29 Division War Diary, WO 95/4304; 87 Brigade War Diary 25/4/15, WO 95/4311, and a translation of a very valuable Turkish account, 'The Gallant 3rd Bn. 26th Regiment in the Operations at Tekke Burnu', summarized by Captain M. Yurdakular in the Rayfield Papers, 69/61/7, Imperial War Museum, London.
31. Aspinall-Oglander, *Gallipoli V1*, p. 225.
32. 1 Borders War Diary 25/4/15, WO 95/4311.

33. 1 Royal Inniskilling Fusiliers War Diary 25/4/15, WO 95/4311.
34. See the account in 'The Gallant 3rd Bn.' in the Rayfield Papers for this view.
35. 29 Division 'Report on Landing.'
36. 'Notes of landing "W" Beach—25th April 1915' by Major Striedeger in GHQ War Diary April 1915, WO 95/4304.
37. Mitchell Committee Report, p. 155.
38. Ibid., p. 156.
39. In general, Turkish accounts do not mention that there were machine guns at Seddelbahr. However, the clinical precision with which the British were cut down and the high casualty rate indicate that machine guns were present. Some eyewitnesses such as Captain Geddes were able to locate the exact position from where these guns were firing.
40. Aspinall-Oglander, *Gallipoli V1*, p. 232.
41. Mitchell Committee Report, p. 156.
42. Ibid.
43. Captain Geddes, 'The Landing of the River Clyde'.
44. Yurdakular, 'Gallant 3rd Bn'.
45. 88 Brigade War Diary 25/4/15, WO 95/4312.
46. Aspinall-Oglander, *Gallipoli V1*, p. 238. I have not been able to trace the source of this signal.
47. Ibid.
48. Mitchell Committee Report, p. 156. It is difficult to credit that the *Queen Elizabeth* fired just 9 of its 15-inch shells during the whole of 25 April.
49. GHQ War Diary 25/4/15, WO 95/4302.
50. See *Turkish Staff History*, p. 101 and Map 26, and Yurdakular, 'Gallant 3rd Bn'.
51. 'Dardanelles' by GSO 3, 29 Division, CAB 45/259. I am grateful to Dr Elizabeth Greenhalgh for this reference. The staff officer is probably incorrect about the time at which the bombardment started, although he might be referring to the moment the *Euryalis* opened fire.
52. Mitchell Committee Report, pp. 157–8.
53. 'Dardanelles' by GSO 3, 29 Division Staff Officer.
54. Yurdakular, 'Gallant 3rd Bn'.
55. Most of this narrative comes from 86 Brigade Report 25/4/15 in their War Diary, WO 95/4310.
56. 86 Brigade War Diary 25/5/15 (note that Guezji Baba is mistakenly called Hill 141 throughout) and 4 Worcesters War Diary 25/4/15, WO 95/4312.
57. Yurdakular, 'Gallant 3rd Bn'.
58. Mitchell Committee Report, p. 156.
59. *Turkish Staff History*, pp. 110–12 and 29 Division Report.
60. Ibid.
61. Establishing exact casualty figures for a particular battle is fraught with difficulty. The British kept them by the month and later by the week. We know, however, that Hamilton required 3,800 reinforcements on 27 April (Hamilton to War Office 28/4/15, Hamilton Papers 15/17) and that British casualties for the whole of April were 4,300. The Turkish figure for 3/26 Company comes from Yurdakular; other casualties are what I consider to be a reasonable estimate.

Chapter 8: A Perfect Hail of Bullets: Landing and Consolidation at Anzac

1. Birdwood, 'Operation Order No 1' 17/4/15, *Gallipoli Maps and Appendices V1*, Appendix 14, pp. 37–41.
2. Ibid.
3. Thursby, 'Orders for 2nd Squadron' 10/4/15, in Mitchell Committee Report, p. 129. Emphasis added.

4. Birdwood, 'Operation Order No 1', *Gallipoli Maps and Appendices V1*, Appendix 14, pp. 37–41.
5. Birdwood, Instructions to GOC 1 Australian Division, in ibid., Appendix 15, pp. 42–3.
6. 3 Brigade Orders, 3 Brigade War Diary, AWM 4/23/3/1, Australian War Memorial, Canberra.
7. See Admiralty Papers, ADM 116/1434, National Archives, Kew for Thursby's alteration.
8. Birdwood to Hamilton 28/4/15, Cabinet Papers, CAB 45/233, National Archives, Kew.
9. See their evidence in CAB 19/33.
10. Thursby, 'Orders for 2nd Squadron' 10/4/15, pp. 124–32.
11. Ibid.
12. 2 Australian Brigade, 'Operation Order No. 5' 21/4/15, Anzac Corps War Diary April 1915, Australian War Memorial AWM 4/1/25/1, Part 7, Canberra.
13. 'General Birdwood's Instructions to GOC 1st Australian Division' 18/4/15, *Gallipoli Maps and Appendices V1*, Appendix 15, pp. 42–3.
14. Anzac Corps War Diary 25/4/15, AWM 4/1/25/1, Part 2.
15. 10 Battalion War Diary 25/4/15, War Office Papers, WO 95/4344, National Archives, Kew.
16. Anzac Corps War Diary 25/4/15, AWM 4/1/25/1, Part 2. The author can attest that the stones off Anzac Cove are still slimy. This makes standing difficult even when unencumbered with rifle and pack.
17. Robert Rhodes James, *Gallipoli* (London: Batsford, 1965), pp. 104–7, rehearses most of the theories.
18. 10 Battalion War Diary 25/4/15, WO 95/4344; 7 Battalion War Diary 25/5/15, AWM 4/23/2/1. At 5.00 a.m. 120 men of B Company, 7 Battalion drifted north of Anzac Cove and were almost wiped out by a machine gun near Fisherman's Hut. It was probably the same gun that opposed the original landing.
19. Untitled account of the landing in the Imperial War Museum, IWM Misc 262, Box 12.
20. 3 Brigade War Diary 25/4/15, AWM 4/23/3/1.
21. 1 Australian Division Report 7/5/15, AWM 4/1/42/3, Part 2.
22. C.E.W. Bean, *The Story of Anzac: From the Outbreak of War to the End of the First Phase of the Gallipoli Campaign, May 4, 1915*, vol. 1 (Sydney: Angus & Robertson, 1942) 3rd edition, Chapters XII to XVI. (Hereafter, Bean, *Story of Anzac V1*.) The great amount of detail in Bean's account may make it daunting. His maps on pp. 256, 268, 288 and 356, however, will be found useful in illustrating how the covering force became split into the groups described above.
23. 2 Brigade War Diary 25/4/15, AWM 4/1/25/1. Note that this War Diary is to be found in the June section of this brigade's papers. In fact it consists of notes made by a regimental officer, Major Cass, and found in his haversack. They were copied 'in case the original War Diary is not found'. Apparently it never was.
24. 2 Brigade, 'Operation Order No. 5' 21/4/15, 2 Brigade War Diary AWM 4/1/25/1, Part 7.
25. Bean, *Story of Anzac V1*, p. 363.
26. Ibid., p. 360.
27. *Turkish Staff History*, pp. 69–70.
28. Ibid., p. 71.
29. See Bean, *Story of Anzac V1*, Chapters XVI and XVII, for these extremely confused events.
30. General Godley, 'Report on Operations', WO 158/600.
31. *Turkish Staff History*, pp. 71–2.
32. Wellington Battalion War Diary 25/4/15, AWM 4/35/20/1; 16 Battalion War Diary 25/4/15, AWM 4/23/33/6.
33. 15 Battalion War Diary 25/4/15, AWM 4/23/32/6.
34. 14 Battalion War Diary 25/4/15, AWM 4/23/31/7.
35. Ibid.
36. *Turkish Staff History*, p. 75.
37. Bean, *Story of Anzac V1*, pp. 452–3.

38. Anzac Corps War Diary 25/4/15.
39. Ibid.
40. Quoted in Bean, *Story of Anzac V1*, p. 458.
41. Ibid., pp. 460–1. There are many accounts of this dramatic episode but all agree on the essentials.
42. Birdwood to Hamilton 28/4/15, CAB 45/233.
43. For a discussion of the tortuous historiography of this incident, see Tim Travers, *Gallipoli 1915* (Stroud, Gloucestershire: Tempus, 2001), pp. 77–9.
44. GHQ War Diary 2/5/15.
45. The details of this operation are to be found in 15 Battalion War Diary 15/5/15, AWM 4/23/32/7.
46. *Turkish Staff History*, p. 88.
47. Ibid., pp. 89–90.
48. C.E.W. Bean, Questions put to the Turkish General Staff and their Answers, CAB 45/236.
49. H.A. Jones, *The War in the Air*, vol. 2 (London: Hamish Hamilton, 1969; reprint of 1928 edition), p. 51.
50. 14 Battalion War Diary 19/5/15, AWM 4/23/31/8.
51. Ibid.
52. Ibid.
53. 3 Battalion War Diary 19/5/15, AWM 4/23/20/1.
54. 4 Battalion War Diary 19/5/15, AWM 4/23/12/2.
55. C.E.W. Bean, *Official History of Australia in the War of 1914–1918: The Story of Anzac*, vol. 2 (Sydney: Angus & Robertson, 1928), p. 161. (Hereafter *Story of Anzac V2*.)
56. Ibid.
57. Ammunition statistics come from Anzac Corps War Diary 22/5/15.

Chapter 9: The Killing Fields of Krithia

1. This account is based on von Sanders *Five Years in Turkey* (London: Ballière, Tindall & Cox, 1928), pp. 57–64, modified by the useful account by Rayfield, 'The Landing from the Turkish Aspect', Rayfield Papers 69/61/2, Imperial War Museum, London and the *Turkish Staff History*, Chapter 5.
2. The Gendarmerie battalions were raised from the police force, which was trained along military lines in Turkey. On mobilization one third of each battalion continued to carry out police duties while the remaining two thirds were taken into the army. They were mainly composed of middle-aged men but had a reputation for steadiness. They were named for the area in which they were recruited. See Rayfield, 'Notes on the Turkish Army in 1914', Rayfield Papers 69/61/5.
3. Hamilton's views were communicated to Major S. Miles who reproduced them in his 'Notes on the Dardanelles Campaign of 1915', *The Coast Artillery Journal*, Vol. 62, 1925, p. 30.
4. 'Notes on the Landing near Cape Helles', by Brigadier-General R.A. Roper 10/5/15, 29 Division War Diary, War Office Papers, WO 95/4264, National Archives, Kew.
5. General Sir Ian Hamilton, *Gallipoli Diary*, vol. 1 (London: Edward Arnold, 1920), p. 183.
6. Translation of French Official Account, Rayfield Papers 69/61/6.
7. Aspinall-Oglander, *Gallipoli V1*, p. 283.
8. 29 Division Operation Order No. 3, 27/4/15, *Gallipoli Maps and Appendices V1*, Appendix 22, p. 60.
9. Aspinall-Oglander, *Gallipoli V1*, p. 284.
10. 87 Brigade War Diary 28/4/15, WO 95/4311.
11. Aspinall-Oglander, *Gallipoli V1*, pp. 289–91.

12. 87 Brigade War Diary 28/4/15.
13. Mitchell Committee Report, p. 175.
14. 88 Brigade War Diary 28/4/15, WO 95/4312.
15. 'Information from Colonel Carr, Worcestershire Regt, about Part played by 4/29th at Gallipoli—April 25—May 2nd.', Cabinet Papers, CAB 45/241, National Archives, Kew.
16. Ibid.
17. 86 Brigade War Diary 28/4/15.
18. Diary of GSO3, 29 Division, CAB 45/259.
19. 87 Brigade War Diary 28/4/15.
20. Diary of GSO3, 29 Division, CAB 45/259
21. Aspinall-Oglander, *Gallipoli V1*, p. 317.
22. Ibid., p. 316.
23. *Turkish Staff History*, p. 125.
24. Rayfield, 'The Turkish Counter-Offensive at Helles—1st to 4th May, 1915', Rayfield Papers 69/61/2.
25. 'Report of Operations 29th Division 1st–5th May, 29 Division War Diary, WO 95/4304; Rayfield, 'Turkish Counter-Offensive'.
26. 29 Division, 'Report or Landing'.
27. *Turkish Staff History*, p. 127; Rayfield, 'Turkish Counter-Offensive'.
28. 4 Worcesters War Diary 1/5/15, WO 95/4312.
29. Rayfield, 'Turkish Counter-Offensive'.
30. Ibid.
31. *Turkish Staff History*, p. 132.
32. Ibid., p. 133.
33. Kitchener to Maxwell 28/4/15, WO 158/574. Emphasis added.
34. Hamilton to Kitchener 28/4/15, WO 159/13.
35. 29 Division Operation Order No. 4, 6/5/15, *Gallipoli Maps and Appendices V1*, Appendix 25, pp. 66–70.
36. Aspinall-Oglander, *Gallipoli V1*, p. 323.
37. Translation of French Official Account in Rayfield Papers 69/61/6.
38. 29 Division, 'Report of Operations on the 6th and 7th May, 1915', 29 Division War Diary, WO 95/4305.
39. *Turkish Staff History*, p. 140. This account confirms that the British were stopped by the Turkish outpost line.
40. 29 Division, 'Report on Operations from 8th to 11th May 1915,' 29 Division War Diary, WO 95/4305.
41. C. G. Brereton, *Tales of Three Campaigns* (London: Selwyn & Blount, 1926), pp. 116–17.
42. New Zealand Brigade War Diary 8/5/15, Australian War Memorial AWM 4/35/17/3, Canberra.
43. 29 Division Report, 8–11 May.
44. Lt-Col Bolton's Report 13/5/15 in AWM 4/23/2/1.
45. 7 Battalion Report, AWM 4/23/2/1.
46. Bolton Report 13/5/15.
47. C.E.W. Bean, *Gallipoli Mission* (Canberra: Australian War Memorial, 1948), pp. 301–2.
48. 7 Battalion Report.

Chapter 10: Last Throw in the South

1. MEF (Mediterranean Expeditionary Force) War Diary, Force Order No. 8, 11/5/15, War Office Papers, WO 95/4263, National Archives, Kew.
2. C. F. Aspinall-Oglander, *Military Operations: Gallipoli*, vol. 2 (London: Heinemann, 1932), p. 33. (Hereafter, *Gallipoli V2*.)

3. Robin Prior and Trevor Wilson, *Command on the Western Front* (Oxford: Basil Blackwell, 1992), p. 33.
4. Figures are in WO 162/69.
5. Corbett, *Naval Operations V2*, pp. 406–8.
6. Mitchell Committee Report, p. 233.
7. Ibid., pp. 230–3.
8. These details can be found in VIII Corps, 'Report on Operations of 8th Army Corps: May 24th to June 7th', VIII Corps War Diary June 1915, WO 95/4274.
9. Ibid.
10. French Official Account translated by Rayfield, Rayfield Papers 69/61/6, Imperial War Museum, London.
11. Ibid.
12. Braithwaite, 'Instructions to General Officers Commanding Corps', 2/6/15, in VIII Corps War Diary June 1915, WO 95/4273.
13. *Turkish Staff History*, pp. 149–50.
14. Ibid.
15. Royal Naval Division, 'Report on Operations, 4th June', Royal Naval Division War Diary June 1915, WO 95/4291.
16. VIII Corps War Diary June 1915.
17. 29 Indian Brigade War Diary, 'An account of the part taken by the 14th Sikhs in the action of the 4th–6th June', WO 95/4272.
18. Lt-Col H.F.L. Grant (Royal Artillery) to Aspinall-Oglander 2/3/29, Cabinet Papers, CAB 45/242, National Archives, Kew.
19. 4 Worcesters War Diary 4/6/15, WO 95/4312.
20. VIII Corps War Diary June 1915.
21. Ibid.
22. See, for example, the War Diary of 1/6 Manchesters 4/6/15, in WO 95/4316.
23. French Official Account translated by Rayfield, Rayfield Papers 69/61/6.
24. *Turkish Staff History*, p. 162.
25. French Official Account translated by Rayfield, Rayfield Papers 69/61/6.
26. Ibid.
27. Ibid.
28. VIII Corps, 'Report on Operations 8th Army Corps from 7th June to 6th July, 1915', VIII Corps War Diary June 1915, WO 95/4274.
29. Martin Middlebrook, *Your Country Needs You* (Barnsley: Pen & Sword, 2000), p. 111.
30. 'Notes on Battle of 28th June 1915 [by] Capt. C.M. Weir 1/7 Cameronians, 156 Brigade', CAB 45/242.
31. See VIII Corps, 'Report on Operations', and Aspinall-Oglander, *Gallipoli V2*, p. 85.
32. VIII Corps, 'Report on Operations 8th Army Corps from 7th to 1st August, 1915', VIII Corps War Diary July 1915, WO 95/4274.
33. General Sir George Egerton (Commander 52 Division) Diary 12/7/15, CAB 45/249.
34. Aspinall-Oglander, *Gallipoli V2*, p. 105.
35. Egerton Diary 12/7/15.
36. Aspinall-Oglander, *Gallipoli V2*, pp. 107–8.
37. RND, 'Report of Operations Royal Naval Division, 13th–16th July', RND War Diary July 1915, WO 95/4290.
38. Aspinall-Oglander, *Gallipoli V2*, p. 111.
39. Egerton Diary 13/7/15.

Chapter 11: The Plans of August

1. John [Jack] Churchill to Winston Churchill 27/4/15, *CV3*, p. 824.
2. Churchill to John Churchill 27/4/15, in ibid., p. 830.

3. War Council Minutes 14/5/15, Cabinet Papers, CAB 42/2/19, National Archives, Kew.
4. Ibid.
5. This paragraph relies on Trevor Wilson, *The Myriad Faces of War* (Oxford: Basil Blackwell, 1986), Chapter 18, 'From Liberal Government to First Coalition', pp. 192–206.
6. Hamilton to Kitchener 17/5/15, Lt-Gen Guy Dawnay Papers, Box 17, Imperial War Museum, London.
7. Dardanelles Committee Conclusions 7/6/15, CAB 42/3/1.
8. Hamilton to Kitchener 8/6/15, Dawnay Papers, Box 17.
9. Dardanelles Committee Minutes 17/6/15, CAB 42/3/4.
10. Dardanelles Committee Minutes 5/7/15, CAB 42/3/7.
11. Hamilton to Kitchener 9/7/15, in ibid.
12. Bean, *Story of Anzac V2*, p. 439.
13. 1 Anzac Corps War Diary 13/5/15, War Office Papers, WO 95/4281, National Archives, Kew.
14. Birdwood to Hamilton 16/5/15, in ibid.
15. Birdwood to Hamilton 30/5/15, in ibid.
16. Birdwood to Hamilton 8/6/15, in ibid.
17. Aspinall-Oglander, *Gallipoli V2*, p. 130, note 1.
18. Birdwood to Hamilton 1/7/15, in Anzac Corps War Diary, WO 95/4821.
19. Birdwood to Hamilton 10/7/15, in ibid.
20. Birdwood to Hamilton 30/7/15, in ibid.
21. Ibid.
22. Hamilton to General G. Ellison 10/7/15, Hamilton Papers 15/17, Liddell Hart Centre, King's College, London.
23. Hamilton to General James Wolfe-Murray, 1/7/15, in ibid 5/7.
24. Note by Braithwaite 22/7/15, WO 158/576.
25. Memorandum by Stopford 31/7/15, WO 158/576.
26. GHQ to Stopford 31/7/15, in ibid.
27. IX Corps Operational Order No. 1, 3/8/15, WO 32/5119.

Chapter 12: The Assault on Sari Bair

1. 'Report on Operations Carried out by the 29th Division on 6th August, 1915', 29 Division War Diary, War Office Papers, WO 95/4305, National Archives, Kew.
2. 1 Australian Division Artillery War Diary 6/8/15, Australian War Memorial AWM 4/1/42/8, Canberra; Bean, *Story of Anzac V2*, p. 500.
3. 2 Battalion War Diary 6/8/15, AWM 4/23/32/1.
4. Bean, *Story of Anzac V2*, p. 566.
5. *Turkish Staff History*, pp. 190–1.
6. Ibid., p. 191.
7. See Michael B. Tyquin, *Gallipoli: The Medical War* (Sydney: University of New South Wales Press, 1993), for the state of the Australian Imperial Force in August.
8. 'Report on Operations against the Sari Bair Position: 6–10th August 1915', NZ & A Division War Diary August 1915, AWM 4/1/53/5, Part 2.
9. 13 Battalion War Diary 6/8/15, AWM 4/23/30/10.
10. 15 Battalion War Diary 6/8/15, AWM 4/23/32/10.
11. 13 Battalion War Diary 6/8/15, AWM 4/23/30/10.
12. 15 Battalion War Diary 6 & 7/8/15, AWM 4/23/32/10.
13. 29 Indian Brigade War Diary 6 & 7/8/15, WO 95/4272.
14. Ibid.
15. Temperley, 'Chunuk Bair'; uncatalogued account in the Imperial War Museum, London.
16. *Turkish Staff History*, pp. 194–5.

17. Birdwood, Report to Hamilton, September 1915, Anzac Corps War Diary August 1915, AWM 4/1/25/5, Part 5. Emphasis added.
18. The Nek is the best known of the attacks made from the Anzac that day, no doubt because of the film *Gallipoli*, which incidentally misrepresents the entire episode. Other attacks were carried out from Quinn's and Pope's. The total casualties were 650 out of the 1,250 who went into action. See Aspinall-Oglander, *Gallipoli V2*, p. 198.
19. W.H. Cunningham et al., *The Wellington Regiment* (Wellington: Ferguson & Osborn, 1928), p. 62.
20. O.E. Burton, *The Auckland Regiment* (Auckland: Whitcombe & Tombs, n.d.), p. 56.
21. C. Malthus, *Anzac: A Retrospect* (Auckland: Whitcombe & Tombs, 1965), pp. 116–17.
22. NZ & A Divisional Order No. 12, 7/8/15, in Aspinall-Oglander, *Gallipoli: Maps and Appendices V2*, pp. 54–5.
23. Rayfield, 'The Battle of Sari Bair from the Turkish Side', Rayfield Papers, 69/61/4, Imperial War Museum, London.
24. 14 Battalion War Diary 8/8/15, AWM 4/23/32/10.
25. 15 Battalion War Diary 8/8/15, AWM 4/23/31/10.
26. 7 North Stafford War Diary 8/8/15, WO 95/4302.
27. Ibid.; Aspinall-Oglander, *Gallipoli V2*, p. 212.
28. New Zealand Brigade War Diary 8/8/15.
29. This account has been assembled from the *Turkish Staff History*, pp. 197–201, the war diaries of the British units involved and Rayfield's 'Sari Bair from the Turkish Side'.
30. New Zealand Brigade War Diary 8/8/15; 'History of the Wellington Battalion', WO 95/4352. Temperley, the brigade staff officer, had a theory that Malone, the commander of the Wellingtons on the summit, had read a pamphlet that stated reverse slope positions were always to be preferred for the protection they gave against artillery. Temperley points out that the Turks were not directing artillery fire on Chunuk Bair at this time, and therefore Malone had given up the summit unnecessarily. (See Temperley's uncatalogued account in the Imperial War Museum, London.) However, it is clear from the war diaries that Malone was not guided by theoretical concerns in withdrawing his forces to the reverse slope.
31. 'History of the Wellington Battalion'.
32. Ibid; Rayfield, 'The Battle of Sari Bair from the Turkish Side'.
33. 'History of the Wellington Battalion'.
34. Godley Report, AWM 4/1/53/5, Part 2.
35. New Zealand Brigade War Diary 9/8/15; Bean, *Story of Anzac V2*, p. 692.
36. Dardanelles Commission, Lt-Col Allanson's Evidence 19/1/17, Q11,792, Cabinet Papers, CAB 19/33, National Archives, Kew.
37. 29 Indian Brigade War Diary 9/8/15.
38. Allanson to Cox 6.30 a.m., 9/8/15, in ibid.
39. Allanson to his brother 8/3/16, DS/Misc/69, Imperial War Museum, London. Allanson does not mention in this letter that the shells were naval.
40. The *Bacchante* opened fire in support of this attack at 5.20 a.m. (see its Log for 9/8/15 in Admiralty Papers, ADM 53/34469, National Archives, Kew.) and Allanson's force was hit at 5.25 a.m. However, it is by no means certain that the flat trajectory of ships' guns could have reached the position on Hill Q occupied by Allanson's force.
41. The legend that the navy denied the army an important lodgement on the ridge was spread about by Allanson himself, probably to suggest the brave actions of his troops constituted a critical turning point in the whole Dardanelles campaign.
42. 13 Division War Diary 9/8/15, WO 95/4300.
43. Ibid.
44. See CAB 45/242 for the experiences of the Royal Irish Rifles in this fiasco.
45. New Zealand Brigade War Diary 9/10/8/15.

46. For these movements see the very useful map (31) accompanying the Mitchell Committee Report.
47. *Turkish Staff History*, p. 206.
48. NZ & A War Diary 10/8/15.
49. Malthus, *Anzac: A Retrospect*, p. 119.
50. Dardanelles Commission, Evidence by Brigadier-General G. N. Johnston (RA), 2/5/17, Q 26,647, CAB 19/33.
51. Ibid. See also questions 26,644 to 26,646.
52. Bean, *Story of Anzac V2*, p. 700.
53. Major W.R.E. Harrison, 'Gallipoli Revisited', *Journal of the Royal Artillery*, vol. 49, October 1932, pp. 293–4.

Chapter 13: Suvla Bay: The Scapegoat Battle

1. 11 Division Operation Order No. 1, 5/8/15, in Aspinall-Oglander, *Gallipoli Maps and Appendices V2*, Appendix 5, pp. 34–7.
2. 31 Brigade War Diary 5/8/15, War Office Papers, WO 95/4296, National Archives, Kew comments on the absence of orders.
3. Aspinall-Oglander seems to make this assumption on p. 144 of *Gallipoli V2*.
4. M. Middlebrook, *Your Country Needs You* (Barnsley: Pen & Sword, 2000), p. 50.
5. See 'Operations of IX Corps' in their War Diary August 1915, WO 95/4276.
6. Ibid.
7. Ibid.
8. Middlebrook, *Your Country Needs You*, p. 50.
9. Bean, *Story of Anzac V2*, p. 648.
10. Robert Rhodes James, 'A Visit to Gallipoli, 1962', *Stand-To*, Vol. 9, No. 2, 1964, p. 5.
11. A.J. Murray (9 Sherwood Foresters) to Aspinall-Oglander 20/7/29, Cabinet Papers, CAB 45/243, National Archives, Kew.
12. Ibid.
13. Gibson Diary 6–7/8/15, uncatalogued manuscript, Imperial War Museum, London.
14. 'Operations of IX Corps' WO 95/4276.
15. 'Suvla Bay Landing' by Major C. O. Ibbotson, 9 Lancashire Fusiliers, CAB 45/242.
16. 31 Brigade War Diary 7/8/15, WO 95/4296.
17. 'Suvla Bay', Notes by Admiral Christian 7/8/15, de Robeck Papers, 4/34, Churchill College, Cambridge.
18. 'Operations of IX Corps'.
19. 'Operations of IX Corps'; Captain J.F. Coleridge, 'The 11th Division at Suvla Bay', CAB 45/243.
20. 'Operations of IX Corps'.
21. 31 Brigade War Diary 7/8/15, WO 95/4297; Captain A.C. Croydon, 6 Battalion. Lincolnshire Regiment, 'The Suvla Landing—August 6th–7th', CAB 45/228.
22. Rayfield, 'The Battle for Sari Bair on the Turkish Side', Rayfield Papers, 69/61/4, Imperial War Museum, London.
23. Coleridge, 'The 11th Division at Suvla Bay', CAB 45/243.
24. 32 Brigade War Diary 8/8/15, WO 95/4322.
25. GHQ War Diary 7/8/15, WO 95/4264.
26. Ibid., 8/8/15.
27. Ibid.
28. Ibid.
29. Ibid.
30. 'Operations of IX Corps'.
31. Ibid.

32. Ibid.
33. 33 Brigade War Diary 9/8/15, WO 95/4297.
34. Dardanelles Commission, Testimony of Lt-Commander Roger Keyes 15/7/17, Q 27,023 and 27,036, CAB 19/33.
35. Ibid., Testimony of Lt-Col F.A.K. White (68th Field Company Royal Engineers) 20/8/17, Q30, 237 to 30, 257 and testimony of Major-General J. Poett (Q M G IX Corps) 9/3/17, Q21, 946.
36. Dardanelles Commission, Statement by Colonel Aspinall, CAB 19/28.
37. Lt-Col A. Murray, 'A Short Account of the Landing at Suvla Bay, Gallipoli, in August, 1915', CAB 45/243.
38. Rayfield, 'The Battle of Sari Bair from the Turkish Side'. This account has relied heavily on Rayfield for this episode where he clearly had access to many Turkish sources. It is desperately sad that his work, at least in part, was never published because for the action described above it is still far and away the best account. For a strongly pro-Kemal account see the *Turkish Staff History*, pp. 212–18.
39. For descriptions of these actions see 158 Brigade War Diary for a letter by A.E.R Jelf-Reveley, WO 95/4232, and a memorandum by Frank Watney of 160 Brigade in their War Diary, WO 95/4232.
40. For these actions see an account by one of the British Yeomen (2 Mounted Division) in CAB 45/241. For the Anzacs see Bean, *Story of Anzac V2*, pp. 718–62.
41. See the letter by Lt-Col A. Williams in CAB 45/242.
42. Major Sherman Miles, 'Notes on the Dardanelles Campaign 1915', *Coast Artillery Journal*, Part III, vol. 62, p. 143.

Chapter 14: 'War as we must': The Political Debate

1. Hamilton to Kitchener 17/8/15, War Office Papers, WO 32/5119, National Archives, Kew.
2. Dardanelles Committee Minutes 20/8/15, Cabinet Papers, CAB 42/3/16, National Archives, Kew.
3. Bean, *Story of Anzac V2*, pp. 781–2.
4. 'Copy of a letter from Mr. K. A. Murdoch to the Prime Minister of the Australian Commonwealth', presented to the Cabinet 23/9/15, CAB 42/3/33.
5. Dardanelles Committee Minutes 6/10/15, CAB 42/4/3.
6. Orlo Williams Diary 21/7/15, Williams Papers, 69/78/1, Imperial War Museum, London.
7. The above account mainly rests on Dawnay's Diary and an appreciation he wrote, 'Situation in the Aegean', 12/9/15. All are in the Dawnay Papers, Box 17, Imperial War Museum, London.
8. Dardanelles Committee Minutes 11/10/15, CAB 42/4/6.
9. Ibid., 14/10/15, CAB 42/4/9.
10. 'Lord Kitchener's Instructions for General Sir Charles Monro', 20/10/15, in *Gallipoli Maps and Appendices V2*, Appendix 17, pp. 69–70.
11. Dardanelles Committee Minutes 31/8/15, CAB 42/3/20.
12. For these discussions see Dardanelles Committee Minutes 3/9/15 and 23/9/15 in CAB 42/3/23 and 42/3/33 respectively.
13. Keyes to his wife 13/6/15, Keyes Papers 2/12, Churchill College, Cambridge.
14. Admiral Guido von Usedom to the Kaiser 20/7/15, CAB 45/215.
15. These are rough estimates using the figures in von Usedom's list and comparing them with the list in Plan 4 in Corbett, *Naval Operations V2*.
16. Mitchell Committee Report, p. 457.
17. The details of the Keyes/Godfrey plan can be found in *The Keyes Papers, 1914–1918*, vol. 1, ed. Paul G. Halpern (London: Navy Records Society, 1972), pp. 194–201 (Godfrey's version), or in Keyes to de Robeck 18/10/15, Keyes Papers 5/17.

18. HMS *Implacable* Gunnery Report 29/9/15, Admiralty Papers, ADM 1/8440/335, National Archives, Kew.
19. B.H.S., 'Dardanelles Detail', *Naval Review*, vol. 24, 1936, p. 89.
20. De Robeck to Sir Henry Jackson Jackson 20/10/15, *Keyes Papers*, vol. 1, pp. 232–3.
21. Wemyss to Keyes 25-30/11/15, in ibid., p. 257.
22. Monro to the War Office 28/10/15, GHQ War Diary WO 95/4265.
23. Dardanelles Committee Minutes 11/10/15, CAB 42/4/6.
24. Monro Report 31/10/15, CAB 42/5/20.
25. Monro to Kitchener 2/11/15, in ibid.
26. War Committee Minutes 3/11/15, CAB 42/5/2.
27. Kitchener to Birdwood 4/11/15, quoted in Aspinall-Oglander, *Gallipoli V2*, p. 410.
28. Kitchener to Asquith 5/11/15, CAB 42/5/5.
29. Kitchener to Asquith 10/11/15, CAB 42/5/20.
30. Kitchener to Asquith 15/11/15, in ibid.
31. War Committee Minutes 16/11/15, CAB 42/5/14.
32. Robertson's Paper of 8/11/15 is to be found in CAB 42/5/6, Murray's Paper of 21/11/15 in CAB 42/5/10.
33. War Committee Minutes 23/11/15, CAB 42/5/20.
34. Curzon to Churchill 30/11/15, *CV3*, pp. 1,294–7.
35. Curzon memorandum 27/11/15, CAB 42/5/24.
36. Hankey memorandum 29/11/15, in ibid.
37. War Committee Minutes 2/12/15, CAB 42/6/2.
38. ibid., 6/12/15, CAB 42/6/4.
39. Monro to the War Office 4/12/15, WO 158/580.
40. Kitchener to Monro 8/12/15, in ibid.

Chapter 15: A Campaign not Won

1. These comments and the proceedings of the inquiry can be found in 52 Division War Diary September 1915, War Office Papers, WO 95/4273, National Archives, Kew. All quotations used above come from this document.
2. Aspinall-Oglander, *Gallipoli V2*, p. 392.
3. Sir Ronald East (ed.), *The Gallipoli Diary of Sergeant Lawrence* (Melbourne: Melbourne University Press, 1981), p. 87.
4. Major W. F. Duncan Nuttall, Letter 6/11/15, uncatalogued, Imperial War Museum, London.
5. Ibid.
6. See the GHQ War Diary for the respective dates of these incidents.
7. Aspinall-Oglander, *Gallipoli V2*, p. 432.
8. 1 Lancashire Fusiliers War Diary 26–27/11/15, WO 95/4310.
9. Rayfield, 'Planning & the Evacuation of Anzac and Suvla', Rayfield Papers, 69/61/4, Imperial War Museum, London.
10. Bean, *Story of Anzac V2*, pp. 863, 870, 881.
11. IX Corps, 'Notes on Evacuation', IX Corps War Diary December 1915, WO 95/4276.
12. Ibid.
13. Ibid.
14. Rayfield, 'Planning & Evacuation of Anzac and Suvla'.
15. Bean, *Story of Anzac V2*, p. 883.
16. Ibid., p. 868.
17. 2 Australian Battalion War Diary December 1915, Australian War Memorial AWM 4/23/32/1, Canberra.
18. Arthur Lynden-Bell to Charles Callwell 21/12/15, Lynden-Bell Papers 90/1/1, Imperial War Museum, London.

19. 2 Australian Battalion War Diary December 1915.
20. General F. H. Davies, 'Report on Evacuation of Cape Helles Position', WO 158/594.
21. Ibid.
22. J.K. Reynolds Papers, Con Shelf, Imperial War Museum, London.
23. Ibid.
24. Davies is clearly wrong in his report in stating that the Turks made a 'determined' attack. Aspinall-Oglander, *Gallipoli V2*, p. 473, is possibly gullible in believing von Sanders' account (*Five Years in Turkey*, pp. 130–2) that the Turks could not be induced to leave their trenches. The real purpose of the Turks on that evening remains a mystery.
25. Robert Rhodes James, *Gallipoli* (London: Batsford, 1965), p. 343.

Reflections on Gallipoli

1. These figures have been taken from: *History of the Great War: Medical Services: Casualties and Medical Statistics of the Great War*, compiled by Major T. J. Mitchell and Miss G. M. Smith (London: HMSO, 1931), Chapter XIII. Other authorities vary slightly in their figures but this compilation has the advantage of providing a common source for Dominion and Indian troops as well as British. The French figures are my own estimates based on the total number of casualties given in the French official account.
2. See Aspinall-Oglander, *Gallipoli V2*, p. 484. The official historian reaches the same conclusion as that above, only to reject it, and states that the Turks suffered 100,000 more casualties than the Allies. His sources for the higher figure are 'other Turkish authorities'.
3. Enver Bey to the Mitchell Committee. See Mitchell Committee Report, p. 382.
4. Von Sanders, *Five Years in Turkey*, p. 47.
5. GHQ Constantinople—Answers to Questions given to the Mitchell Committee, Admiralty Papers, ADM 116/1714, National Archives, Kew.
6. H. Morganthau, *Ambassador Morganthau's Story* (New York: Doubleday, 1919), pp. 199–200.
7. Dardanelles Commission—Admiral Hall's Evidence, Q 4906, 24/10/16, Cabinet Papers, CAB 19/33, National Archives, Kew.
8. Answers Given to the Mitchell Committee, ADM 116/17/4.
9. Winston Churchill, *The World Crisis* (London: Odhams, 1951), pp. 849.
10. For the Rumanian Army, see C. Kiritescu, *La Roumanie dans la Guerre mondiale 1916–1919* (Paris: Payot, 1936), pp. 54, 265, and Pamfil Seicaru, *La Roumanie dans la Grande Guerre* (Paris: Minard, 1968), pp. 289, 346. I have had the relevant sections of these works translated.
11. T.M. Cunninghame 'The Greek Army and the Dardanelles', *National Review*, vol. 92, 1928, p. 122.

Bibliography

National Archives, Kew

Admiralty Papers

ADM 1 Admiralty and Secretariat Papers
ADM 53 Ships' Logs
ADM 116 Case Papers on Special Subjects
ADM 137 War History Papers

Cabinet Papers

CAB 19 Dardanelles Commission Evidence and Correspondence
CAB 37 Microfilm copies of Cabinet Memoranda
CAB 42 Microfilm copies of War Council, Dardanelles Committee and War Committee minutes and papers
CAB 45 Postwar Official History Correspondence
CAB 63 Hankey Papers

Foreign Office Papers

FO 371 General Correspondence (Political) Files
FO 800 Papers of Sir Edward Grey

War Office Papers

WO 32 Registered Files
WO 95 Operational War Diaries
WO 106 Directorate of Military Operations Files
WO 157 Directorate of Military Intelligence Files
WO 158 Military Headquarters Correspondence and Papers
WO 162 Adjutant General Files

Private Papers

   NA 30 Papers of Lord Kitchener

Australian War Memorial, Canberra

   AWM 4 Operational War Diaries
   AWM 26 Operational Files
   AWM 124 Mitchell Committee Report
   DRL Series, General Birdwood Papers

Churchill College, Cambridge

   Churchill Papers
   Admiral de Robeck Papers
   Admiral J.H. Godfrey Papers
   Admiral of the Fleet, Lord Keyes Papers

Imperial War Museum, London

   Colonel C.J.L. Allanson Papers
   Major General G.P. Dawnay Papers
   Rear Admiral I.W. Gibson Papers
   Captain Godfrey Papers
   Lt D.H. Hepburn Diary
   General Lynden-Bell Papers
   Captain H.C. Lockyer Papers
   Major W.F. Dixon Nuttall Papers
   J.K. Reynolds Papers
   Col F.A. Rayfield Papers
   Swaby Papers
   Major General A.C. Temperley Papers
   Dr O.C. Williams Papers
   Commander H.M. Wilson Papers
   Anonymous account of the Anzac landing in Misc 262, Box 12

Liddell Hart Centre, King's College, London

   General Sir Ian Hamilton Papers

National Maritime Museum, Greenwich

   Graham Greene Papers
   Admiral Sir David Beatty Papers
   Admiral Sir Frederick Hamilton Papers
   Admiral Limpus Papers
   Admiral Sir Henry Oliver Papers
   Admiral Sir Herbert Richmond Papers

Books and Articles

E. Ashmead-Bartlett, *The Uncensored Dardanelles* (London: Hutchinson, 1928)
Brigadier-General C.F. Aspinall-Oglander, *Military Operations: Gallipoli*, 2 vols and appendices
   (London: Heinemann, 1929–32)

C.E.W. Bean, *Official History of Australia in the War of 1914–1918: The Story of Anzac*, 2 vols (Sydney: Angus & Robertson, 1938–42)

——, *Gallipoli Mission* (Canberra: Australian War Memorial, 1948)

B.H.S., 'Dardanelles Details', *Naval Review*, vol. 24, 1936, pp. 81–91, 310–19, 480–8

Field Marshal Lord Birdwood, *Khaki and Gown: An Autobiography* (London: Ward Lock, 1942)

C.G. Brereton, *Tales of Three Campaigns* (London: Selwyn & Blount, 1926)

Peter Burness, *The Nek* (Canberra: Kangaroo Press, 1996)

Lt O.E. Burton, *The Auckland Regiment* (Auckland: Whitcombe & Tombs, n.d.)

——, *The Silent Division: New Zealanders at the Front 1914–18* (Sydney: Angus & Robertson, 1935)

Eric Bush, *Gallipoli* (London: Allen & Unwin, 1975)

Major-General Sir Charles E. Calwell, *The Dardanelles* (London: Constable, 1920)

George H. Cassar, *The French and the Dardanelles: A Study in the Failure of the Conduct of War* (London: Allen & Unwin, 1971)

——, *Kitchener* (London: Kimber, 1977)

E. Keble Chatterton, *Dardanelles Dilemma: The Story of the Naval Operations* (London: Rich & Cowan, 1935)

Peter Chausseaud and Peter Doyle, *Grasping Gallipoli: Terrain, Maps and the Failure at the Dardanelles 1915* (Staplehurst: Spellmont, 2005)

Winston S. Churchill, *The World Crisis*, vol. 2 (London: Odhams, 1951)

Bryan Cooper, *The Tenth (Irish) Division in Gallipoli* (London: Herbert Jenkins, 1918)

Sir Julian Corbett, *Naval Operations*, vol. 2 (London: Longmans, 1921)

W.H. Cunningham et al., *The Wellington Regiment* (Wellington: Ferguson & Osborn, 1928)

T.M. Cunninghame, 'The Greek Army and the Dardanelles', *National Review*, vol. 92, 1928, pp. 121–32 and pp. 270–81

G. Davidson, *The Incomparable 29th and the River Clyde* (Edinburgh: Bisset, 1919)

H.M. Denham, *Dardanelles: A Midshipman's Diary, 1915–16* (London: John Murray, 1981)

Sir Ronald East (ed.), *The Gallipoli Diary of Sergeant Lawrence* (Melbourne: Melbourne University Press, 1983)

Edward E. Erikson, *Ordered to Die: A History of the Ottoman Army in the First World War* (Westport, Conn.: Greenwood, 2001)

——, 'One More Push, Forcing the Dardanelles in March 1915', *Journal of Strategic Studies*, vol. 24, 2001

Lt Mehmed Fasih, *Gallipoli 1915: Bloody Ridge (Lone Pine) Diary* (Istanbul: Denizler Kitabevi, 2001)

Kevin Fewster (ed.), *Gallipoli Correspondent: The Frontline Diary of C.E.W. Bean* (Melbourne: Allen & Unwin, 1983)

Lord Fisher of Kilverstone, *Memories* (London: Hodder & Stoughton, 1919)

——, *Records* (London: Hodder & Stoughton, 1919)

Tom Frame, *The Shores of Gallipoli: Naval Aspects of the Anzac Campaign* (Sydney: Hale & Iremonger, 2000)

Martin Gilbert, *Winston S. Churchill, Vol. 3, 1914–1916* (London: Heinemann, 1971)

——, *Winston S. Churchill, Vol. 3, Companion: Documents July 1914–December 1916*, 2 vols (London: Heinemann, 1972)

Captain S. Gillon, *The Story of the 29th Division* (London: Nelson, 1925)

Frank Glen, *Bowler of Gallipoli* (Canberra: Army History Unit, 2004)

Great Britain Parliament, *Dardanelles Commission First Report and Supplement*, Command 8490 and 8502 (London: H.M.S.O., 1917)

——, *Dardanelles Commission Final Report, Conduct of Operations etc*, Command 371 (London: H.M.S.O., 1919)

Viscount Grey of Falloden, *Twenty-Five Years, 1892–1916*, 2 vols (London: Hodder & Stoughton, 1925)

Paul Guinn, *British Strategy and Politics 1914 to 1918* (London: Oxford University Press, 1965)

General Sir Ian Hamilton, *Gallipoli Diary*, 2 vols (London: Edward Arnold, 1920)

Ian Hamilton, *The Happy Warrior: A Life of General Sir Ian Hamilton* (London: Cassell, 1966)

Lord Hankey, *The Supreme Command*, 2 vols (London: Allen & Unwin, 1961)

H. Hanna, *The Pals at Suvla Bay: Being the Record of "D" Company of the 7th Royal Dublin Fusiliers* (Dublin: Ponsonby, 1917)

John Hargrave, *The Suvla Bay Landing* (London: Macdonald, 1964)

Major W.R.E. Harrison, 'Gallipoli Revisited', *Journal of the Royal Artillery*, vol. 49, 1932, pp. 293–4

Lt-Colonel C.O. Head, *A Glance at Gallipoli* (London: Eyre & Spottiswoode, 1931)

Michael Hickey, *Gallipoli* (London: John Murray, 1995)

Trumbull Higgins, *Winston Churchill and the Dardanelles* (London: Heinemann, 1963)

Richard Hough, *First Sea Lord: An Authorised Biography of Admiral Lord Fisher* (London: Allen & Unwin, 1969)

H.V. Howe, 'The Anzac Landing—A Belated Query', *Stand To*, vol. 107, 1962, pp. 1–3

Robert Rhodes James, *Gallipoli* (London: Batsford, 1965)

——, 'A Visit to Gallipoli', *Stand To*, vol. 109, 1964, pp. 4–6

H.A. Jones, *The War in the Air*, vol. 2 (London: Hamish Hamilton, 1969). Reprint of 1928 edition

Hans Kannengiesser, *Campaign in Gallipoli* (London: Hutchinson, 1928)

Admiral of the Fleet Baron Keyes, *The Keyes Papers* vol. 1, 1914–1918 (London: Navy Records Society, 1972)

——, *The Naval Memoirs of Admiral of the Fleet Sir Roger Keyes: The Narrow Sea to the Dardanelles*, vol. 2 (London: Thornton Butterworth, 1934)

C. Kiretscu, *La Roumanie dans la Guerre mondiale 1916–1919* (Paris: Payot, 1934)

John Lee, *A Soldier's Life: General Sir Ian Hamilton 1853–1947* (London: Macmillan, 2000)

Peter Liddle, *Men of Gallipoli: The Dardanelles and Gallipoli Experience, August 1914 to January 1916* (London: Allen Lane, 1976)

Ruddock Mackay, *Fisher of Kilverstone* (Oxford: Clarendon Press, 1973)

Jenny Macleod, *Reconsidering Gallipoli* (Manchester: Manchester University Press, 2004)

Compton Mackenzie, *Gallipoli Memories* (London: Cassell, 1929)

Cecil Malthus, *Anzac: A Retrospect* (Auckland: Whitcombe & Tombs, 1965)

Arthur Marder, *Portrait of an Admiral: The Life and Papers of Sir Herbert Richmond* (London: Cape, 1952)

——, *Fear God and Dreadnought: The Correspondence of Admiral of the Fleet Lord Fisher of Kilverstone*, vol. 3 (London: Cape, 1959)

——, *From the Dreadnought to Scapa Flow: The Royal Navy in the Fisher Era 1904–1919*, 5 vols (London: Oxford University Press, 1961–72)

——, *From the Dardanelles to Oran: Studies in the Royal Navy in War and Peace 1915–1940* (London: Oxford University Press, 1974)

Martin Middlebrook, *Your Country Needs You* (Barnsley: Pen & Sword, 2000)

Major Sherman Miles, 'Notes on the Dardanelles Campaign of 1915', *The Coast Artillery Journal*, vol. 61, 1924, pp. 506–21; vol. 62, 1925, pp. 23–42, 119–43, 207–25

Major T.J. Mitchell and G.M. Smith, *Casualties and Medical Statistics of the Great War* (London: H.M.S.O., 1931)

Alan Moorehead, *Gallipoli* (London: Hamish Hamilton, 1956)

Henry Morganthau, *Ambassador Morganthau's Story* (New York: Doubleday, 1919)

Joseph Murray, *Gallipoli As I Saw It* (London: Kimber, 1965)

Lt-Col H.D. Napier, *The Experiences of a Military Attaché in the Balkans* (London: Dranes, 1924)

H.W. Nevinson, *The Dardanelles Campaign* (London: Nisbit, 1918)

John North, *Gallipoli: The Fading Vision* (London: Faber, 1966)

Anthony Preston, *Battleships of World War 1* (London: Galahad Books, 1972)

Robin Prior, *Churchill's 'World Crisis' As History* (London: Croom Helm, 1983)

Robin Prior and Trevor Wilson, *Command on the Western Front* (Oxford: Blackwell, 1992)

Christopher Pugsley, *Gallipoli: The New Zealand Story* (London: Hodder & Stoughton, 1984)

Admiral Sir Herbert Richmond, *Statesmen and Sea Power* (Oxford: Clarendon Press, 1946)

John Robertson, *Anzac and Empire* (Sydney: Hamlyn, 1990)

Stephen Roskill, *Hankey: Man of Secrets*, vol. 1 (London: Collins, 1970)

——, *Churchill and the Admirals* (London: Collins, 1977)

Otto Liman von Sanders, *Five Years in Turkey* (London: Baillière, Tindall & Cox, 1927)

P. Seicaru, *La Roumanie dans La Grande Guerre* (Paris: Minard, 1968)

Nigel Steel and Peter Hart, *Defeat at Gallipoli* (London: Macmillan, 1985)

A.T. Stewart and C.J.E. Pershall, *The Immortal Gamble: And the part played in it by H.M.S. Cornwallis* (London: Black, 1918)

Tim Travers, *Gallipoli 1915* (Stroud: Tempus, 2001)

Ulrich Trumpener, *Germany and the Ottoman Empire 1914–1918* (Princeton: Princeton University Press, 1968)

Turkish General Staff, *A Brief History of the Canakkale Campaign in the First World War (June 1914–January 1916)* (Ankara: Turkish General Staff Printing House, 2004)

Michael Tyquin, *Gallipoli: The Medical War* (Sydney: University of New South Wales Press, 1993)

Admiral of the Fleet Lord Wester Wemyss, *The Navy in the Dardanelles Campaign* (London: Hodder & Stoughton, 1924)

Trevor Wilson, *The Myriad Faces of War* (Oxford: Blackwell, 1986)

Denis Winter, *25 April 1915* (St Lucia: Queensland University Press, 1994)

Index